IS WOMEN'S PHILOSOPHY POSSIBLE?

New Feminist Perspectives Series

General Editor: Rosemarie Tong, Davidson College

Beyond Domination: New Perspectives on Women and Philosophy
  Edited by Carol C. Gould, Stevens Institute of Technology

Claiming Reality: Phenomenology and Women's Experience
  by Louise Levesque-Lopman, Regis College

Dehumanizing Women: Treating Persons as Sex Objects
  by Linda LeMoncheck

Evidence on Her Own Behalf: Women's Narrative as Theological Voice
  by Elizabeth Say Virgili, California State University, Northridge

Gendercide: The Implications of Sex Selection
  by Mary Anne Warren, San Francisco State University

Is Women's Philosophy Possible?
  by Nancy J. Holland, Hamline University

Manhood and Politics: A Feminist Reading in Political Theory
  by Wendy L. Brown, University of California, Santa Cruz

Mothering: Essays in Feminist Theory
  Edited by Joyce Treblicot, Washington University

Toward A Feminist Epistemology
  by Jane Duran, University of California, Santa Barbara

Uneasy Access: Privacy for Women in a Free Society
  by Anita L. Allen, Georgetown University

Women and Spirituality
  by Carol Ochs, Simmons College

Women, Militarism, and War: Essays in History, Politics, and Social Theory
  Edited by Jean Bethke Elshtain, Vanderbilt University, and Sheila Tobias, University of Arizona

Women, Sex, and the Law
  by Rosemarie Tong, Davidson College

IS WOMEN'S PHILOSOPHY POSSIBLE?

Nancy J. Holland

Rowman & Littlefield Publishers, Inc.

ROWMAN & LITTLEFIELD PUBLISHERS, INC.

Published in the United States of America
by Rowman & Littlefield Publishers, Inc.
8705 Bollman Place, Savage, Maryland 20763

Copyright © 1990 by Rowman & Littlefield Publishers, Inc.

All rights reserved. No part of this publication may
be reproduced, stored in a retrieval system, or transmitted
in any form or by any means, electronic, mechanical,
photocopying, recording, or otherwise, without the prior
permission of the publisher.

British Cataloging in Publication Information Available

Library of Congress Cataloging-in-Publication Data

Holland, Nancy J.
    Is woman's philosophy possible? / Nancy J. Holland.
    p.   cm. — (New feminist perspectives series)
    Includes bibliographical references and index.
    1. Feminist theory.   2. Philosophy.
I. Title. II. Series.
HQ1190.H65   1990   305.42'01—dc20   90–9006 CIP

ISBN 0–8476–7620–X (cloth : alk. paper)

5   4   3   2   1

Printed in the United States of America

∞ ™ The paper used in this publication meets the minimum requirements of
American National Standard for Information Sciences—Permanence of
Paper for Printed Library Materials, ANSI Z39.48–1984.

*For Gwendolyn Rose Koon
and her generation*

Contents

Acknowledgments   xi

Introduction   1

   Some Basic Definitions   1
   Feminist Philosophy as Critique   5
   Deconstruction as a Method   9
   Some Historical Assumptions   16
   A General Outline   19
   Notes   20

PART ONE

   1. Gender and the Generic in Locke   27

      The Limits of "Human" Understanding   27
      Locke's *Essay*   29
      Substance and Solipsism   32
      Monsters and Women   37
      Ethics and Shared Simple Ideas   40
      Notes   44

   2. "Betwixt a False Reason and None at All"   47

      Atomism, Scepticism, Psychology   47
      Sidestepping Descartes   49

Reconnecting the Pieces 51
A Self Divided 58
Ethical Considerations 61
Notes 65

3. The Feminist and the Individual 69

　　The Political Individual 69
　　Applications of Individualism 73
　　The Construction of Gender 79
　　The Knowing Individual 82
　　Hierarchical Dualism 85
　　Notes 89

PART TWO

4. Feminism and Phenomenology 95

　　Alternatives to Individualism 95
　　Heidegger's Hermeneutics of Modernity 98
　　Merleau-Ponty's Phenomenology of the Body 104
　　Sartre's Existential Individualism 109
　　De Beauvoir in Context 112
　　Notes 116

5. Women's Philosophy After the End of Metaphysics 121

　　Semiotics and Structuralism 121
　　Barthes on Signs and Systems 124
　　Lacan on Freud on Women 128
　　Foucault and the Post-Structuralist Opening 133
　　Derrida, Women, and Politics 137
　　Notes 142

6. Feminine Writing/The Writing of Women   145

    The "French Feminists" in Context   145
    Wittig and the Female Body   148
    Kristeva and the Freudian Mother   151
    Cixous's Middle Path   156
    Irigaray and Language   159
    Notes   163

7. Conclusion   167

    A Recommendation   167
    The Problem of Abortion   170
    The Wrong of Nuclear War   173
    Notes   177

References   179

Index   189

Acknowledgments

As is so often the case with feminist scholarship, this is in many ways a collective work, drawing on the knowledge and wisdom of more people than I can mention. Where possible, I have listed specific contributions to my thinking in the footnotes, but other influences are more widely dispersed throughout the text. Many of the ideas expressed here developed out of discussions with other members of an interdisciplinary study group at the University of Minnesota, including Susan McClary, John Mowitt, Marty Roth, and Eileen Sivert. I would also like to express great appreciation to my colleagues in the Women's Studies Workshop and the Faculty Seminar on Gender Issues at Hamline University. The editorial support of Rowman and Littlefield, especially Rosemarie Tong of Williams College and copy editor Kelli Gilbert, was, of course, vital to the completion of this project. I am also deeply grateful to Duane Cady of Hamline, Naomi Scheman of the University of Minnesota, and Bert Dreyfus of the University of California at Berkeley, not only for their intellectual contributions, but, more importantly, for their continuing confidence in me and my work.

The writing of this book was greatly facilitated by generous gifts given to Hamline University by the late Paul and Jean Shulman Hanna. My initial research and a major portion of the writing were supported by Hanna Summer Faculty Research Grants from Hamline in 1985 and 1987, and the early stages of the project benefited from the encouragement of Huston Smith, who at that time held the Hanna Chair in Philosophy at Hamline. My research also relied heavily on books purchased with faculty development funds provided to Hamline by the Bush Foundation.

Finally, I would like to thank my husband, Jeff Koon, for constant encouragement, as well as for sharing the computer; Wendy for love and hope; and Justis for waiting that final week to be born.

Introduction

Participating in an interdisciplinary study group that discusses women's scholarship has taught me that philosophy is unlike many other academic disciplines in one important respect. There is women's literature, women's music, women's history, and so on, and there is philosophy done by women and even feminist critiques of the philosophical tradition, but there is little that could unequivocally be called women's philosophy. A musicologist friend once said that surely there must be women's philosophy somewhere out there, unknown to academic philosophers, just as women's music and women's art had always existed. My immediate reaction, however, was to say that if there was such women's philosophy, such a folk wisdom, it just wouldn't be *philosophy,* as if the very nature of philosophy would exclude such a possibility. Why that response still seems to me to be a correct one will form the basic argument of this book.

Some Basic Definitions

Before asking whether women's philosophy is possible, however, it seems best to offer at least a partial definition of what women's philosophy might be. By women's philosophy I mean philosophical work (i.e., discussion of traditional philosophical issues) that arises from, explicitly refers to, and attempts to account for the experience of women. This need not exclude the possibility that such philosophical work might arise from, explicitly refer to, and attempt to account for the experience of men as well, but women's philosophy seems to entail a healthy scepticism about easy universalizations. This is part of what makes it women's philosophy, a realization that reality is more complex and more diverse than traditional philosophy often seems to recognize. More deeply, however, women's philosophy, as a reflection of women's experience, must always be aware of the power hidden in universalization, the power to say who and what other people are, and the power to ignore their self-definitions and their own experience of themselves and the world.[1]

As this definition makes clear, men's philosophy will be, and is, philosophy that arises from, explicitly refers to, and attempts to account for the experience of men. Sometimes, perhaps often, men's philosophy does describe a more general human experience. Thus, there is nothing wrong with men's philosophy *per se,* but only with men's philosophy that considers itself to be the only philosophy, the philosophy of humanity as a whole, when it is not. The first and most basic claim that I would like to make here is that virtually all the philosophy done in the past has been men's philosophy in the above sense.[2] At the same time, however, I am not suggesting that the differences between men's and women's experience referred to here are biological, "natural," transhistorical, or inevitable. On the contrary, my claim will be that the differences between men's and women's lives and experiences under modern industrial capitalism are themselves artifacts of a certain social, economic, political, religious, and philosophical configuration that is unique to a particular period of time in specific areas of the world. Therefore, my analysis, like its object, will necessarily be historically and culturally specific.

It is for this reason that I have chosen to focus my inquiries on the history of Anglo-American philosophy—it is the tradition in which I was primarily trained, and the one in which I live. I have further chosen to focus primarily on the work of John Locke and David Hume as philosophers whose historical importance and continuing influence on Anglo-American thought are clear to all. Historically, they played a central role in establishing the basic methods that define British Empiricism, and also in establishing the limitations of those methods— the failure of British Empiricism to solve the problems it sets for itself in the terms that it allows itself to use. One focus of this investigation will be the relationship between that failure and the fact that Empiricism is an especially powerful (quite literally) form of men's philosophy. Since analytic philosophy in the twentieth century continues to claim the methods of the Empiricists, and to make virtues of their failures—as A. J. Ayer does in *Language, Truth and Logic* by arguing that Locke, Hume, et al., rejected metaphysics in favor of analysis and psychology, rightly refusing to answer many traditional philosophical questions in traditional terms—the discussion that follows will, in general, apply to much of contemporary Anglo-American philosophy as well.[3] Thus, I hope indirectly to show how contemporary analytic philosophy, by remaining within the Empiricist tradition, inherits not only the problems of that tradition, but also a self-definition that identifies it as necessarily men's philosophy.

What is wrong with men's philosophy? Since most philosophers are men, it is certainly not surprising that philosophy should arise from, make explicit reference to, and try to account for men's experience. The problem is not merely that British Empiricism innocently offered itself as human philosophy, as arising from, making explicit reference to, and accounting for all of human experience, while at the same time generally ignoring, or remaining ignorant of, the experience of women (and of large numbers of men as well). Rather, and this is what makes it men's philosophy rather than middle-class white men's philosophy, this philosophy defines itself throughout its history in such a way as to exclude what our culture defines as women's experience from what is considered to be properly philosophical. Thus, my second claim would be that there is no women's philosophy, in the above sense, within the Empiricist tradition because philosophy in that tradition has been defined in a way that makes women's philosophy logically impossible.

To see the outlines of this definitional exclusion, one need only look at the political and moral Individualism so central to the Empiricist tradition. The historical roots of this Individualism in the political philosophy of Thomas Hobbes do not actually define the unit of analysis as the individual, but rather the head of a household. Note the equivocation on the generic "man" in this quotation from *Leviathan:*

> So that in the nature of man we find three principal causes of quarrel: first, competition; secondly, diffidence; thirdly, glory.
>
> The first makes men invade for gain, the second for safety, and the third for reputation. The first use violence to make themselves masters of other men's persons, wives, children, and cattle.[4]

Given this use of "man," it is important to remember that traditionally women may often have been single parents, but they were never heads of households, a role usually assumed by the nearest male relative, or more recently by the welfare state. Thus, women could never be "men," that is, individuals or persons, as that term appears in Hobbes. Persons, as Naomi Scheman has pointed out, have wives; women do not.[5]

This form of Individualism does not explicitly deny that women are persons or individuals as classically defined, or offer arguments for such a position. Rather, women are not treated or perceived as persons because the definition of personhood is put entirely in terms of the male experience as the head of a family, and so is not a question of women at all. That is, women are not perceived as persons or classical individuals just *because* an individual is defined in a way that is outside of women's experience or, more accurately, outside men's experience of women. Generally, such Individualism only describes the situation of a subset of men in a society (most often property-owners) and thus limits philosophy to the concerns of that class of men. Women are not excluded for lacking some essential qualification that they can then later be proven to possess, as might be the case with excluded groups of men, but are excluded by definition because they do not conform to any of the male-defined norms of personhood. Ultimately, men's philosophy can consider itself the philosophy of all humanity because its own definition of the human denies full personhood to women.

Men's philosophy traditionally accomplishes this denial of women's personhood, in part at least, by defining philosophical problems in terms that reflect a primarily male sense of self, that is, in the early Modern period through an overemphasis on the metaphysical, epistemological, and moral Individualism just noted; by using a metaphysical system that relies excessively on hierarchical dualisms (all of which are isomorphic with the male/female dichotomy) as the basic conceptual categories; and by putting the burden of proof on women to show that this system yields only a partial picture of human reality, while denying us the tools to do so (even when the male-oriented educational system makes those tools available to women) because the tools themselves are defined in the same male-oriented terms. The Empiricist tradition then represents any feminist argument as a question of induction at infinity, requiring that we establish our unjust exclusion from the philosophical in an infinite number of specific cases, rather than acknowledging philosophy to be a structural unity in which that exclusion is inscribed as a logical necessity. This atomism that is basic to the Empiricist tradition, and the political and moral Individualism that are correlated with it, therefore, go beyond a mere methodology that excludes women's experience from philosophy, and become part of a strategy to protect that philosophy from any feminist criticism.

Therefore, my final claim here will be that in order to create women's philosophy it will be necessary for those of us who work within the Anglo-American tradition (at least) to rethink the philosophical from the beginning, to rethink the questions that philosophy asks, and to rethink what counts as an answer to these questions. I will not, however, pretend to do that rethinking myself. Instead, I hope to make a contribution to the preliminary ground clearing now being done by many feminists by showing the systematic nature of the problem and the ways in which it leads to the failure of philosophy in the Empiricist tradition to answer basic philosophical questions adequately, even in its own terms. At the same time, I will attempt to correlate these feminist criticisms with similar criticisms found in twentieth-century Continental philosophy.

Before fully developing my argument, however, it will be necessary to outline the basic assumptions on which it is based. As I have already suggested, my first set of assumptions is borrowed from the work being done by many other feminist philosophers. The second set of assumptions is derived from what may seem to be an entirely different philosophical enterprise, which I will call, for want of a better name, deconstruction, primarily as found in the work of Jacques Derrida. The third set of assumptions I will draw on can be vaguely described as "historical," as the term is applied in the history of philosophy, but also as it is used in a loosely Hegelian concept of the philosophy of history. The rest of this introduction, therefore, will be devoted to brief explanations of each of these three sets of assumptions, after which it will be possible to begin to develop a reading of key texts by Locke and Hume that relies on insights derived from all three of these philosophical "methods."

Feminist Philosophy as Critique

In thinking about a project entitled "Is Women's Philosophy Possible?" an obvious objection arises. As Immanuel Kant says of mathematics, how can one question the possibility of something when it actually exists? The existence of a considerable body of feminist philosophy and of philosophical works written by women certainly cannot be denied. My next step, therefore, will be to address Kant's companion question of *how* feminist philosophy is possible by suggesting that it is possible, and hence actual, at least in large part as a critique of one specific theme in the Anglo-American philosophical tradition. Since many of the earliest feminist criticisms of the Empiricist tradition came from the field of political philosophy, the "Individualism" noted above (or, in Alison Jaggar's more telling terms, "abstract individualism") is the basis for a wide variety of criticisms that provide the grounding for my own analysis. However, the recurring critique of Individualism in feminist texts is often hidden to some extent because it is addressed to a configuration of deeply interrelated problems that may not seem, on the surface, to be related at all. While I intend to deal more fully with this body of literature later, here I would like to draw on two of the most recent feminist critiques of philosophy in the Anglo-American tradition to give a preliminary outline of the constellation of problems/concepts that are the basic assumptions of the feminist methodology (if there is such a thing) of my own investigations. At the same time, it should become clearer how this "method" developed specifically as a critique of the British Empiricist roots of contemporary Anglo-American philosophy.

In *Feminist Politics and Human Nature,* Jaggar defines, compares, and criticizes four "schools" of (Anglo-American) feminist political thought—liberal, Marxist, radical, and socialist—and correlates each with a specific doctrine about what constitutes human personhood.[6] In the cases of liberal and Marxist feminisms (and to some extent socialist feminism as well, which Jaggar believes to be the most viable basis for feminist politics), these theories of human nature developed from the traditional political theories of the same kind. Thus, liberal feminism is based on the assumptions of liberalism in general, and therefore on the political philosophy of the British Empiricists, so that both are also tied to an Empiricist epistemology and metaphysics. One of the basic problems that Jaggar finds with this position is precisely its belief in "abstract individualism," that is, the belief that

> Logically if not empirically, human individuals could exist outside a social context; their essential characteristics, their needs and interests, their capacities and desires, are given independently of their social context and are not created or even fundamentally altered by that context. (p. 29)

What this Individualism is abstracted from, on her account, is the concrete social and biological realities that make strict equality of opportunity problematic for those with special needs, due to problems such as a physical limitation or the possibility of pregnancy. This abstraction thus undermines the fairness of a social system, even where social problems such as overt racism or sexism have been eliminated.

This is not an issue for feminism, however, simply because of sexism. Rather, Jaggar emphasizes, this abstract individualism itself incorporates a male bias. The focus on the individual as the basic unit of social analysis may accurately reflect the experience of adult, white, middle-class males, who are in a position to consider themselves self-motivated, self-defined, and "self-made" within the norms of our culture, but it is immediately problematic for those who experience their socially defined "essential characteristics," needs, interests, capacities, and desires both as alienated from their own self-understanding *and* as absolutely inescapable facts about themselves as social beings in our society. Not all women can or care to be mothers, for instance, but all are affected by work place rules intended to protect pregnant women from exposure to toxic agents. For the victims of stereotyping, the concept of abstract individualism can cause more problems (both practical and philosophical) than it solves. Thus, abstract individualism reflects a specifically (European) male experience of the world.

What becomes much clearer in Locke, however, is the foundation of this political Individualism in a metaphysical and epistemological Individualism that is basic to the Empiricist enterprise. Sandra Harding's *The Science Question in Feminism* approaches this issue in epistemology and the philosophy of science, finding three feminist responses to the "science question."[7] First there is what she calls feminist empiricism (very similar to Jaggar's liberal feminism), which asks whether male-dominated science in our culture succeeds by its own standards of objectivity. This question, in turn, raises the issue of whether "feminist" science has any advantage over the traditional kind, and then to what Harding calls "feminist standpoint" theories, which have their roots in Marxist and socialist feminist thought. These state that the status of women as oppressed people gives them greater objectivity than can be found in the science of more privileged groups. In looking at the parallel claims of an "African standpoint" epistemology, however, Harding sees that women and Africans describe themselves in very similar ways, especially in contrast to European males, suggesting a common source in their oppressed status. This leads to a plea for diversity and even a degree of incoherence in feminist theory, and to the suggestion that "post-modernism" (i.e., Continental philosophy) might provide the best model for a "successor science."

Harding's argument is that one way Empiricism rules women out of philosophy is by ruling them out of science, which is the standard of rationality for Empiricism and for all of Anglo-American philosophy.

> Science affirms the unique contributions to culture to be made by transhistorical egos that reflect a reality only of abstract entities; by the administrative mode of interacting with nature and other inquirers; by impersonal and universal forms of communication; and by an ethic of elaborating rules for absolute adjudications of competing rights between socially autonomous—that is, value-free—pieces of evidence. These are exactly the social characteristics necessary to become gendered as a man in our society. (p. 238)

At the same time, they are also the characteristics of moral personhood that are assumed in our political system, so that Jaggar and Harding's analyses converge on a common problem that is not fully within the scope of either book.[8] It is that problem, which lies in the metaphysical roots of the political and epistemological Individualism they explore, that I hope to clarify and situate by a careful and detailed look at the historical roots of current Anglo-American empiricism.

One way in which feminists—and others—have undertaken the kind of metaphysical critique I am developing here is by focusing on an underlying schema of European metaphysics, one that is, as noted above, both dualistic and hierarchical. Behind the subject vs. object of scientific investigation and the individual vs. society of political thought lies a mind that also sees the world in terms of man/woman, culture/nature, rational/irrational, mind/body, public/private, and so on. Not only are metaphysical categories dualistic in this way, but each pair is hierarchically arranged, with the first term valued and the second de-valued. Within each pair, the de-valued concept is always defined differentially, for example, my body is what is not my mind, nature is what is not culture, etc. Usually no attempt is made to provide a positive definition of the de-valued side in its own terms, so that it serves as a place-holder for whatever is not attributed to the self. (Compare the predicates that refer to "mind" for René Descartes with the analogous list in Gilbert Ryle, for instance.) Of course, the valued half of each pair is correlated with the male, the de-valued with the female.

Beyond the evaluation these hierarchical dualisms import into any discussion, they are also used within philosophy to limit discourse to what can be captured in terms of such dualisms. This means that philosophical discourse is limited *a priori* to the experience of those who have defined these dualistic categories and whose lives they reflect, that is, it is limited to the realm of male experience. As Catherine MacKinnon puts it in "Feminism, Marxism, Method, and the State,"

> Feminism does not see its view as subjective, partial, or undetermined but as a critique of the purported generality, disinterestedness, and universality of prior accounts. These have not been half right but have invoked the wrong whole. . . .
> . . . men *create* the world from their own point of view, which then *becomes* the reality to be described.[9]

Moreover, what cannot be captured in terms of these dualisms (e.g., the relationship between a pregnant woman and the fetus she carries, which violates all rules of inner/outer, self/other, etc.[10]) is not part of what philosophy, which thinks only in terms of these dichotomies, is prepared to discuss. This then puts into question the very possibility of something that might be called "women's philosophy."

Therefore, what I hope to have suggested by evoking Jaggar and Harding here is that the problem may be more serious than a superficial reading of their work might suggest. This is because the same problems they find in abstract individualism and traditional empiricism may also lie at the root of the internal limitations of British Empiricism as a philosophical system. That is, women's philosophy might be impossible within the Anglo-American tradition for exactly the same reasons that philosophy itself eventually comes to be seen as impossible. This is where this analysis converges with those made by such internal critics of the Anglo-American tradition as Ludwig Wittgenstein and J. L. Austin.

More importantly for our present purposes, this is also where the feminist critique converges with the critiques of Empiricism that have been made in the Continental tradition. Deconstruction itself, interestingly, has seldom been applied in a systematic way to the Empiricist tradition, possibly because the classical rationalist and Kantian criticisms of it were taken as conclusive, perhaps because Empiricism was regarded as both naïve and politically conservative in the intellectual circles in which deconstruction arose, for reasons I will try to make clearer later.[11] Before undertaking deconstructive "reading" of the Empiricists, therefore, I will need to clarify the second set of assumptions that will be guiding my investigations.

Deconstruction as a Method

> It is no longer possible to go looking for woman, or for the femininity of woman, or for feminine sexuality. At least, they cannot be found by any

familiar mode of thought, or knowledge—even if one cannot stop looking for them.—Jacques Derrida ("The Question of Style," p. 182)

It is common in deconstructive readings of texts to begin with an often seemingly irrelevant quotation. I have compromised here by providing a seemingly relevant one. When I describe myself as a feminist and as someone who does deconstruction, I meet with one of two responses. The first is, "But deconstructionists are such sexists," usually meaning in their manner and/or personal lives. For those who would respond to the juxtaposition of feminism and deconstruction in this way, the above quotation is intended to at least open the question of what might count as sexism outside of anything that might offer itself as a "master" text. If deconstruction not only notes, but even underscores, the extent to which women lie outside of the philosophical realm, that might carry more weight than the admittedly sexist innuendo in the last clause of the quotation. On the other hand, it might not. The second response I encounter asks "Do you do mostly deconstruction or mostly feminism?" To these people the above quotation might suggest why my most frequent answer is to say, "Are they two different things?" Most American readers, however, would think I owe a more detailed account of the relationship between feminism and deconstruction than that.

One common way of misunderstanding deconstruction is not to distinguish it clearly enough from classical textual analysis. The key point here is that deconstruction not only takes a text apart (the linguistic core it shares with "analysis"), but takes it apart in a way that is based on its prior construction, that is, by deconstructing the "cornerstones" on which it has been built and that make its construction possible. Interestingly, in the last few years, more and more deconstructive readings have discovered that one of the major cornerstones that can be found in virtually every text, especially "master" texts, is a mystification of the problem of gender. Thus, a deconstructive reading of a text will also always already be a feminist reading, or open the way for a feminist reading, of that text.

This is perhaps clearest in the work of Jacques Derrida, and may reach its most complete form in the work of the French feminists who have been influenced by Derrida and the psychoanalyst Jacques Lacan. Therefore, I will begin my account of deconstruction as a "method" (a problematic term here as it is for feminism) with another quote from Derrida's *Memoires* (in which "deconstruction" is also problematic).

Deconstruction as Method

> The best spot for efficiently inserting the deconstructive lever is a cornerstone. There may be other analogous places but this one derives its privilege from the fact that it is indispensable to the completeness of the edifice. A condition of erection, holding up the walls of an established edifice, it also can be said to maintain it, to contain it, and to be tantamount to the *generality* of the architectonic system, "of the entire system."[12]

This quotation brings out two points that are of special importance here. The first is a partial answer to the objection many feminists raise to the possibility that deconstruction might be applied to recent texts (usually literary) by feminist and/or minority writers.[13] This may be an important issue in American literary theory, but deconstruction, as it has been done by Derrida and other philosophers, is almost invariably addressed either to "master texts," cornerstones of the system, or to "near misses," that is, texts that are themselves deconstructive but (necessarily) incompletely so. (Derrida often deconstructs "Derrida.") The second point I would like to mention is Derrida's belief that, once one has deconstructed the cornerstone argument of a text, it is unnecessary to repeat the operation for each stone, since the cornerstone reproduces the system of the entire structure. (This reliance on a prior concept of structure is part of what marks deconstruction as "post-structuralist" thought.) Thus, deconstruction gives us the ability to deconstruct traditional texts, including philosophical texts, as a whole, rather than piecemeal, as Empiricism requires.

To make this "method" clearer, I will offer three examples of how it is used in reading master texts. The first is embodied in the concept of "differ*a*nce." The French verb *différer* means both to differ and to defer, so this neologism refers to the fact that structures such as language, according to Ferdinand de Saussure, (a) establish meaning, not in the elements of the structure itself, but by the *difference* between elements (i.e., between the sounds or signs in a language), and (b) infinitely *defer* the final referent of the linguistic act, since one can never actually include non-linguistic elements (i.e., "real" things) in the linguistic system.[14] Both aspects of differance are captured in Sigmund Freud's account of what is necessary for an infant to become even minimally socialized: (a) it must learn that it is distinct and different from the other things around it, especially its mother, and (b) it must learn to delay gratification and eventually to substitute socially acceptable pleasures for its original desires, which are therefore permanently deferred because they are excluded from the (conscious) system.[15] For deconstruction, differance is the organizing principle for all systems, although they constantly deny it.[16]

A second deconstructive "technique," or clue to where the cornerstone of a text might be located, is found in another concept borrowed from Freud, that of "cauldron dream logic." Freud reports a dream of having a borrowed cauldron returned with holes in it by a borrower who claims: (a) "The holes were in the cauldron when you loaned it to me"; (b) "There are no holes in the cauldron"; and (c) "I never borrowed your cauldron."[17] Freud sees in this "logic" a basic structure of psychoanalytic denial, although deconstructions of his own work illustrate its use as well as any.[18] Feminists might use this logic in reading the Biblical account of Adam and Eve, which seems to assert: (a) that women are external "add ons" to men, who have no real need for them (Adam had no mother); (b) that women are dangerous to men, and so must somehow also be internal to the male economy; and (c) that women are helpmates for men, and so are not so bad after all. Such a reading might suggest that this story, as it appears in the current canon at least, covers over some basic reality about women and their relationship to men that its "authors" (who are no more historical, anonymous, or numerous than the "author" of a psychological denial) are so deeply anxious about that they contradict themselves in trying to hide it.

A third way in which deconstruction approaches the reading of a text is by looking for what is called a privileged example.[19] This is an example that is presented as one among many, but which implicitly introduces evaluative standards into the analysis. The most famous case of this common feature of philosophical discourse is Plato's use of mathematics, first as an example of knowledge, and then as the standard with which all other forms of knowledge must agree, so that in the end the objects of all knowledge must have the same metaphysical status as numbers. The most obvious case in feminism is the way that male norms or experiences are offered as examples of human behavior, but also function as standards that exclude those with different experiences from the realm of the human. Why, for instance, is hormonal constancy considered the "normal" way for humans to be, while female hormonal fluctuations are perceived as a problem? This approach to the question, coupled with an awareness of cauldron logic, might lead us to ask why, if female hormonal changes are "abnormal," post-menopausal women aren't regarded as "normal" again. Recognizing that they are in fact considered doubly "abnormal," one might begin to think that women can never be "normal" by the standards of our culture.

All three of these examples of how one might approach the deconstructive reading of a text converge immediately on the most prevalent shared assumption of the two "methodologies" that I will be using: What the denial of differance, cauldron logic, and privileged examples do is to establish, disguise, and provide arguments that pretend to support exactly the kind of hierarchical dualisms referred to in the last section.[20] Differance accentuates, and "master" texts try to hide, the fact that both sides of any hierarchical dualism stand in a reciprocal relationship of difference and deferral, so neither side can be taken as a "reality" independent of the other. (The interdependence between the sides of these oppositions and how they can change their value over time can be seen by comparing the significance of the pair aristocrat/bourgeois in Molière and Jean Jacques Rousseau.) Cauldron logic provides a "cover-up" of the fact of differance, and privileged examples further disguise it while seeming to provide a logical reason for judging the male, rational, objective, and so on, to be superior to their opposites, without really having to do so, or even purporting to make such an argument. What deconstruction adds to feminism then, at a minimum, is a vocabulary and "techniques" for reading texts that can help us find the male bias built so deeply into our culture. (What it might add at a maximum will be the topic for a later discussion.)

This is not to say important criticisms of Derrida's work cannot be made from a feminist perspective. Two major groups of such criticisms were well represented by a panel at the National Women's Studies Association meeting held in June, 1988.[21] The first such group might loosely be called the "Marxist/critical theory" group, represented on the panel by Judith Grant, who offered three basic points against postmodernism. First, it can be seen as insufficiently subjective and too impersonal and alienating, subordinating the agent to historical or linguistic forces over which she can have little or no control and thus undermining the possibility of meaningful political action. On the other hand, work such as Derrida's can also easily be seen as *too* subjective, as idealistic and purely intellectual, a theoretical fiction bordering on the romantic. In either case, such a position is problematic for feminism because it leads to ambiguity and arbitrary analyses, leaving us no foundation from which we can criticize domination or even identify relevant cases of what domination *is*. A second, more strictly feminist group of criticisms was presented by Joan Tronto. From this perspective, deconstruction universalizes and rejects traditional theory too quickly (e.g., argues against a nonexistent, unified concept of Reason in the Enlightenment), while at the same time being too closely tied to a Eurocentric concept of language and the linguistic. Thus, it does both too much and too little for a practical feminist criticism, leaving us in a relatively weak argumentative position *vis à vis* our more traditional intellectual adversaries, and depriving us of the authority we need to do our work because of its inherently anti-authoritarian basis.

Clearly, there is a large overlap of concern between these two criticisms, but each seems somewhat distinct as well. What may be more interesting is their structural overlap, that is, the fact that they both attribute contradictory attributes to a deconstructive method such as Derrida's: it is too subjective and not subjective enough; it does too much and too little; it destroys old foundations and old authorities but leaves none for our own use. That is why I have been trying to emphasize Derrida's work as a tool, not a theory. As a theory, it will inevitably end in paradox, because it is always involved in swallowing its own tail, destroying its own metaphysical attachments, being now too much one way and now too much another. As a tool, however, it can be adapted to our needs as feminists, becoming more sweeping and perhaps even universalizing when we wish to criticize the broad outlines of the patriarchal tradition, becoming more narrow and perhaps even ethnocentric when we confront a particular piece of language that has been turned into a transcendental "Truth" of male philosophy. The alternatives suggested by Grant and Tronto, that we turn to Marxism or to critical theory for our conceptual tools, or that we insist as feminists on making our own, are as valid claims as any I would wish to make for deconstruction, but they are claims and tools that may be better suited to other theorists and to other theoretical realms. Derrida, unlike the other structuralists and post-structuralists I will discuss, and unlike the critical theorists or most feminists, is a philosopher, and it is as a philosopher that I find his method both most accurate and most useful as a feminist tool.

One advantage of this particular tool in the present context is that it allows me to look beyond the content of a philosopher's texts to the way in which that content is presented, to the philosopher's rhetoric, if you will. This will become most apparent in my reading of Hume, partially because it is there that his male bias is often most apparent (in what he takes to be natural or even "dead" metaphors, for instance) and partially because he is a very literary writer, relying much more on his own rhetoric to make part of his point for him than is the case, most notably, in Locke. What deconstruction makes clear here is that metaphors are never "innocent," but rather always carry part of the meaning of the text in which they appear, and gender metaphors perhaps more so than others—especially the "dead" ones. The one I just used, for example: if metaphors can be "innocent," they must be female (only Rousseau speaks of male innocence), and since they are not really innocent, they must be "guilty" women, and one would do well to avoid them. This implies, in turn, that guilt, metaphors, and women are something that one *could* avoid, if one wished.

One final benefit of a deconstructive approach for this investigation is that it has allowed me to make what I consider to be a vital distinction between the history of philosophy and the ideology based on that history. I am not an historian of philosophy, nor am I an expert on the British Empiricists—my object of concern is not the "real" meaning of the Lockean or Humean text in their own terms, although I firmly believe that such investigations form a significant part, perhaps the most significant part, of the philosophical enterprise. My own concern, rather, is with the role that "Locke" and "Hume," as they are traditionally interpreted, have played and continue to play in Anglo-American philosophy and in the gender ideology of our culture. (One might wish to make a similar distinction between the Christian Bible and Christian doctrine, or between Plato and Platonism.) At the same time, I do not feel myself compelled to argue either for the primacy and importance of Locke and Hume's work within the Empiricist tradition, or for a strong continuity either within that tradition (including Hobbes) or between that tradition and contemporary Anglo-American philosophy, since it is contemporary Anglo-American philosophers such as Ayer who themselves assign those values and trace those lines of filiation.

Therefore, I consider myself subject to correction on strictly historical grounds, but not simply on the basis that I am not being fair to what Locke or Hume "really meant." Deconstruction questions the concept of "author-ity" (the author's "ownership" of the work) in many ways, as well as the relationship between an author's intention and what is actually read in the text (a concern many feminists share). One could look at Shakespeare's need to have his women played by men as something beyond his power and incidental to his plays, for instance, but one could also look at the effect it has on his characterizations of women, as well as on the gender confusion on which so many of the plots of his comedies rest. Generally, I will try to tread a thin line between ignoring the historical context of a philosopher's thought completely and undertaking what would count as a serious historical study. Instead of offering a detailed justification of this approach, however, I will simply stipulate that one can read quotes around the names of Locke and Hume in almost every instance of their use here, a few biographical references aside. It is exactly the difference, the differance, between Hume and "Hume" that makes the realm of ideology.

Some Historical Assumptions

One further set of more-or-less historical assumptions must be discussed before I move to the full body of my argument. These assumptions have grown up more slowly over the course of my philosophical education, and so are more difficult both to attribute to specific sources and to justify as fully as I might like. They are, however, essential to my enterprise here, and I obviously believe that they are defensible, if not conclusively proven, or I would not rely on them. In many ways they are similar to, or compatible with, the historical assumptions that underline Susan Bordo's rereading of Descartes's *Meditations, The Flight to Objectivity*.[22] Bordo, however, takes a backwards-looking perspective—how modern philosophy is related to "the waning of the Middle Ages"—while I adopt more of a forward-looking perspecitve—how modern philosophy is related to contemporary Anglo-American feminist thought. Thus, Bordo sees the exclusion of "the feminine" from modern philosophy primarily as a reaction to the new scientific world view of the early Modern period, although she also discusses the way in which that reaction became an active defense, while I emphasize the active side of the exclusion and largely ignore its reactive aspects.

One way to understand the general structure of my own historical assumptions is to look carefully at the metaphysical atomism that is basic to British Empiricism. Once our knowledge of the world is seen as based entirely on perceptual experience, and perceptual experience has been reduced to simple, atomic givens, as it is in Empiricism, it would seem to become difficult, if not impossible, to recreate our experience of a unified pre-philosophical world.[23] This is not strictly a feminist thought. It is, rather, a criticism of Anglo-American philosophy that is shared by off-shoots of that tradition such as process philosophy, alien philosophical traditions such as those of Asia and Africa, and closely related traditions such as Continental philosophy, as well as feminist variants on all three. (It is important to understand that male bias is only part of what is wrong with British Empiricism, although I would also argue that male bias is closely related to much of what else is wrong with it.)

To see how Empiricist atomism undoes our pre-philisophical understanding of the world, consider the problem of material substance. If one assumes, on the one hand, that the perceived world is composed of atomic, unrelated realities but without an empiricist epistemology, there can still be unperceived relationships that exist as innate ideas or as analytic or *a priori* synthetic knowledge and that can account for our experience of material objects. Or, on the other hand, if all ideas come from sense experience, but that experience need not be atomistic and may include experience of relationships in the empirical world (certain "natural" categories, for instance), there is also no problem explaining our belief in material substance. With the powerful combination of the male bias toward seeing the world as composed of atomistic givens and a commitment to a "tabula rasa" epistemology, however, we can use neither of these expedients and have no way to develop a coherent concept of substance, or any substitute for one.

The problem with British Empiricism, then, is not just that it reflects male thinking, but that it reflects atomistic, empiricist male thinking.[24] It would be far beyond my powers here to further prove that empiricism itself reflects a male philosophical bias, but British Empiricism is correlated both historically and intellectually with four other developments in the seventeenth and eighteenth centuries that help to mark the beginning of the Modern era in Britain.[25] This specific configuration of historical factors, including philosophical Empiricism itself, strongly suggests a male bias in the conception of what constitutes a human person, and also helps in part to make the kind of distinction between Anglo-American and Continental philosophy that is necessary for my argument.[26]

One aspect of this configuration, the emergence of a limited democracy in the context of a limited monarchy, is a political development that can literally be traced in the philosophy of the same men who are the founders of the Empiricist movement (Hobbes being a transitional figure in both cases). Therefore, it reflects, but also reinforces, the male bias of "abstract individualism" in the political realm that Jaggar discusses in her analysis of liberal feminism in *Feminist Politics and Human Nature,* as well as the focus on the (male) head of household noted above. The history, and male bias, of a second development in this period, the "rise of modern science," (specifically Baconian empiricism, as opposed to Cartesian mathmatical rationalism), is thoroughly discussed in Harding's *The Science Question in Feminism,* as well as in Evelyn Fox Keller's *Reflections on Gender and Science,* and many other works in feminist philosophy of science.[27] A third factor is modern industrial capitalism, the limits and biases of which are the topic of many discussions in both feminist and non-feminist socialist and Marxist literature, of which Jaggar's book and Zillah Eisenstein's *The Radical Future of Liberal Feminism* provide excellent examples.[28] The least discussed, perhaps, is the unique Protestantism of the Anglican church with its quasi-Catholic doctrine and its Calvinist subconscious.[29]

These five factors—Empiricism, limited democracy, Baconian/Newtonian science, capitalism, and Anglicanism—form a system capable of generating a specifically British ideology that was in many ways more powerful and more coherent than its Continental rivals—also capitalist and scientific, but statist, rationalist, and Catholic/Lutheran—and that was also more inclusive (in potential, at least) of powerless groups of men, and more exclusive (in theory, I would claim, if not necessarily in fact) of women. This unified ideological configuration parallels the relative cultural and political unity of Britain in this period and lacks, to take just a few examples, the precarious balance of Catholic faith and scientific rationality embodied in Cartesian thought (and underscored by Blaise Pascal's early form of Christian existentialism), the conflict between statist politics and individualistic morality found in Kant, and the paradoxes of absolute democracy and collective will that undermine Rousseau's texts.[30]

The element that unites the five elements of British, or Anglo-American modernity is the kind of person they postulate as the agent of the activity they address. That is, they share a common, coherent, heavily male-biased conception of human nature. Moreover, this uniquely modern and Anglo-American concept of human nature can be easily summarized and is familiar to us all. The ideal philosopher, citizen, voter, scientist, businessman, or Christian is objective, rational, independent, sceptical of authority, unswayed by emotion or sentimental morality, concerned with the concrete and the "bottom line." These are all virtues, of course, except perhaps to a King or Pope, but even within the British context, one must ask, virtues for whom? For women, these are in fact not virtues, but vices or synonyms of vices: cold, calculating, hard, rebellious, unfeeling, materialistic—in a word, unfeminine. Therefore it seems that the ideal philosopher, citizen, voter, scientist, businessman, Christian within the

British tradition has always already been defined as a man: the man who is both created and described by the ideology built on these five "cornerstones," the man whose understanding is, for Locke and Hume, generically human.

A General Outline

All of this remains rather schematic, of course. Full development of the argument will be done in five stages. In Part One, I will first discuss Locke and Hume in some detail in order both to illustrate men's philosophy more fully and to establish my claim that philosophy is defined in these two bodies of texts in such a way as to make women's philosophy impossible. The section on Locke is somewhat briefer because his work seems to lack the complexity of Hume's, and his political thought is so well known that one can merely allude to key portions of it and avoid detailed explanations of basic points. It is necessary to look at Hume at greater length, not only because some areas of his thought are less well known and arguably more complex, but also because he questions some of the central tenets of the tradition that Locke represents. I especially intend to look at the nature and extent of Hume's "deviance" and its implications, if any, for the possibility of women's philosophy within the tradition of which he is a part. At that point, I will begin a double task: to offer a detailed critique of men's philosophy as exemplified in Locke and Hume, and to place my own thought in the context of an extensive body of feminist writings that address the same or similar points. I will attempt to demonstrate not only the feelings of traditional Anglo-American philosophy but also the validity of a feminist critique as an explanation of these failures. In so doing, I will also indicate paths within the tradition, in addition to Hume's, which might provide a basis within Empiricist thought itself, at its most radical, for a feminist critique, and ways in which these avenues have in fact been used by feminist philosophers in their work.

In Part Two, I will turn to the Continental philosophical tradition as a source of insights and analytical tools that might also be useful in a feminist re-thinking of philosophy. First I will focus on the hermeneutical approach of Martin Heidegger and the more traditional phenomenology of Maurice Merleau-Ponty, not only because of the centrality of their thought to contemporary European philosophy, but also because of the connections between their work and the deconstruction and feminist analyses being done within post-structuralist thought. I will also consider in some detail Jean Paul Sartre's existentialism and the related, but quite unique, feminism of Simone de Beauvoir's *The Second Sex*. In all four cases, I will be looking for the roots of the more recent developments in French thought that will be the focus of the next two chapters. There I will begin with structuralism and semiotics, seen primarily through the work of Roland Barthes, after which I will return to post-structuralism in general and deconstruction in particular to explain more fully some of the themes common to the work of Lacan, Michel Foucault, and Derrida, especially the decentering of the Self and the "end of metaphysics."

The final stage will be to consider what I will call "French feminism," although some of the women whose work I will discuss—Luce Irigaray, Hélène Cixous, Julia Kristeva, and Monique Wittig—would explicitly reject the label of "feminist" for themselves. This rejection, as well as several other difficulties in interpreting "French feminism" to an American audience, will be discussed, as will the relationships between the different views these women represent, and between their work and that of the male post-structuralist thinkers discussed in the previous chapter. My conclusion will then offer some examples of how Anglo-American feminists might draw resources from the various aspects of the Continental tradition in preparing ourselves to do women's philosophy and, perhaps more importantly, how we might avoid simply doing more men's philosophy under another name.

Notes

1. See, for instance, the interesting discussion in Maria C. Lugones and Elizabeth V. Spelman, "Have We Got a Theory for You," *Women's Studies International Forum* 6, no. 6 (1983): 573–81, and the comments on this topic throughout Bell Hooks's *Feminist Theory: From Margin to Center* (Boston: South End Press, 1984).

2. This is not meant to deny, by the way, that many women have done much good philosophy over the history of the discipline. Mary Ellen Waithe, however, in her Introduction to the series she edited, *A History of Women Philosophers,* vol. 1 (Dordrecht, The Netherlands: Martinus Nijhoff, 1987), says that the philosophy women have done throughout the centuries tends, by and large, to be very much the same as the philosophy being done by men at the same time, although some did apply philosophical insights to issues of special interest to women. Her explanation for this fact is much like my own: not only were men and women trained in the same way, but anything that

exceeded the realm designated by that training as "philosophical," that is, anything that referred too directly to women's experience except as an application of "gender-neutral" basic principles, would not be considered philosophy and so had not come down to us as such, and probably has not come down to us at all. (See especially p. xii of Waithe's Introduction.)

3. A. J. Ayer, *Language, Truth, and Logic* (New York: Dover, 1952), pp. 52–55.

4. Thomas Hobbes, *Leviathan,* Parts I and II, ed. Herbert W. Schneider (New York: Bobbs-Merrill, 1958), p. 106. This apt quotation is cited in Helen E. Longino's "Rethinking Philosophy," in *Women's Place in the Academy,* ed. Marilyn R. Schuster and Susan R. Van Dyne (Totowa, N.J.: Rowman and Allanheld, 1985), p. 191.

5. In a talk delivered at the University of Minnesota, November, 1983.

6. Allison Jagger, *Feminist Politics and Human Nature* (Totowa, N.J.: Rowman and Allanheld, 1983).

7. Sandra Harding, *The Science Question in Feminism* (Ithaca, N.Y.: Cornell University Press, 1986).

8. Both Jaggar and Harding are well aware of this connection. See, for instance, Jaggar's *Feminist Politics and Human Nature,* pp. 356–58, and Harding's "The Social Function of the Empiricist Conception of Mind," *Metaphilosophy* 10, no. 1 (January 1979): 38–47.

9. Catherine MacKinnon, "Feminism, Marxism, Method, and the State," in *Feminist Theory,* ed. Nannerl O. Keohane, Michelle Z. Rosaldo, and Barbara C. Gelpi (Chicago: University of Chicago Press, 1982), p. 23.

10. This point is brought out in Iris Young's interesting paper "Pregnant Embodiment: Subjectivity and Alienation," *The Journal of Medicine and Philosophy* 9 (1984): 45–62; and the politics of it are made clear in Elizabeth Wolgast's "Wrong Rights," *Hypatia* 2, no. 1 (Winter 1987): 25–43.

11. In an unusual and very early book on Hume, *Empirisme et Subjectivité* (Paris: Presses Universitaires de France, 1953), Gilles Deleuze, now one of the more radical post-structuralist thinkers, makes the distinction between Empiricism and "Critical" (i.e., Continental) philosophy a matter of whether one starts with the Self and asks how experience must be ordered for such a Self to exist, or starts with atomic experiential givens and asks how one might construct a Self from such material. The second enterprise is, needless to say, doomed: "Hume doesn't create an atomistic psychology, he shows that atomism is a state of mind that doesn't allow a psychology" (pp. 9–10). Deleuze's argument, and especially his critique of Empiricist atomism, bears comparison with the one by Barry Stroud referred to below. (Thanks are due to Joelle Proust for bringing this book to my attention.)

12. Jacques Derrida, *Memoires,* trans. Cecile Lindsay, Jonathan Culler, and Eduardo Cavada (New York: Columbia University Press, 1986), p. 72.

13. For a fuller discussion of the relationship between American feminism, especially in literary theory, and deconstruction, see Alice Jardine's fascinat-

ing book *Gynesis* (Ithaca, N.Y.: Cornell University Press, 1985), especially chapter two.

14. Ferdinand de Saussure, *Course on General Linguistics,* trans. Wade Baskin (New York: Philosophical Library, 1959), pp. 117–18, 120. (Cited by Derrida in *Margins of Philosophy,* trans. Alan Bass (Chicago: University of Chicago Press, 1982), p. 11.)

15. Sigmund Freud, *Beyond the Pleasure Principle: The Standard Edition of the Complete Psychological Works of Sigmund Freud,* vol. 18, trans. and ed. James Strachey (London: The Hogarth Press, 1953). (Cited by Derrida in *Margins of Philosophy,* p. 19.)

16. This concept receives its fullest development in *"Differance"* in *Margins of Philosophy*.

17. See Derrida's "Plato's Pharmacy" in *Dissemination,* trans. Barbara Johnson (Chicago: University of Chicago Press, 1981), pp. 110–11.

18. In addition to Derrida's work in this area, there are several feminist versions of the argument, for instance, Sarah Kofman's *The Enigma of Women,* trans. Catherine Porter (Ithaca, N.Y.: Cornell University Press, 1985).

19. This concept is developed, among other places, in Derrida's *Speech and Phenomena,* trans. David B. Allison (Evanston, Ill.: Northwestern University Press, 1973).

20. One version of Derrida's argument on hierarchical oppositions can be found in his "Plato's Pharmacy" in *Dissemination*.

21. The panel was entitled "Post-modernism as a New Direction in Feminist Theory," and an able defense of feminist uses of "post-modernism" (primarily Foucault's concept of "geneology") was offered by Kathy Ferguson of the University of Hawaii.

With regard to both sets of criticisms discussed here, see also Nancy Fraser and Linda Nicholson's "Social Criticism Without Philosophy: An Encounter Between Feminism and Postmodernism," in *Universal Abandon? The Politics of Postmodernism,* ed. Andrew Ross (Minneapolis: University of Minnesota Press, 1988).

22. Susan R. Bordo, *The Flight to Objectivity* (Albany: State University of New York Press, 1987).

23. This basic problem in Anglo-American philosophy was pointed out to me many years ago by the late Philip Rhinelander of Stanford University and has been one of the organizing principles of my philosophical work since long before I realized that it was a women's issue.

24. Interestingly, Stroud, in his critical study *Hume* (London: Routledge and Kegan Paul, 1977), realizes both that atomism (p. 225) and Individualism (pp. 217–18) are central problems in Hume's philosophy (as does Hume himself) and that Kant's reliance on synthetic judgment, rather than atomistic perception, was responsible for the advances he was able to make on Hume's "problems" (p. 237), independently of any feminist concerns in the matter.

25. The relationship between philosophy, especially modern philosophy,

and the socio-historical ground on which it arose was just one of many important lessons in the history of philosophy that I learned from John Mothershead, also of Stanford University.

26. The following discussion has benefited greatly from conversations with Glenn Holland of Allegheny College. A similar discussion appears in Jagger's *Feminist Politics and Human Nature,* pp. 355–58.

27. Evelyn Fox Keller, *Reflections on Gender and Science* (New Haven, Conn.: Yale University Press, 1985).

28. Zillah Eisenstein, *The Radical Future of Liberal Feminism* (Boston: Northeastern University Press, 1981).

29. Zillah Eisenstein's chapter on Locke also includes excellent references that link Protestantism with both liberal political thought and the rise of capitalism (notably the vital work by Max Weber on "the Protestant work ethic").

30. Carole Pateman's work on Rousseau, both as an alternative to Locke ("Sublimation and Reification: Locke, Wolin, and the Liberal Democratic Conception of the Political," *Politics and Society* 4 (1975): 441–62) and in relationship to feminist thought ("The Disorder of Women," *Ethics* 91 (October 1980): 20–34) seems complementary to my own.

Part One

Chapter 1

Gender and the Generic in Locke[1]

The Limits of "Human" Understanding

Consider the following examples of predication from Locke's *Essay Concerning Human Understanding:*

> *A man is white* signifies that the thing that has the essence of a man has also in it the essence of whiteness . . ; or *A man is rational* signifies that the same thing, that hath the essence of a man, hath also in it the essence of rationality, i.e. a power of reasoning.[2]

What man is the subject here? In an essay that concerns itself with human understanding, who counts as human? Rationality serves as an absolute criterion of personhood for John Locke. Are we to assume the same about whiteness? Most likely not, for a sympathetic reading would find in Locke references to (native) Americans as examples in various arguments he makes about early man.[3] Still, a non-white reader of Locke might begin to wonder exactly what audience this text addresses.

A similar point could be made about women. Every anthology of negative philosophical comments about women includes its quota of passages from Locke. For example, there is the claim in the *Second Treatise* that the ultimate power to decide within a marriage must be placed somewhere and hence must be placed with the man "as the abler and the stronger" or, more subtly, there is his support for divorce in an age when such an arrangement could have only worked to make the lives of divorced women miserable while leaving their husbands free to start new families.[4] These specific statements about women seem less offensive, however, because they are embedded in a work

27

that is intended to undermine patriarchy (in its literal sense) and in many ways seems sympathetic to women's status as parents and to their rights as property owners, that is, to women's needs and experience insofar as they are the same as men's.[5]

More disturbing, however, is the background on which the specific claims are made, a background in which human seems by and large to mean male and in which human knowledge and moral discourse is couched in terms of male experience and male categories. That some accommodation for the obvious characteristics of women insofar as they are relevant to the male enterprise of maintaining a civil society can be made on this background is not surprising, nor should it blind us to the deeper implications here. Traditionally, philosophy has addressed the so-called generically human and, if pressed for a reason why women appear not at all in the *Essay* and only briefly in the *Second Treatise,* Locke would no doubt appeal to the universality of his claims about human reason as a defense. As a woman reader of Locke, however, the number of times that one is drawn up short in trying to read oneself as the subject of "human" understanding is illustrative of the extent to which Locke, like the philosophical tradition of which he is a part, fails to include the experience and understanding of at least half of humanity.

Locke's thought is basic to our own in many ways. The importance he has for our political philosophy is obvious, but in our epistemology and metaphysics as well he seems to hold a central place when we move, as we must, from the questioning of perceptual and religious belief in Descartes, through Locke's agnosticism about essence and substance, to George Berkeley's phenomenalism and Hume's radical empiricism, and from there to Anglo-American philosophy in its present form. The question of the gendered use of masculine pronouns in Locke, therefore can be seen as a question about the place of women not only in his text, but in the Anglo-American philosophy of the last few centuries as well.

In this chapter, I will look closely at Locke's *Essay* and *Second Treatise* in an attempt to gauge the extent to which his use of the word "man" and masculine pronouns must be seen to indicate a male subject of philosophy. Traditionally, the description of male experience as generically human is the opposite face of gender-specific language and other means of excluding women from certain central arenas of human life, both in theory and in practice. Women, and others, whose lives are limited on the basis of linguistic and social conventions that define the human as (European) male will not in fact have the kind of education and other experiences that are normative for humans so defined, thereby justifying the initial exclusion. The question here will be the degree to which Locke's philosophy is a repetition of, and a contribution to, this phenomenon within Western thought, and the effect that this limited view of human understanding and experience has on his general philosophical enterprise.

Locke's *Essay*

Locke's stated intention in writing the *Essay,* similar to the intention I stated above, is one of "clearing ground a little, and removing some of the rubbish that lies in the way to knowledge" (Vol. 1, p. xxxv). That rubbish seems to arise from two main sources, one stated and one more implicit. The stated source is Descartes, whose doctrines of innate ideas as a basis (and ultimately the only basis) for knowledge, and of clear and distinct ideas as the criterion of truth are directly and effectively attacked in the *Essay*. The other source, which he inherits as part of Hobbes's legacy, is Scholasticism. (This is not, of course, an entirely separate issue from the criticisms Locke makes of Descartes, but the relationship between Descartes and the Scholastic tradition falls far outside the scope of this discussion.) Locke's enterprise is not only negative, however, but also involves providing an alternative to the Cartesian account based on a *"tabula rasa"* theory of the origins of human knowledge. At the same time, Locke's work must be seen as alternative answers to Descartes's own questions, and so is neither a complete rejection of Descartes nor a radical examination of the philosophical status quo. Thus, we can investigate the extent to which Locke is able to answer the questions posed by Descartes within a strictly Empiricist framework.

Not all of the Cartesian questions, however, are directly relevant to a feminist reading of Locke. Therefore, we will focus on those issues that are both highly controversial, either in Locke or in his successors, *and* most clearly tied to the male bias built into Empiricist philosophy. Primary among these will be the concept of substance, the problem of solipsism, the rejection of essentialism, the nature of moral reasoning, and the justification of the political state. (These last two are, of course, legacies from Hobbes rather than Descartes, but are closely tied to the first three in Locke's thought.) Descartes himself relies heavily on both his rationalism (the belief that reason, rather than sense experience, is the primary source of human knowledge) and his doctrine of innate ideas in developing both the proof(s) of God's existence on which the rest of his philosophy depends, and the specific accounts he gives of substance, other minds, and so on. Part of the problem for Locke is how to avoid saying there are no answers to these questions (although he often comes close to saying this, and Hume comes closer still), while denying the premises on which Descartes answered them. Therefore, the positive and negative aspects of Locke's account are closely, if not always successfully, intertwined.

The structure of the *Essay* reflects its double enterprise by beginning with the argument against innate ideas. In a sense, as suggested above, the entire *Essay* is an argument against innates, since Locke's purpose is to convince his readers that they are unnecessary because he can demonstrate "how men, barely by the use of their natural faculties, may attain to all the knowledge they have, without the help of any innate impression" (Vol. 1, p. 9). In addition to being unnecessary, however, Locke finds the doctrine of innate ideas incoherent, for a variety of reasons. First of all, not everyone exhibits knowledge of the same innate ideas, and to the extent that they do, the "general assent" could as well be based on a commonality of experience. Furthermore, the ideas Descartes considers to be innate are not the first ideas that come to us, but rather come later, as if they were the result of some process of reasoning. Therefore, Locke believes, based on considerations of parsimony and consistency with the facts, we must reject innate ideas.

The question of a replacement is addressed next with Locke's own doctrine of simple ideas, atomic perceptual givens, which he then undertakes to build, slowly but surely, into all of the large and complex ideas that Descartes relies on innatism to provide, such as time and space, pleasure and pain, and cause and effect. (Descartes's reliance on hierarchical dualisms is clearly not part of what is being put in question by Locke.) Here it is important to note two basic, but not always obvious, tenets of the Empiricist enterprise. The first is that sense impressions include what are called impressions of reflection. This turns out to be a key point, since the simple ideas these impressions result in, notably those of substance and "power," are central in Locke's defense of the adequacy of the Empiricist account. The second important point here is the Empiricists' belief that their strongest, and simplest argument is the inability of the human mind to come up with any ideas that are not, in fact, borrowed in some way from our sense experience. (This point, of course, refers back to the above argument against innate ideas—one example of how the positive and negative accounts are interrelated.)

In Book III of the *Essay*, (Volume 2) Locke turns, interestingly, to an explicit consideration of language, which leads him both to make early efforts at some of the same arguments found in twentieth-century linguistic philosophy and to develop some deep contradictions in his own work, especially the contradiction between foundationalism (his belief that all knowledge is based on sense perception) and an accurate understanding of language (which always gives us both more and less than sense perception itself). If one might say that all that prevents Berkeley from achieving the stature of a Hume or Kant is his inability to see the logical consequences of his own arguments, one might also say that what keeps Locke from being a linguistic philosopher of the stature of Wittgenstein or Austin is his inability to see the inconsistencies his account of language introduces into Empiricism.

In any event, having discussed language, Locke then moves to knowledge per se, building a system of what Hume would call mitigated scepticism on the basis of simple ideas drawn from sense perception. For Locke, knowledge is "the perception of the connexion and agreement, or disagreement and repugnancy, of any of our ideas" (Vol. 2, p. 133). This agreement can be of four sorts: identity or diversity, relation, co-existence (substantial relations), and real existence, in an apparently ascending order of importance. The account, however, remains one of mitigated scepticism because much of this book concerns what we do not or cannot know (the relationship between primary and secondary qualities, for instance), and ways in which we can be led into error (e.g., by religious "enthusiasm"). Interestingly, the account of the division of the sciences with which Locke concludes the *Essay* consists of physics (i.e., the natural sciences), practical philosophy (i.e., ethics and political philosophy), and "semiotics," by which he means logic and the philosophy of language. In some ways, as we will see, Locke shows signs of being a deconstructionist *manqué*.

In addition to the potentially radical, if largely ignored, contradictions that Locke's concern for language introduces into British Empiricism, it must be remembered that his political philosophy was not only relatively radical and liberatory for the time at which it was written (and even liberatory for women, at least as compared to the patriarchal political philosophy it was meant to replace), but became literally revolutionary in the ensuing hundred years, both in the thirteen American colonies and in France. At the same time, this political philosophy is deeply tied to the same metaphysical and epistemological commitments that mark both the male bias and the limitations of Locke's philosophy. As Jaggar has shown, to reject "abstract individualism" is to reject the liberalism based on it, and hence many of our most basic political beliefs.[6] An American might say that this only proves that what is liberatory at one time and place can cease to be so as conditions change. For deconstruction, on the other hand, the basic conservativism of Locke's political theory is present from the moment in the *Second Treatise* when he violates the logic of his own "labor theory of value" to allow for the alienation of labor through money and thus for the rise of capitalism (p. 29). His atomistic account of the relative situations of labor and capital in the period of early industrialism is reaffirmed in its bourgeois bias when Locke ultimately follows Hobbes in saying that, in the end, the only recourse of an oppressed people is an appeal to God (p. 123). In a revolution, God often seems to be on the side of the rich and powerful, even—or especially—if that sometimes includes the revolutionaries themselves. (As the descendent of Jacobite refugees from Scotland, I tend to see Locke's "Glorious Rebellion" as just the first of many such bourgeois revolutions.)

Substance and Solipsism

As has been noted, Locke's epistemology is atomistic in structure: Our mental contents are composed of simple ideas that are not themselves subject to further explanation or analysis—they are givens "which, being each in itself uncompounded, contains in it nothing but *one uniform* appearance or conception in the mind" (*Essay,* Vol. 1, p. 90). These simple ideas are connected into the larger structures called complex ideas through external relations that have no impact on the simple ideas themselves. Even abstract general ideas are actually simple ideas with enough specific content removed to allow them to refer indifferently to several things of the same kind. Simple ideas are not only the basis of all our knowledge and thought, but are also the ultimate referents of language because, for Locke, words refer not to things but to ideas. Moreover, simple ideas themselves are not intrinsically meaningful, but derive their (linguistic) meaning from their accumulation into aggregates of similar ideas to which language refers—"all (except proper) names are general" (*Essay* Vol. 2, p. 11). That is, simple ideas get their meaning through their mutual relations of resemblance and difference. It would seem to follow that language can never return us to the simple ideas themselves, since it only refers to the general aggregates, so that reference to the basic atoms of perceptual experience is always deferred. Clearly, such an account could provide the basis for a radical questioning of Empiricism itself.

What Locke is approaching here is the conflict between the reality of differance and the Empiricist attempt to ground philosophy on irrefutable perceptual givens. Locke is forced to admit that

> All the knowledge we have being only of particular or general truths, it is evident that whatever may be done in the former of these, the latter, which is that which with reason is most sought after, can never be well made known and is very seldom apprehended but as conceived and expressed in words. (*Essay,* Vol. 2, p. 181)

That is, most of the knowledge that matters is linguistically formulated, meaning that it can, by Locke's own account, refer only indirectly to the perceptual givens on which knowledge is supposedly based. And Locke also develops his own version of the "private language" argument famous in Wittgenstein.[7] In explaining why "the greatest part of terms" are general, rather than referring directly to simple ideas, Locke cites not only principles of parsimony and utility, but also the fact that, if names referred directly and exclusively to one's own simple ideas, "the names of them could not be significant or intelligible to another who was not acquainted with those very particular things which had fallen under my notice" (*Essay,* Vol. 2, pp. 15–16). This argument seems to entail both a radical rejection of Individualism in all its forms by illustrating that any verbalization even to oneself of basic wants and needs is dependent on our language and hence on our status as members of a social group, and a radical division between sense experience (which is always in terms of simple ideas) and the scientific knowledge that Empiricism would claim to build from it.[8]

Furthermore, Locke's atomism—the logical correlate of his Individualism—brings in its wake many of the problems that mark the limitations, or the failure, of British Empiricism as a philosophical enterprise. These problems, entailed by the very atomism of the account, appear as soon as Locke leaves the level of simple ideas to address complex ideas. He acknowledges, for instance, the inability of Empiricism to explain the concept of substance.

> Whatever therefore be the secret and abstract nature of *substance* in general, all *the* ideas *we have of particular distinct sorts of substance* are nothing but several combinations of simple *ideas,* co-existing in such,

though unknown, cause of their union as makes the whole subsist of itself. (*Essay*, Vol. 1, p. 247)

While Locke himself is willing to accept this occult account of substance, other philosophers, notably Berkeley, were less complacent about building philosophy on a belief in "this inconceivable Somewhat," as Berleley terms it in his *Three Dialogues*.[9]

All that Berkeley must do to undermine Locke's belief in material substance (and lay the groundwork for Hume's rejection of mental substance as well—see *Three Dialogues*, p. 67) is to ask the most basic Empiricist question: From what sense experience does belief in a concept such as material objects arise?

> Whatever we perceive, is perceived immediately or mediately: by sense, or by reason and reflection. But as you have excluded sense, pray show me what reason you have to believe their existence; or what *medium* you can possibly make use of, to prove it either to mine or your own understanding. (p. 40)

What Berkeley himself offers to replace the concept of substance as the cause of the union of our several combinations of simple ideas into what we take to be externally existing material objects is the concept of a God in whose mind perceptual objects can have permanence and reality independent of all human minds. Hume, and most contemporary Anglo-American philosophers, find this solution at least as unsatisfactory as Locke's, which leaves them with no coherent account of substance at all.

What Berkeley has done, however, is to prove that the commitment to atomistic Empiricism *necessarily* leads to a phenomenalism (i.e., a belief that objects exist only insofar as they are perceived) that can be defended only be re-introducing religious beliefs into the recently secularized philosophical realm and by violating our commonly held pre-philosophical notions about reality. The resurgence of phenomenalism (without God and hence even more powerfully counter-intuitive) in contemporary Anglo-American philosophers such as Ayer only underscores the extent to which that philosophy is continuous with the tradition marked by this problem in Locke's account, as well as the inability of two centuries of philosophy to find any way, within the limits of the Empiricist paradigm, in which to account for the experience of reality that the concept of substance represents. The point I have tried to make here with regard to substance is, moreover, repeated throughout Anglo-American philosophy. (A complete deconstruction of this tradition would reconsider all the "re's" in the recounting of this failure. For deconstruction, Empiricism is the oldest and most naïve of errors.)

To see just one way in which Locke's problem, or Empiricism's problem, with substance multiplies itself, consider the implications of Berkeley's phenomenalism for the problem of other minds.[10] If objects are logical constructs out of our sense contents and the postulation of actually existing external objects beyond these constructs represents a logical error (to call upon Ayer's contemporary, linguistic version of the phenomenalists' argument[11]), what is meant when we say that another person has a mind like our own? At best, it can only mean that the object we logically construct out of our sense impressions as a human body engages in behavior that we logically construct (through analogy or whatever) to be evidence of the presence of a mind—but where? "Behind" the behavior? What could such a claim mean, if external objects are our own logical constructs? Is the mind "in" the sense impressions themselves? Does that mean we experience the other's mind directly? How can we logically construct a mind based on the behavior of a body that is itself a logical construct out of our own mental contents? More significantly, does it even make sense, as Wittgenstein might ask, to say we have *evidence* of other human minds?[12] Or that we *only* have evidence of them? As soon as one tries to make sense of our experience of other people's minds within a phenomenalistic framework, that is, within a rigorously Empiricist framework, the atomism of the account inevitably leads to a necessary and deeply seated solipsism. And clearly this is not only a "women's problem" with Locke's work.

Even without Berkeley's phenomenalism to evoke this solipsism, Locke's own text seems to suggest it already when he claims in the *Essay* that our words refer only to our ideas (Vol. 2, p. 12), and to become mired in it when he limits our knowledge, as Empiricism must, to what we can directly perceive or logically demonstrate:

> [W]e have an intuitive knowledge of our own *existence,* a demonstrative knowledge of the *existence* of a god; of the *existence* of anything else, we have no other but a sensitive knowledge, which extends not beyond the objects present to our sense. (Vol. 2, pp. 157–58)

On this account, we cannot know that any other minds exist. We cannot know it from our sense experience, unless one accepts Ayer's form of logical behaviorism, as outlined above, which Locke (if not necessarily Hume) probably never thought of and could not easily accept. We cannot know it through any logical demonstration, except the kind of innatist argument that Descartes uses and that Locke could accept even less. As Locke himself points out with regard to the problem of personal identity (Vol. 1, pp. 288–89), there is a large gulf between my own experience of myself as a continuous entity based on memory and others' experience of me as a discontinuous entity based on sense perceptions. This gulf means that, within Empiricism, not only the mental states of others, but their very existence as knowing subjects like myself must remain radically unknowable.

In fact, the "argument" for solipsism Locke seems to offer is a good example of how his work reflects a specifically male view of the world. Assuming that the knowledge of our own existence for Locke includes knowledge of our own physical as well as mental states (Vol. 1, p. 82), one can ask at what point a woman's knowledge of her unborn child's existence ceases to be knowledge of her own existence, that is her own bodily states, and becomes only "sensitive" knowledge based on what is present to her senses. Does her child's existence suddenly become problematic for her at its birth? I am not proposing this as a solution to the problem of other minds, but this question does not even occur to Locke (or to the rest of philosophy), not because the answer is self-evident, but because the question itself embodies two assumptions philosophy discounts: that a woman might have experiences and knowledge that are not routinely available to men, and that the hierarchical dualisms of inner/out and self/other may not exhaust all of the possible ways in which such a question might be addressed. Again, women's experience is ruled out of the philosophical realm before the questions, much less the answers, are even formulated. And the answers that are formulated on that basis are once again inadequate.

This is another area where my own analysis comes very close to Harding's (and several other works by feminist philosophers of science and epistemologists as well). The solipsism that seems inherent in British Empiricist philosophy is neither innocent nor entirely accidental. A certain degree of solipsism, a certain ability to see the minds of others solely as objects of one's own knowledge, is also inherent in modern science, and not only the social sciences. In her article on "The Social Function of the Empiricist Conception of Mind," Harding points out that much modern science is possible based only on a model that gives the scientist a conception of mind that is "tacitly understood as a view of *others'* minds"[13]. Moreover, this kind of "methodological solipsism"—the ability to make a qualitative distinction between one's own mental states and those one attributes to others—can provide another link between the five "cornerstones" of Anglo-American modernity postulated above. While one might imagine that Jonathan Edwards truly believed he was as damned as his parishioners, the history of British colonialism and American expansionism in the nineteenth century, not to mention slavery and the growth of industrial capitalism in the same period, shows a deep-seated tendency to make very strong distinctions between the mental states of the powerful and those of the people whose lives they came to control.

Monsters and Women[14]

Another line of thought within Locke's metaphysics seems in a similar, lateral way, to throw into question the universality of the human subject he claims to describe in the *Essay*. As important to Locke's thought as his atomism is his anti-essentialism, with its roots in the rejection of Cartesian innatism, Protestantism, modern empirical science, and a bourgeois political bias. Locke's anti-essentialism, however, bears in it not only the mark of the male bias of these "cornerstones," but also an explicit rejection of female experience, which he reiterates frequently and with a strange vehemence.

According to Locke's *Essay,* there are no natural kinds: "Whereby it is evident that the *essence of* the *sorts or . . . species* of things are nothing else but abstract ideas" (Vol. 2, p. 20). He admits that in living things there is a relationship of resemblance between parent and child, but insists that the sorting into species is a human convention based on that resemblance, which itself carries no epistemological weight. In any event, natural kinds are not sharply divided, as there are always borderline cases and types that don't fit clearly into one species or the other (e.g., mules), so whatever genetic connection there may be is not definitive. Rather, the species of each individual must be decided on the basis of its conformity to the conventional definition of that species, not on the basis of its ancestry.

The example Locke repeats several times throughout the *Essay,* however, is not mules or other truly borderline cases, but rather human "changlings" and "monsters." In these cases, being the child of human parents does not mean that the infant is itself human for Locke. "But it is the issue of rational parents, and must therefore be concluded to have a rational soul. I know not by what logic you must so conclude" (Vol. 2, p. 174). Rather than accept the fact of parentage as proof of an infant's humanity, Locke seems rather inclined to leave it up to the judgment of the priests as to whether the child is to be baptized, at least as a preliminary move. Recognizing that priests can be wrong about these things, as in the case of the Abbot of St. Martin, which he cites (Vol. 2, p. 56), Locke later gives rationality as a more definitive criterion of humanity (Vol. 2, p. 113), but one that can, of course, only be exhibited at a later stage of life.

What does this have to do with women? Most obviously, it shifts the determination of the humanity of a child from its birth mother to the male mothers of the priesthood.[15] Politically, this has always been a powerful move, but more insidiously, and on a level that Locke probably would not recognize, his version of the argument also provides the basis for a solution to Aristotle's problem of how men and women can share the essence of humanity and still be so different in their intrinsic value. Locke solves the problem by saying that there is no essence of humanity—one has to prove one's humanity on an Individualist, Empiricist, case-by-case basis, with no benefit of a doubt based merely on one's human parentage. And this may be a common oppressive move in the history of "man." Some feminist historians have wondered why it is that, when a culture becomes more democratic, the status of women in that culture often goes down. A frequent answer is that women lose the status they had because of their class membership and are prevented from achieving an equivalent status through any other means.[16] Locke's anti-essentialism might be seen to function in the same way: Women are set "free" from their "class" status as humans to prove themselves the equals of men, without being provided with any of the tools to do so, and hence can be held individually accountable for their failure to measure up to male standards of rationality, etc. This, in turn, leads back to Jaggar's criticisms of "abstract individualism" cited above, and suggests that the liberal feminism of Mary Wollstonecraft or Harriet Taylor and John Stuart Mill may amount to "proving" that women are really equal, that is, really human after all.

Interestingly, Rom Harré's *Personal Being,* in attempting to establish the social definition of mental characteristics, traces the level of rationality attributed to women in English literature from the time of Shakespeare to the present.[17] What Harré discovered was that in sixteenth- and early seventeenth-century literature, women were held "accountable" for their opinions and beliefs, that is, they were expected to provide rational justifications of them. After the Glorious

Rebellion, however, in eighteenth- and nineteenth-century literature, "women's intuition" was no longer considered to be rationally based and women were considered to be highly irrational. As Harré asks, "Does this change in literary conventions represent a change in the cognitive processes of half the human race or are we seeing a reflection of one set of conventions in another?" (p. 122). Locke's work, of course, is the main philosophical text in the transition between the two periods. This suggests two possibilities. First, that the *Essay* may have played a causal role, however small, in the cultural shift that Harré documents, and secondly, that the greater ease with which Hume can dismiss women's intellectual achievements reflects the success of the same social devaluation of women's rationality in the following century.

If any of this is true, the modern debates about such issues as affirmative action are merely the latest variant on an old argument about women's status in the world of male rationality, that is, about our status as humans. In *The Politics of Reality,* Marilyn Frye offers an unusually acute account of how one can come to deny human personhood to someone who is clearly exhibiting "person behavior."[18] One way is simply not to notice the behavior; another is to underestimate the extent to which a particular behavior, such as secretarial work, requires "person characteristics." Most relevant here, however, is the third case that she discusses, the possibility that

> One may observe circumstances that are adverse to the manifestation of the relevant abilities, judge these circumstances to have been optimal, and conclude from the nonappearance of the abilities in these "optimal" circumstances that they are not present. (p. 46)

Frye goes on to consider the education of black children in white schools and women in the university as examples of situations where this last manipulation is especially obvious, but the same might well be said of women's perceived rationality in any male-defined area where women and men have very different life experiences, but are judged "equally" by male standards.

In the case of both metaphysical and political equality, the question seems to be one of why, if we are all equally persons, we don't all think the same way and exhibit the same beliefs and behavior? Since we don't, those who meet the standards of rationality established by the privileged example of the (European) male philosopher are surely justified in relegating women to an inferior position, as they do with other deviant thinkers such as Asians, Africans, or (native) Americans. And once excluded, the ability of these groups to develop the skills and have the experiences that will allow them to think in the "normal" way is severely impaired, if only by the threat of being "unfeminine." Surely any "normal" human being would think as Locke did and, while Locke would not want to deny that women might possess a rational human soul, the failure to fully conform to (European) male standards of rationality is certainly opened as a reason for women's exclusion from the wider civil society.

Ethics and Shared Simple Ideas

This exclusionary tendency in Locke's text is reinforced by his assumption that all people will not only have a similar rationality, but will also have experiences that are sufficiently similar to supply them with an identical stock of simple ideas. "For I am apt to think that men, when they come to examine them, find their simple *ideas* all generally to agree, though in discourse with one another they perhaps confound one another with different names" (*Essay,* Vol. 1, p. 145). Locke is aware of the problems with such an assumption, noting both that it may not be true and that, if it were not true, there would be no way to tell, since we can never compare our ideas with another person's (*Essay,* Vol. 1, p. 330). As was discussed earlier, the wedge that this drives between one person's ideas and the words with which they must be described *and* between the ideas of any two different people are in themselves de-stabilizing to the Empiricist tradition. The doctrine of shared ideas, however, also has powerful political implications.

How does the assumption of shared ideas work within Locke's more general philosophical enterprise? To take an especially clear example, the following is a key step in Locke's version of the first cause argument for the existence of God from the *Essay:* "And I appeal to everyone's own thoughts whether he cannot as easily conceive matter produced by *nothing* as thought produced by pure matter, when before there was no such thing as thought or an intelligent being existing" (Vol. 2, p. 222). Since to be unable to think of thought as arising from pure matter is tantamount to believing either in the eternal existence of thought and hence in a god, or in the creation of thought and hence also in god, this argument begs the question of whether a god exists rather directly. Other examples of this fallacy are not common in

Locke, but there is a tendency throughout his work to rely on shared ideas and common experience in making arguments that are only seemingly self-evident. As the above quotation shows, this form of argument is by nature conservative—it is easy for us now to conceive of thought arising from matter and yet would have been all but inconceivable to Locke's contemporaries. In philosophy, it is best to avoid arguments that rely on the limits of human imagination, but assuming that all men, much less all people, share the same basic stock of simple ideas infects Locke's work with just that kind of error.

Since morality, as with mathematics for Locke, consists of complex ideas that do not reflect any external reality by which they might be measured, his belief in shared simple ideas plays an especially important role in moral reasoning, and the political consensus built upon it. It is significant, therefore, that when Locke does consider the possibility that men might have different simple ideas, he regards it as an absolute bar to communication: "But if it should happen that any two thinking men should really have different *ideas,* I do not see how they could discourse or argue one with another" (Vol. 1, p. 145). On this view, what would happen if men and women (or any other two groups in a society) had life experiences that were sufficiently different that, while most of their simple ideas were the same, some were not, and therefore there were corresponding differences between their complex ideas, especially those involved in political thought and the moral reasoning that underlies it?

The result might be very much like the situation that Carol Gilligan describes in her book, *In A Different Voice.*[19] Based on her studies of the moral reasoning used by women, Gilligan concludes that women's life experiences, especially the centrality of relationships in their lives, leads them to reason differently from men about moral problems, since men's participation in the "public sphere" means that they tend to think primarily in terms of conflict. In general, women focus more on balancing positive outcomes for everyone in moral dilemmas and men reason in terms of rules and strict considerations of justice. She calls for a redefinition of our usual methods of evaluating moral reasoning in ways that would reflect these differences between men and women without assuming that, since women's moral reasoning is different, we are less morally mature than men. She also argues that the best moral position might well be a combination of the two, rather than any hierarchical opposition between them. What is intriguing about this account here is that Locke would have to agree that men and women would find it difficult to communicate about morality insofar as each might be tracing their moral concepts back to different simple ideas based on culturally determined differences in their life experience:

> [H]aving by *sensation* and *reflection* stored our minds with simple *ideas,* and by use got the names that stand for them, we can by those names represent to another any complex idea we would have him conceive so that it has in it no simple *ideas* but what he knows and has with us the same name for. (*Essay,* Vol. 1, p. 242)

Where one of the parties has simple ideas that are not common to both, it follows, moral communications obviously become problematic.

Now, my claim here is not that either Gilligan or Locke has correctly or incorrectly described an independent, pre-existing reason for differences in male and female reasoning. Rather, I would like to suggest that Locke's own moral and epistemological atomism, and the sharp distinction between the public and the private in his political thought, might themselves be causal factors in the way in which men and women perceive the world and each other. That is, the normative Individualism that is common to all five "cornerstones" of the system at issue here means that: (a) women, traditionally devalued, are excluded from public life and relegated to the home, where (b) they are perceived to be, and perceive themselves to be, less individuals than partners in various sorts of relationships, especially relationships with men, so that (c) they do not exhibit the sort of moral, and other, reasoning correlated with Individualism, and hence are devalued (see a). Thus, Gilligan might describe a reality for which Locke's philosophy provides part of the ideological justification. And, if Claudia Card and other critics of Gilligan are correct in saying that women's—and men's—moral reasoning as it currently exists may be the reasoning of "damaged" persons, the role that Locke's philosophy played in doing that damage, in justifying the sex-segregation of our society, is itself part of the argument I am trying to make here.[20]

Moreover, Locke's work helps to create this reality just because of the assumption of shared simple ideas. The devaluation of women's moral reasoning, as I have already suggested, might reflect the fact that men will regard women's different moral reasoning as necessarily inferior because it seems irrational on the assumption that it is based on the same "simple ideas" as men's moral reasoning. The role that Locke in particular, and Empiricism in general, may have played in marking women's (and other non-standard) reasoning as an error based on sameness, rather than correct reasoning based on difference, is not the least of the subtle ways in which it has supported (European) male power in the world for the last three hundred years. It is only those who need not take the reality of others seriously, whose lives do not depend on understanding how others see the world, who can assume that all lives, and all simple ideas, are basically the same—and that very assumption perpetuates their power.[21]

This problem in Locke is also important because the ability to reach agreements on basic issues of Natural Law that will turn out to be necessary for a civil society depend on the communication of shared simple ideas, and thus on the assumption of shared experience. The "abnormal" experience, and hence perhaps ideas, of women, for instance, might mean that they would not "properly" regard contracts as creating absolute and inviolable obligations, but instead might emphasize the need for a balanced outcome in disputed cases. Such disregard for as basic a Natural Law as promise-keeping would, in turn, undermine the authority of the state that is based on a contractarian theory. Similarly, members of obvious minorities, racial and otherwise, might be less willing to abdicate their wills to majority rule than members of the dominant group. Indeed, John Rawls created the fiction of an "original position" to avoid precisely this problem in his own contractarian theory of government.[22] Equality itself, as has been noted, can have different meanings for those who have more or less ability to act on that equality. Or, as Victor Hugo noted, the law, in its wisdom, keeps the rich and poor alike from sleeping under bridges.

Barbara Herrnstein Smith has pointed out that political consensus of the sort required by Locke and other contractarian political theorists is often achieved by excluding from the polity those whose status might lead them to reject the self-interested collective will of those for whose benefit the polity was formed,[23] and Carole Pateman has clarified the extent to which liberal political theory was developed in part as an exclusionary alternative to radical democracy.[24] Iris Young argues, in "Impartiality and the Civic Public," that liberal political theory defined rationality as opposed to bodily sensation, which led to a racist and sexist exclusionary attitude toward those whose "wildness" represents the body in early modern discourse: "In practice this assumption [about rationality] forces a homogeneity of citizens upon the civic public. It excludes from the public those individuals and groups that do not fit the model of the rational citizen who can transcend body and sentiment."[25] What we have been tracing here in Locke, on this account, is the basic rationale that has been put to use to justify such exclusions, on both an epistemological and a political level, in the Empiricist tradition. A familiar pattern reappears here: To the extent that women, and other groups, are excluded from key areas of what is defined as "human" experience, such as education and the marketplace, they will lack the experiences needed to become part of the moral consensus that underlies civil society and so will also be excluded from the political realm. This will, in turn, justify their exclusion from other areas of "human" experience, and so on.

Locke's atomistic epistemology bears the stamp of male experience in our culture and also generates certain kinds of problems in making sense of our perceptions, the existence of a Self, or other minds, and his reliance on shared simple ideas seems to make it more difficult for those with significantly different life experiences (women and those from other cultures) to become part of the civil community. Locke, however, does not himself draw these sorts of conclusions. Why does the Lockean text provoke such an analysis? Surely Locke did as much as, or more than, any thinker to create our great modern democracies, with all the opportunities they offer to people of all races, genders, etc. One may well ask, however, how much of that equality of opportunity is due to a genuine desire to have civil society, with its challenges and rewards, be an arena of activity for women and non-European men, and how much to Locke's inability to see these people as even potentially equal competitors with the dominant group, as full participants in "human understanding?" What I hope to have suggested so far is that Locke's epistemological and metaphysical positions at least open up the possibility that the latter is a much more likely explanation of the "openness" of his society, and that some of the problems in both our current epistemology and our attempts as a society to become more inclusive in our political thought can be traced back to elements in Locke, and in many others, that would simply equate human knowledge with (European) male experience.

Notes

1. Parts of this chapter were presented as a paper under this title at the Pacific Division meeting of the American Philosophical Association held March, 1986. The response to that paper, by Jean Hampton of the University of California at Los Angeles, raised many important issues I have tried to address in my subsequent thinking about this project.

2. John Locke, *An Essay Concerning Human Understanding,* ed. John W. Yolton (New York: Everyman's Library, 1974), vol. 2, p. 75.

3. For example, see Locke's *Essay*, vol. 1, p. 169, or *Second Treatise on Government*, ed. C. B. Macpherson (Indianapolis: Hackett, 1980), p. 36.
4. Locke, *Second Treatise*, p. 44.
5. Melissa Butler, in her "Early Liberal Roots of Feminism: John Locke and the Attack on Patriarchy," *American Political Science Review* 72, no. 1 (March 1978): 135–50, takes a more positive view of Locke's writings on women that is based primarily on his political thought. Part of my point here is that taking Locke's political work in the context of his metaphysics and epistemology and of British Empiricism as a whole might allow us to draw more critical conclusions about his ideas.
6. See chapter seven of Jagger's *Feminist Politics and Human Nature*.
7. Ludwig Wittgenstein, *Philosophical Investigations*, trans. G. E. M. Anscombe (New York: MacMillan, 1968), pp. 94–97.
8. Naomi Scheman, "Individualism and the Objects of Psychology," in *Discovering Reality*, ed. Sandra Harding and Merrill B. Hintikka (Boston: D. Reidel, 1983).
9. George Berkeley, *Three Dialogues Between Hylas and Philonous*, ed. Robert M. Adams (Indianapolis: Hackett, 1979), pp. 52–53.
10. This argument is based on a very similar one made by John Searle in a class at the University of California at Berkeley.
11. This version can be found in A. J. Ayer, *Language, Truth, and Logic*, pp. 63–65.
12. See, for instance, Wittgenstein's *Logical Investigations*, p. 228.
13. Sandra Harding, "The Social Function of the Empiricist Conception of Mind," pp. 38–47.
14. This heading is due to Barbara Johnson who, in *A World of Difference* (Baltimore: Johns Hopkins University Press, 1987), cites the close juxtaposition of the discussion of "monsters" in Locke with a figurative reference to women to argue that women are themselves figured as monsters in this text, or rather are monsters *because* they are figures for the seductive and yet monstrous disfigurement of literal speech in the figures of rhetoric (p. 38—the reference is to page 105 of Volume Two of the *Essay*). Deconstruction emphasizes the extent to which women and figurative language represent something that the "pure" speech of the male world always seeks to exclude, but from which it in fact draws its own existence. Locke would be just one example.
15. Julia Kristeva refers to the Christian transfer of birthing from mothers to priests in a section of *Chinese Women* reprinted in *The Kristeva Reader*, ed. Toril Moi (New York: Columbia University Press, 1986), p. 146.
16. See Marilyn Arthur, "'Liberated' Women: The Classical Era," in *Becoming Visible: Women in European History*, ed. Renate Bridenthal and Claudia Koonz (Boston: Houghton Mifflin, 1977).
17. Rom Harré, *Personal Being* (Cambridge, Mass.: Harvard University Press, 1984).
18. Marilyn Frye, *The Politics of Reality* (Trumanburg, N.Y.: The Crossing Press, 1983).

19. Carol Gilligan, *In a Different Voice* (Cambridge, Mass.: Harvard University Press, 1982).

20. In her response to the paper on which this chapter is based, Hampton reported hearing Card argue this point against Gilligan at a conference on "The Virtues" held at the University of San Diego in February, 1986.

21. Gary Shapiro discusses "the repression and sublimation of power" to be found in the transition from discourse about power to discourse about representation in the development of British Empiricism in his "British Hermeneutics and the Genesis of Empiricism," *Phenomenological Inquiry* (October 1985): 29–44. Although Shapiro does not mention it, Carole Pateman's "Sublimation and Reification: Locke, Wolin, and the Liberal Democratic Conception of the Political" would provide a link between Foucault's sense of representation, to which Shapiro refers, and political representation, which is also a "repression" of power in Locke. Shapiro does raise the issue of "canonicity" in British Empiricism, asking both why Hobbes is usually excluded and why we read only Locke's *SECOND Treatise* (not to mention only Parts I and II of *Leviathan*).

22. See, for instance, John Rawls, *A Theory of Justice* (Cambridge, Mass.: Harvard University Press, 1971), p. 18.

23. Smith made this comment at a conference on "Critical Philosophy and Critical Theory," held at the University of Minnesota in April, 1986.

24. See Pateman's "Sublimation and Reification: Locke, Wolin and the Liberal Democratic Conception of the Political."

25. Iris Marion Young, "Impartiality and the Civic Public: Some Implications of Feminist Critiques of Moral and Political Theory," *Praxis International* 5, no. 4 (January 1986): 389.

Chapter 2

"Betwixt a False Reason and None at All"

Atomism, Scepticism, Psychology

Let's begin in the middle, about two-thirds of the way through Book II of *A Treatise of Human Nature*. There we come to the following "human" trait: "One who is inflam'd with lust, feels at least a momentary kindness towards the object of it, and at the same time fancies her more beautiful than ordinary."[1] Leaving aside the assumption that all "human" lust has a female object for the moment, what sort of situation does this imagery suggest? That is, what seems to be the paradigm case of "love betwixt the sexes" for Hume? And what gender implications does such a paradigm carry with it? Even if Hume insists elsewhere that lust, as defined above, is a trait common to men and women, and hence is not in itself male-biased, to take relatively casual sex (as we would say now) or even prostitution (more likely in Hume's time) as the paradigm case for the analysis of it, rather than the presumably more common case of love in a continuing relationship, suggests a stereotypically male sense of the way the world basically is. On such a reading, one might take this passage as an indication of the extent to which Hume continues to do men's philosophy.

As in Locke, Hume's thought is extremely atomistic, and it is just this atomism, the lack of any intrinsic connection between our emotions (or our experiences in general), that leads to the complex account of the "amorous passion" quoted above. This passion combines lust, admiration of beauty, and benevolence, which

> are evidently distinct, and has each of them its distinct object. 'Tis certain, therefore, that 'tis only by their relation they produce each other.

47

> But the relation of passions alone is not sufficient. 'Tis likewise necessary there shou'd be a relation of ideas. The beauty of one person never inspires us with love for another. (pp. 395–96).

Thus, "love betwixt the sexes" is not a unitary emotion, but occurs when "we" see a beautiful woman who can inspire lust and benevolent feelings, or have lust for a woman who is close to beautiful and merits at least temporary benevolence, or have benevolent feelings for a woman who can pass for beautiful and inspires lust. The three emotions can exist separately, but most often occur together because they reinforce each other, forming a powerful "double relation," even though, as Hume explains, for no particular reason, in a footnote to *An Enquiry Concerning the Principles of Morals*, "the same beauty, transferred to a different sex, excites no amorous passion where nature is not extremely perverted."[2]

The heterosexism of this is not, however, the only thing about Hume's account that might be considered problematic. Are lust and beauty really distinct passions, combined only in certain favorable cases? On the other hand, is lust impossible in the absence of beauty, or can it lead to a new conception of the nature of beauty itself? What *is* the relationship between "benevolence" (perhaps what we might call love) and lust—and in whose thinking in this culture is it considered to be an accidental and external one? Perhaps what seems most wrong here is the attempt to glue something back together that should never have been broken into atomic components in the first place, at least not if we are concerned as philosophers with recreating the full richness of our pre-philosophic experience of the world. Clearly, this atomistic approach is at least as much a problem for Hume as for Locke.

This account also provides one example of how Hume in some ways goes beyond the narrower confines of the Empiricist tradition, and in so doing is able to more adequately solve the problems Empiricism set for itself.[3] To put it very briefly for now, in many cases, of which "the amorous passion" is one, Hume seems to use what we would now call psychology to fill in the gaps left by the atomism of his purely philosophical account. Thus, in our example, we have three distinct, irreducible emotions: lust, admiration of beauty, and benevolence. How do they come to be combined in the way that they are, not only to bring men and women together, but also, with the help of love for their mutual offspring, to keep them together over the years? According to Hume, two different relations are involved. First, these three distinct emotions are all pleasant, so they all move in the same direction and reinforce each other. For instance, since lust and benevolence attract, and deformity repels, a certain degree of beauty is needed to draw the three emotions together. Secondly, the emotions must all be related as ideas, that is, they must all be caused by the same person. (Both can be seen in Rostand's *Cyrano de Bergerac*—Roxanne's passions are not flowing in the same direction with regard to Cyrano nor, as it happens, are they being caused by the same person in the case of Christian.)

This is not as minor a point as it may seem in Hume. The tendency of the mind to combine emotions that resemble each other in being pleasant and causally related to the same object, this biological or psychological fact about human beings, forms the basis for the human family, which Hume in turn sees as the basis for all human society. He implies that a similar species without this tendency would not form permanent breeding pairs, and so would lack the advantages that family life brings to humans.[4] Moreover, in this chapter I will try to show that the structure of this account of one passion—atomism, scepticism, psychology—is repeated thoughout Hume's work, and further that both the problems that lead to his scepticism, and the use of what we now consider to be psychology that sometimes provides the response to it, are deeply intertwined with the same self-definition of British Empiricism that makes women's philosophy problematic within that tradition.

Sidestepping Descartes

Perhaps even more than Locke, Hume perceived his own work as radical. Not politically radical, but epistemologically radical. What it is a radicalization of, however, is the Lockean model of Empiricist philosophy, as already radicalized by Berkeley's phenomenalism. That is, there is a deep continuity between Locke and Hume in which Hume's scepticism emerges directly out of simply making Locke's philosophy consistent. In Hume, the same direct Empiricist questioning of other basic concepts (causality, the Self, and God) that Berkeley applies to material substance—from what sense perception does such a concept arise?—serves to undermine the possibility of providing any rational account of these other concepts, and thus, the possibility of doing philosophy at all. At the same time, the continuity between Locke and Hume also shows the limits of Hume's radicalism, making it clear that Hume is still relying on the same Empiricist concept of what philosophy is as Locke and Berkeley, and still trying to answer the same Cartesian questions that Locke addressed. That is, Hume's stated concern in the *Enquiry Concerning Human Understanding* continues to be how we can step outside the confines of the isolated Cartesian Self, how "we can go beyond the evidence of our memory and senses."[5] Unfortunately, of course, Hume's work establishes that we can only go beyond these limits through cause and effect reasoning, and that a belief in causal necessity cannot be rationally justified. After a hundred years of modern philosophy, the answer to Descartes's question of whether there can be true knowledge of the external world appears, in the Empiricist tradition at least, to be "No."

From the beginning of Book I of the *Treatise,* it is clear that Hume is very much in the Empiricist tradition, especially with regard to its *"tabula rasa"* epistemology— ". . . *all our simple ideas in their first appearance are deriv'd from simple impressions, which are correspondent to them, and which they exactly represent"* (p. 4)—and its atomism—*"As all simple ideas can be separated by the imagination"* (p. 10). Furthermore, the outline of Book I is very similar to that of Locke's *Essay,* if in a more abbreviated form. What is omitted are the discussions of innatism (a dead horse by Hume's time) and of language, arguably the one place in which Hume's work is not more "modern" than Locke's. What is added, of course, is a lengthy discussion of the problem of causal connection (Part III) and Hume's overt, if supposedly mitigated, scepticism. This scepticism extends beyond causality and the knowledge based on it to another problem we will consider in some detail later, that of "mental substance" or the Self. Based on the same argument that he has applied to material substances and causality, Hume develops what has been called a "bucket theory" of the Self, a "deconstruction" of the Self far ahead of its time (and one with important consequences for Hume's religious thought as well).[6]

That very comment should illustrate a major difficulty in the argument of this chapter. I will try to show, on the one hand, that Hume's scepticism does not provide an answer to Empiricism's Cartesian questions *in its own terms,* and, on the other hand, that Hume's account demonstrates in part what is wrong with those terms, and hence provides better "answers," that is, more accurate depictions of our pre-philosophical reality, than any that are possible within a more strictly Empiricist paradigm. Thus, the discussion of the "passions" in Book II of the *Treatise* is necessary to provide Hume with an account of human psychology compatible with his "psychological" solution to the problem of causal reasoning, as well as a basis for the moral and political theory presented in Book III, but it at the same time steps beyond what have been taken to be strictly philosophical questions in the Empiricist tradition (if not in the Cartesian tradition, where the study of the "passions" remains part of philosophy). That these non-philosophical questions are also "women's questions," that is, questions of feeling and relationship, need hardly be mentioned.

What has been often mentioned in feminist readings of Hume, however, is the male bias, or lack of it, in his moral theory.[7] While few of the authors who work in this area would deny that there is some sexism in Hume's moral thought, there seem to be differing opinions on whether his ethics is necessarily sexist or especially well suited to women's moral thinking (as Gilligan describes it). We will return to this issue below, but here I would at least like to offer an initial account of why I find Hume's moral philosophy more traditionally male-biased than not. For Hume, morality is not determined by reason but is based on the "passions," which are immune to the effects of reason. Thus, what Hume does in his moral philosophy, in part, is to establish something like the "is/ought" distinction and to locate morality in the stereotypical women's realm of emotion and irrationality, repeating the traditional devaluation of the right-hand side of all the hierarchical dualisms that are isomorphic with the pair is/ought (and male/female).

Before tracing out this and other key arguments in the *Treatise,* however, it will be necessary to say something about the relationship between the arguments there and those in Hume's other writings. Since I am dealing with "Hume" here, and not as a historian with Hume, I generally will not make much distinction between the *Treatise* and the *Enquiries,* and will also emphasize the continuity in Hume's thought rather than the variations in the different forms his main argument take in his various works. My discussion of Hume's *Dialogues Concerning Natural Religion,*[8] for instance, will stress both how those arguments rely on Hume's more general metaphysical and epistemological commitments and the ways in which they show those commitments to be, in spite of occasional significant deviations, at base still integrally tied into the general schema of British Empiricism and the male-biased cultural world it represents.[9]

Reconnecting the Pieces

We have already discussed the atomism that is basic to British Empiricism, and have correlated that atomism both with the Individualism that builds a strong male bias into Empiricist political thought, and with the ultimate failure of the Empiricist tradition to re-create a unified reality out of atomic simple ideas. A double reading of Hume as both Empiricist and counter-Empiricist would then need to emphasize above all that atomism, and the problem of connection, is the central dilemma of Hume's philosophy, reappearing in his discussions of causal relations, the Self, and even God. In the *Treatise,* Hume himself identifies this atomism as the source of the problem of causal connection:

> Now nothing is more evident, than that the human mind cannot form such an idea of two objects, as to conceive any connexion betwixt them, or comprehend distinctly that power or efficacy, by which they are united. Such a connexion wou'd amount to a demonstration, and wou'd imply the absolute impossibility for the one object not to follow, or to be conceiv'd not to follow upon the other: Which kind of connexion has already been rejected in all cases. (pp. 161–62)

Consider the powerful imagery here. We have, on the one hand, the inconceivability of any connection, a state of absolute atomism and isolation, and, on the other hand, the inconceivability of separation, total absorption with no independent identity. Significantly, this strong dualism is closely tied to one of the basic critical tools of Hume's philosophy, "Hume's fork"—the contrast between empirical, contingent "matters of fact" and logical, necessary "relations of ideas."

This metaphysical atomism found so strongly in the Empiricist tradition, and the corresponding need to explain any kind of connection, is seen by many feminist thinkers as a stereotypically male response to certain socio-psychological factors found in modern industrial capitalism. Nancy Chodorow, for instance, in *The Reproduction of Mothering,* draws upon psychoanalytic "object relations" theory to argue that the pattern of men working outside the home and children being raised exclusively by women produces male children who lack a strong male presence as a role model and so can define themselves as masculine only negatively, by denying their connection to what is present, their mother.[10] Therefore, the argument goes, male children develop rigid ego boundaries and tend to see the world as atomistic, repressing their experience of connection because they see separation (from the M/Other) and lack of relationship as essential to their masculinity. There are many reasons that one might hesitate to read such a psycho-cultural account back into the eighteenth century (or the early death of Hume's father), but if one did consider the similarities between middle-class child-rearing practices then and now as more significant than the differences, the powerful dichotomy represented in the above passage could be seen as a psychologically and historically conditioned "choice" between isolation on the one hand and the total lack of any independent identity on the other.

Drawing on this sort of analysis, several feminist theorists have gone somewhat further and suggested that a sort of theoretical matricide can be traced throughout modern philosophy as a response to these limited alternatives of absorption or atomic separation.[11] In her paper "Othello's Doubt/Desdemona's Death: The Engendering of Scepticism," Naomi Scheman develops this analysis in Descartes, claiming that his argument in the Third Meditation that only God was the true cause of his existence is in effect an attempt to establish that he had only one parent, needless to say a male one.[12] Bordo, in *The Flight to Objectivity,* characterizes seventeenth-century thought as a whole as a move to annihilate the medieval view of the world as female flesh, transfer all creative power to a masculine God, and define the murdered mother as an always already dead mater-ial reality. Seyla Benhabib argues, in her "The Generalized and Concrete Other," that "The early bourgeois individual not only has no mother but no father as well; rather he strives to reconstitute the father in his own self-image."[13] Much the same might be said, of course, of Descartes's God. Thus, as both Bordo and Alice Jardine claim,[14] the modern ethos replaces the patricide of the Oedipus myth with the matricide of the Orestes myth, replacing desire for the mother with desire for masculine self-assertion predicated on her death, that is, on the total denial of any connection with her.[15]

In feminist studies of the British tradition, a similar analysis arises. Christine Di Stefano, in a paper on "Masculinity as Ideology in Political Theory," discovers a matricide in Hobbes's portrayal of the State of Nature as a situation in which men are radically independent and essentially asocial, so that "men are not born of, much less nurtured by, women, or anyone else, for that matter."[16] Jane Flax, in "Political Philosophy and the Patriarchal Unconscious" also notes that the Leviathan Hobbes erects to replace the State of Nature is, like Descartes's God, an omnipotent father without a mother.[17] We have already discussed one way in which Locke might be said to commit a matricide in his belief that the humanity of a human infant does not depend on its birth to a human mother. Moreover, in both Hobbes and Locke, one aspect of the establishment of philosophical and political modernity is a liberating matricide against the scholasticism of the medieval "Mother" church.[18] Hume's discussion of causality, thus, can be seen as an emphasis on atomism and lack of connection that structures philosophy as a realm in which a mother cannot exist, in which no connection is possible. He has, one might say, effectively exorcised the mother's ghost that still haunts Locke's less rigorous Empiricism.

Even independently of such an analysis, however, Hume himself is well aware that atomism is a problem for the Empiricist enterprise, and unlike Locke, he also seems to be aware that empiricism itself reinforces this atomism to create serious problems for philosophy. Just before the passage cited above, Hume repeats the claim that "All ideas are deriv'd from, and represent impressions. We never have any impression, that contains any power or efficacy. We never therefore have any idea of power" (p. 161). Since causality is a species of "power" in Empiricist thought, it follows rather directly that, strictly speaking, we can have no idea of causal necessity, and therefore that whatever we take to be such an idea must be somehow mistaken, at least from a philosophical point of view. Hume's philosophy is both atomistic (and so Individualistic and stereotypically male in our culture) and Empiricist, and it is this combination that generates his famous paradoxes.

Thus, Hume continues to do men's philosophy. The double reading of Hume that I am suggesting, however, while it would place Hume's questions and his basic metaphysical and epistemological commitments squarely within the Empiricist tradition, would also point out that his "answers," to the extent that they do more to resolve the paradoxes that men's philosophy generates than many of the Anglo-American philosophers who followed, are able to accomplish this just because Hume occasionally abandons his male-centered position for one that is, if not non-male, at least in some ways less aggressively male. This double reading of the *Treatise* is based on careful consideration of one "cornerstone" of Hume's argument: the causal biological explanation of our causal beliefs he gives after he has proven that causal accounts cannot be rationally justified. That is, Hume explains in great detail why causal accounts provide no rational justification for belief, and then proceeds to give a causal account of our belief in causality, and of our passions and moral beliefs as well. In his *Hume*, Barry Stroud resolves this apparent paradox by arguing that Hume could claim that it is simply a fact that there is the kind of constant conjunction between our experience and our causal beliefs he describes and, moreover, that any critic must also see a causal relationship there, once the constant conjunction is brought to the critic's attention.[19] Thus, the argument is naturally, but not viciously, circular. On the other hand, deconstruction would suggest that this self-nullifying cornerstone of Hume's work is an attempt to conceal how radical his analysis is, and the extent to which it makes philosophy impossible, at least on the Empiricist model. Such a reading would end where it might have begun, with the dismissal of Empiricism as a naïve and untenable system.

It is not so easy, however, for modern feminists trained in the Anglo-American tradition to simply write off Empiricism. Not only is it the paradigm within which we must ourselves work, but Empiricism and the Utilitarianism that is already appearing as its consequence in Hume have so strongly shaped our political world that our lives outside of the academy—outside of the "study," as Hume would say—require that we take it seriously, if only for our own survival. For us, therefore, there is much still to be said here, especially when we, as feminists, see that Hume's move from what is strictly philosophically justified to something more like a psychological account adds a new dimension to the explanations available to him, and one that seems much more sympathetic to the demands of our own philosophical work. Unlike the atomistic epistemology and metaphysics he inherited from Locke, psychology is, for Hume in the *Treatise,* a realm of connection and intuition.

> 'Tis a common observation, that the mind has a great propensity to spread itself on external objects, and to conjoin with them any internal impressions, which they occasion, and which always make their appearance at the same time that these objects discover themselves to the senses. (p. 167)

Given such a concept of the psychological, it represents an irrational, stereotypically "female" realm as well. I would like to suggest that it is just insofar as he steps beyond the male-defined confines of the Empiricist tradition into the "female" realm of psychology that Hume is able to provide "solutions" to the problems that atomistic Empiricism creates, and just insofar as his heirs in the Anglo-American tradition have returned to a more rigid insistence on atomism and Empiricism that they have fallen into the traps that Hume's arguments set.

We have already seen how Hume uses a psychological explanation, in terms of association of ideas, to overcome some of the difficulties created by his atomistic account of "the amorous passion." A similar form of argument, with a similar implicit evolutionary point of view, can be found in Hume's account of our sense of the necessity of causal relationships. Hume begins his account of causality by showing that we have no rational basis for our feeling that the same cause must always have the same effect, because it is neither a logical truth nor an empirically justified claim, so it belongs on neither side of "Hume's fork." Causal reasoning is not strictly logical for Hume because it is not governed by the law of non-contradiction, that is, the negation of a causal law is always logically possible. On the other hand, there is also no empirical justification for our belief in causal necessity. To say that we believe in causal reasoning is to say that we believe that future/unperceived cases (of causal connection) will be the same as past/perceived cases. If we ask, then, why we believe that to be the case, the answer eventually comes around to saying that it is because, in the past, future cases have been the same as past ones, and so we assume that in the future the same reasoning will apply. Thus the only available argument to justify our belief in causal reasoning turns out to be a circular one.

Hume's psychological account, however, explains our belief in causal reasoning by saying that the sense impression or feeling of a "necessary connexion" in causal reasoning is precisely that—a feeling in the brain that comes from having, as we would now say, the same neural pathway activated by seeing the same cause always followed by the same effect. As in the case of the passions above, psychology ties together what logic and philosophy can only see as distinct realities and thereby comes much closer to recapturing, and even explaining, our pre-philosophical experience of the world. The fact of having seen a causal relationship in the past does not logically or empirically justify our belief that it must occur in the future, but it does lead us to feel the necessity of thinking of the effect every time that we see the cause, and we interpret this as a necessity in the external world rather than a fact about our brains. It is not, on this account, an illusion, but rather a misinterpretation, an example of the mind's tendency to generalize connection outside of its proper sphere.

As with the earlier account of the passion, morever, this kind of explanation has what might be called an "evolutionary" side to it, when used as part of Hume's argument that scepticism is an untenable position outside of the philosopher's "study."

> Nature, by an absolute and uncontroulable necessity has determin'd us to judge as well as to breathe and feel; nor can we any more forbear viewing certain objects in a stronger and fuller light, upon account of their customary connexion with a present impression, than we can hinder ourselves from thinking as long as we are awake. . . .
> My intention . . . is only to make the reader sensible of the truth of my hypothesis, *that all our reasonings concerning causes and effects are deriv'd from nothing but custom; and that belief is more properly an act of the sensitive than of the cogitative part of our natures.* (p. 183)

Thus, atomistic Empiricism leads to conclusions that we cannot, as human animals, accept, and hence it must be supplemented by a psychological account of our undeniable experience of connectedness in the world. Hume's psychology, of course, remains a matter of piecing together a shattered world, rather than capturing the original unity of our lived experience. Still, by leaving the narrowly male-defined realm of philosophy, he is able to do more to restore some connection between what we learn from philosophy and what we believe in our everyday lives than has more recent work in the Anglo-American tradition.

What would be left of Hume's philosophy if he remained within a narrower definition of the philosophical? There would be no concept of causality as a "natural" relation (i.e., no account of "necessary" connection), but only as a "philosophical" relation (i.e., simple correlation of atomic entities). It must be remembered, however, that

> tho' causation be a *philosphical* relation, as implying contiguity, succession, and constant conjunction, yet 'tis only so far as it is a *natural* relation, and produces an union among our ideas, that we are able to reason upon it, or draw any inferences from it. (p. 94)

That is, connectedness is not "philosophical," but without our "irrational," "natural" belief in the "necessary connexion" of cause and effect, we could never think beyond the sensory present because we would have no basis on which to reason forward to future events, backward through memory (which relies on causality as well), or even to contemporary unperceived cases. We would be trapped forever in the solipsistic loneliness of the Cartesian Self which remains, however, the realm of pure philosophy. For Hume, connection is a practical necessity, atomism the philosophical truth. And, for Hume, that constitutes a major criticism of philosophy.

A Self Divided

It is necessary to remember, however, that for Hume, many philosophical problems remain unresolvable, given an atomistic metaphysics and an Empiricist epistemology, because both the philosophical and the psychological solutions are unsatisfying. Most notably, of course, personal identity or the problem of the Self falls into this category—certain things just cannot be glued back together once they are taken apart and the Self appears to have this Humpty-Dumpty character. Hume begins his investigation of personal identity, as he does with causality and most other questions, by asking what sense impression provides us with our concept of a Self. He acknowledges that some philosophers, Descartes perhaps, claim to have not only a direct impression of a Self, but also a constant and enduring one. Hume, however, says that in his own case "when I enter most intimately into what I call *myself*, I always stumble on some particular impression or other" (p. 252). He also points out that we cannot have such an impression of the Self during sleep, and so an explanation is still required of how we know, when we awaken, that the Self we now have an impression of is the same Self we had an impression of when we went to sleep. For these and related reasons, he decides, as in the case of causality, that wherever our concept of the Self might come from, it does not come either from some logical reasoning (since the nonexistence of a Self is logically possible) or from our senses (since we have no such sense impression).

He turns, therefore, to the question of identity per se, and finds that it is one area in which the human mind tends to be inordinately sloppy in its thinking: "tho' we commonly be able to distinguish pretty exactly betwixt numerical and specific identity, yet it sometimes happens that we confound them, and in our thinking and reasoning employ the one for the other" (pp. 257–58). Using the famous case of the ship that is slowly rebuilt piece by piece until it is an entirely different ship, he establishes that we attribute identity, usually out of convenience, to a great many things that are not self-identical at all. It is important to see that when Hume applies this argument to the problem of personal identity, it results in a radically different estimation of the depth of the problem than in the case of causality. Our belief in causal necessity is really based on an internal impression of necessity that we project onto the external world. In the case of the Self, however, "The identity, which we ascribe to the mind of man, is only a fictitious one" (p. 259). There is no impression of the Self at all, only a series of related impressions, to which we erroneously attribute unity. There is, for Hume, no Self, no "mental substance," but merely a "bucket" of unrelated, atomic ideas.

The rejection of the concept of a Self or of "mental substance" in Hume has serious consequence for his views on religion as well. In "natural" theology, that is, proofs of the existence and nature of God through logic alone (another Cartesian question with which all modern philosophers have been forced to grapple), the usual progression from Locke through Berkeley to Hume within the Empricist tradition appears to be broken. Locke's account of our "demonstrative" knowledge of the existence of God is much closer to Hume's than the more idiosyncratic version found in Berkeley. Locke begins with self-knowledge in proving God's existence, but does not rely on a substantial concept of the Self. He gives, rather, a "first cause" proof of God's existence that requires only human rationality, or consciousness, as the basis for establishing that the world requires an intelligent Creator. (This is the question-begging argument noted in the previous chapter.) He also is willing to leave open the issue of what idea, if any, we can be said to have of God, and accepts the divine existence on purely impersonal, abstract grounds. He is, in the *Essay* at least, a sort of proto-deist.

In Berkeley's *Three Dialogues,* however, God tends toward the immanent instead of the transcendent, being intimately involved in our every mental state, as guarantor (if not warehouse) of the existence of material objects independent of human minds. For Berkeley, therefore, it becomes much more important that we have an actual idea of God, since it is the nonexistence of an idea of matter that rules it out as the possible explanation of the independent existence of material objects. (Berkeley also argues that the concept of matter is incoherent, but that seems a more questionable argument, both with regard to matter and with regard to God.) When Hylas asks Philonous, in good Empiricist fashion, what impression the idea of God is based on, Philonous says that it is an extension of our idea of the Self (p. 65). He goes on, of course, to admit that there is something rather mysterious about this idea, since it is not based directly on sense impressions, but seems to regard this as a minor complication. Clearly, therefore, Hume's denial that we have such an idea of the Self immediately puts him on the other side of Locke's "agnosticism" about our idea of God (as in the case of substance) and into a position where God's nature, if not existence, must remain unknown and unknowable. Thus, deism—the belief in an abstract and impersonal God—seems to be a logical implication of Empiricism itself, once it is made entirely self-consistent.

Something very much like this argument appears in a footnote to the Appendix to the *Treatise:*

> The order of the universe proves an omnipotent mind; that is, a mind whose will is *constantly attended* with the obedience of every creature and being. Nothing more is requisite to give a foundation to all the articles of religion, nor is it necessary we shou'd form a distinct idea of the force and energy of the supreme Being. (p. 633)

Earlier, however, in discussing the immateriality of the soul, Hume also makes it clear that any purported first cause argument for God's existence (Locke's, for example) must suffer the severe disability of not being able to give a coherent account of what causality can mean in the absence of any contiguity or constant conjunction. The "philosophical" content of the concept of causality obviously cannot be applied when we are speaking of God, "since our idea of that supreme Being is deriv'd from particular impressions, none of which contain any efficacy, nor seem to have *any* connexion with *any* other existence" (p. 248). So God can be known neither by analogy to the Self nor by causal arguments, and, as with substance in Locke, can only be an "inconceivable Somewhat." Further, this deistic God is inconceivable just because a unified and integrated Self is inconceivable, that is, because connection is inconceivable in the philosophical realm. The apparent conclusion of the *Dialogues Concerning Natural Religion* "that the cause or causes of order in the universe probably bear some remote analogy to human intelligence" (p. 88) would just be another step in the continuing erasure of connection and meaning in the world in favor of mechanism and an Engineer/Creator—a very abstract and impersonal God indeed.

The rejection of a substantial Self in Hume also marks one way in which my own analysis of his work in this area differs significantly from Sandra Harding's in the article already discussed, "The Social Function of the Empiricist Conception of Mind." Harding attributes directly to Hume the differentiation between the mind of the scientist and the mind of those he studies that was noted earlier. This is one case, however, where I think a distinction can be made between history and ideology that might be more beneficial to a feminist analysis of Hume's work. It is certainly true that a strong differentiation between my own experience of myself as a unified entity (in the modern

European world, at least) and Hume's account of the Self as a "bucket" of ideas results in an ideology that radically separates the investigator or the ruler from the object of investigation or the ruled, with the effects, both scientific and political, that Harding describes. What I would take issue with, though, is the claim that this is what Hume himself is doing. In Hume, rather, I think it is unusually clear that Hume's dispersed and divided Self is a self-portrait, as it were, and that this self-disclosure, in conjunction with a number of others, primarily those that mock the "mere" philosopher and the "Pyrrhonian," tell us much more about Hume than he may have intended.

This "self-portrait" would include the strong statement in the preceding section that indicates that the only alternative to atomism is total absorption and loss of identity, and the possible interpretation of Hume's concept of the philosophical as a form of theoretical matricide. There is also the picture of a fractured and incomplete Self and the constant reminders both of our extreme epistemological limitations and of the cruelty with which people treat those who make those limitations clear to them. Finally, there are the possible responses to the necessity of the deistic principle quoted above that he lists at the end of the *Dialogues Concerning Natural Religion,* including ". . . Some melancholy from its obscurity: Some contempt of human reason that it can give no solution more satisfactory with regard to so extraordinary and magnificent a question" (p. 89). Of course, this is only a partial picture of Hume's work, but it is a consistent picture, and one that suggests a mind prone, at the least, to a depressive view of the world—a mind that sees the world as one in which nothing is the way it should be and no one wants to be reminded of that unpleasant fact. This depressive view, moreover, is linked to the atomistic way that Hume sees the world and so to the fact that this world can be defined "philosophically" as one without relationship, a world without a mother and, therefore, also ultimately without any access to the father/God as a source of meaning. Thus, I would argue that Hume does see himself as a victim of a world he would reject if he could and not as an observer privileged to escape the common destiny of men. One might also ask if it is because Hume more clearly exposes, and perhaps more acutely feels, the costs of a purely male-defined philosophy that some aspects of his work reflect what might be considered stereotypically female thinking.

Ethical Considerations

In a certain sense, everything that comes after Book I of the *Treatise* can be regarded more as psychology than as philosophy. In the book on the Passions and the one on Morals, Hume is giving us a quasi-scientific, naturalistic account of how the human mind happens to work, rather than logical, rational explanations of philosophical truths. Moreover, the result of that account is to prove that "Reason is, and ought only to be the slave of the passions, and can never pretend to any other office than to serve and obey them" (p. 415). Let us stop here a moment and look at this famous personification of reason and passion. Why does it seem to violate our normal way of thinking? And what does its "shock value" say about the gender imagery that is built into this powerful sado-masochistic metaphor? In fact, it has retained its "shock value" through two hundred years of more or less "emotivist" moral theory in the Anglo-American world not only because our pre-philosophical experience of the world continues to be at odds with Hume's emotivism, but also *because* of the gender imagery: Reason is male and passion female, so for the former to be slave to the latter remains a radical departure from the way the world "really is." (A more complete feminist deconstruction of the Humean text might then also ask if this gender imagery was "only" a metaphor.)

Parts of the above analysis are based on Annette Baier's recent and very insightful discussion of Hume's gender bias, or lack thereof, in "Hume, The Woman's Moral Theorist?" As her title suggests, Baier draws on Gilligan's account of the differences in men's and women's moral reasoning to argue that Hume's moral theory, with its emphasis on "sympathy" and connection, more closely reflects stereotypically female moral thinking than male thinking. Therefore, Baier thinks that Hume's work can provide a basis for women's ethics because it involves more balancing of claims and stresses the emotional rather than the rational in ethical thought. She contrasts this with the strong emphasis on rules and reason in the Kantian moral theory that provides the basis for the Kohlberg scale of moral development with which Gilligan takes issue. For instance, Hume traces the origin of the political state to the family rather than to a "social contract" (with its gender implications, as suggested above) while seeming to avoid the explicit patriarchal bias such a claim traditionally carried.

As I pointed out earlier, however, one can also read Hume's moral theory not as a valuing of women's moral reasoning, but as a devaluing of morality itself, a "demotion" of it, as it were, to the "merely" emotional and irrational side of things, the "merely" female half of all of the traditional dichotomies, a tendency that continues in contemporary Anglo-American philosophers such as Ayer.[20] For instance, Louise Marcil Lacoste, in "The Consistency of Hume's Position Concerning Women," traces Hume's allocation of women among others of these traditional dualisms, notably the pair public/private and natural/artificial (in which case, she points out, Hume's thinking is extremely complex). Baier's argument here, then, may fit into a common conumdrum of contemporary feminist thought: If we value (or commend those who value) those aspects of human life that have traditionally been given to women, those right-hand sides of the dualisms, we also run the risk of merely restating and thereby reinforcing the traditional identification of women with, and hence their limitation to, only those aspects of life. If we do not do so, however, we risk also de-valuing women by acceding to our culture's preference for the left-hand side of each pair. Therefore, agreement or disagreement with Baier is less the issue here than the need to see and evaluate both sides of Hume's work.

What Lacoste brings out about the gender bias of Hume's moral thought, however, seems to support a less benevolent view of his work than the one Baier presents. She notes, as Baier also suggests, that some of the apparent sexism in Hume's writings are simply reflections of the social world in which he lived. He drew his morality from a quasi-empirical consideration of what was in fact the case in his culture and, not surprisingly, ended up describing women in limited and stereotypical ways. The question Lacoste asks is whether this "empirical" approach to ethical theory does not itself perpetuate the gender bias it discovers in society, and finally end by providing a justification for it.[21] This point returns to one discussed with regard to Locke: Is classical liberal Individualism inherently conservative to the extent that it gives legal equality to persons who are socially quite unequal? That is, if we look "objectively" at people as they now are, with their previous social liabilities, we may find many gender, race, and other differences with regard to intelligence, moral reasoning, and so on, and may see unequal outcomes as the result, not of an unfair system, but of "natural" differences. Lacoste suggests that any quasi-empirical ethical theory might have this kind of structural bias built into it from the start.

Those parts of Hume's moral thought that are more closely tied to his Empiricist epistemology and metaphysics, moreover, are correspondingly less well-suited to women's moral thinking. When Hume applies his account of causality to human behavior, for instance, he develops a rather paradoxical response to the traditional problem of Free Will. On the one hand, we have no more proof of causality in human behavior than elsewhere, so we cannot say that human actions are or are not caused in a strong, metaphysical sense of the term. On the other hand, though, we do have in the case of human behavior exactly the same kind of constant conjunction that we have in the case of physical causation, so that the human will (which we never really understand in any case, Hume reminds us) is no more, and no less, causally determined than events in the physical world.

Two things are of note here. First of all, this concept of Free Will as a "pseudo-problem" remains, like Hume's emotivism, a mainstay of Anglo-American moral thought, so not much progress has been made toward resolving the paradox since Hume first stated it. Second, this dualistic account (which derives its structure from the question itself: Do we have Free Will or not?) excludes a level of causality considered significant by many feminist thinkers (and many others outside the Anglo-American philosophical tradition). Jaggar, for example, argues in *Feminist Politics and Human Nature* that many human actions are neither the acts of a free, autonomous will nor the passive result of strictly physical causality, but are rather choices among a set of options limited by what can be called social necessity—for instance the one Hume himself notes that places far more value on the chastity of women.[22] If a woman is said to have Free Will, she freely chooses to remain chaste or to sin if she does not. If she is said not to have Free Will, her chastity or sin are caused by chains of physical events. To the woman, however, her freedom, or lack of it, might be much more accurately described in terms of the social benefits and costs of her chastity, and those will not in any sense be something over which she herself has control. Her choices, free or determined, are severely constrained by a social context in which she herself is often powerless—and it is this issue, not her metaphysical freedom or lack of it, that is of importance *to her,* and is arguably the most important moral question as well.

What moral Individualism does, both in Locke and in Hume, is to provide the means for those with power to act freely, or at least with what counts as freedom for Hume, while it denies that there is another kind of freedom, the very social freedom that the powerful enjoy and that other groups, notably women and the poor, could also have but are denied. Hume's apparently "objective" account of Free Will effectively obscures this far more complex reality. The issue of gender bias in Hume, therefore, is very subtle. In many ways, Hume is admirable for the consistency with which he works out the logical implications of the basic beliefs of British Empiricism, and demonstrates their inability to solve many of the central philosophical questions Empiricism poses. In many ways, also, Hume is admirable for stepping outside what he considers to be the strictly philosophical to generate alternative answers to those questions that suggest a less gender-biased view of the world. In many other ways, however, Hume is as completely the prisoner of the Empiricist paradigm with regard to gender as he is with regard to other central questions—and his scepticism does not extend to questioning the male bias of the paradigm itself. That critical work has fallen to the recent chorus of feminist voices from a variety of perspectives within Anglo-American philosophy whose analyses in many cases seem to parallel my reading of the Empiricist tradition.

Notes

1. David Hume, *A Treatise of Human Nature,* ed. L. A. Selby-Bigge (New York: Oxford University Press, 1975), p. 395.
2. David Hume, *Hume's Enquiries,* ed. L. A. Selby-Bigge (New York: Oxford University Press, 1975), p. 213.
3. My thinking about Hume, and especially on this point, has been greatly influenced by Annette Baier's paper "Hume, The Women's Moral Theorist?" in *Women and Moral Theory,* ed. Eva Feder Kittay and Diana T. Meyers (Totowa, N.J.: Rowman and Littlefield, 1987), although she would probably not endorse my conclusions.
4. See *Treatise,* p. 486, and *Hume's Enquiries,* pp. 300–01.
5. Hume, *Hume's Enquiries,* p. 213.
6. I first heard the expression "bucket theory of mind" from John Searle.
7. In addition to Baier's paper, noted above, see also Steven Burns, "The Humean Female," *Dialogue* 15, no. 3 (1976): 415–24; and Louise Marcil Lacoste's response, "The Consistency of Hume's Position Concerning Women," *Dialogue* 15, no. 3 (1976): 425–40). Marcia Lind, of Duke University, also argues for a feminist ethics based on Hume's thought, in a paper on "Hume and Feminist Moral Theory" that she read at a conference on "Explorations in Feminist Ethics," held October 7 and 8, 1988, and sponsored by the University of Minnesota at Duluth.
8. David Hume, *Dialogues Concerning Natural Religion,* ed. Richard H. Popkin (Indianapolis: Hackett, 1983).
9. Gary Shapiro, in his "The Man of Letters and the Author of Nature: Hume on Philosophical Discourse," *The Eighteenth Century: Theory and Interpretation* (1985): 115–37, argues for a rhetorical difference between Hume's *Dialogues Concerning Natural Religion* and standard British Empiricist discourse, but the feminist analysis here suggests a greater continuity, at least with regard to gender-relevant content.

10. Nancy Chodorow, *The Reproduction of Mothering* (Berkeley: University of California Press, 1978).

11. Derrida, in the section of *Dissemination* called "Plato's Pharmacy," traces out a similar move in Plato that Derrida describes as a response to the inconceivability of "man's" bisexual origin. I sketch out the matricidal side of the argument in "The Treble Clef/t: Jacques Derrida and the Female Voice," in *Philosophy and Culture: Proceedings of the XVIIth World Congress of Philosophy*, vol. 2 (microfiche), Editions de Montmorency, 1988.

12. Naomi Scheman, "Othello's Doubt/Desdemona's Death: The Engendering of Scepticism," in *Power, Gender, Value*, ed. Judith Genova (Edmonton, Alberta: Academic Printing and Publishing, 1987), pp. 120–21.

13. Seyla Benhabib, "The Generalized and the Concrete Other," in *Feminism as Critique*, ed. Seyla Benhabib and Drucilla Cornell (Minneapolis: University of Minnesota Press, 1987), p. 83.

14. Susan Bordo, *The Flight to Objectivity*, fn. 6, p. 127; Alice Jardine, *Gynesis*, p. 233.

15. In *Moses and Monotheism*, trans. Katherine Jones (New York: Vintage Books, 1939) Freud himself links the Orestes myth with an equation of the pair male/female to the pair reason/sense (pp. 145–46, cited in Hélène Cixous and Catherine Clement's *The Newly Born Woman*, trans. Betsy Wing (Minneapolis: University of Minnesota Press, 1986), p. 100), which closely parallels the present account of Hume as seeing female-defined "psychology" as an alternative to the failures of male-defined "philosophy." Naomi Scheman quotes the same passage from Freud in her "Othello's Doubt/Desdemona's Death," cited in note #12.

16. Christine Di Stefano, "Masculinity as Ideology in Political Theory: Hobbesian Man Considered," *Women's Studies International Forum* 6, no. 6 (1983): 638.

17. Jane Flax, "Political Philosophy and the Patriarchal Unconscious: A Psychoanalytic Perspective on Epistemology and Metaphysics," in *Discovering Reality*, ed. Sandra Harding and Merrill B. Hintikka (Boston: D. Reidel, 1983).

18. This point was developed in conversations with Glenn Holland of Allegheny College, but similar issues are raised both in Bordo's book and in Scheman's paper, which I read subsequently.

19. In fact, it was Stroud who first turned my attention to the analogies between Hume's work and Derrida's that led to the current project. My understanding of Stroud's own work on Hume also benefited from discussions with Janet Broughton of the University of California at Berkeley.

20. Stroud seems to support my view by making a distinction between philosophy and morality in Hume, the later being closer to the psychological "data" just because it is somewhat independent of the theory of ideas, unlike "the more purely intellectual cases" (*Hume*, p. 233).

21. María Brewer, in "A Loosening of Tongues: From Narrative Economy

to Women Writing," *Modern Language Notes* 99, no. 5 (December 1984): 1141–61, uses J. L. Austin's concept of performative speech acts to argue that "when women are told they are silent, they hear the imperative 'do not speak' " (cited by Winnie Woodhull in *Power, Gender, Values,* ed. Judith Genova (Edmonton, Alberta: Academic Printing and Publishing, 1987) pp. 25–26). A similar phenomenon in Hume may explain the intuition that some women philosophers have that his texts tend to be conservative with regard to gender issues.

In fact, Hume goes somewhat further than reporting, or supporting, the sexual status quo in "A Dialogue," which appears in the Selby-Bigge edition of *Hume's Enquiries* (pp. 342–43). There he offers a justification for what Sarah Kofman calls "women's confinement on a reservation" by arguing that adultery is the necessary price "we" pay for the participation of women in the social world. While he does not go so far as Rousseau in recommending sex segregation, his argument could be subjected to an analysis similar to the one in Kofman's "Rousseau's Phallocratic Ends," trans. Mara Dukats, *Hyaptia* 3, no. 3 (Fall 1988): 123–36.

22. See, for instance, *Feminist Politics and Human Nature,* p. 305.

Chapter 3

The Feminist and the Individual[1]

The Political Individual

Contemporary feminist scepticism about male bias in traditional Anglo-American philosophy first became most evident in political philosophy, where the contrast between egalitarian theory and male dominance is more overt, and in the closely related area of ethical thought, where the special ethical dilemmas of women (abortion above all) showed the conceptual limitations of the usual philosophical paradigms. A relatively early collection of feminist philosophy, published as Volume 5, nos. 1–2 of *The Philosophical Forum* (Fall–Winter 1973–1974) and then as *Women and Philosophy,* consists primarily, although far from exclusively, of papers from these two fields.[2] A large number of these papers, moreover, focus precisely on the issue of Individualism within Anglo-American political and moral philosophy as a major example of male bias. As feminist thought has developed since then, it has become increasingly clear that Individualism is part of a much larger problem, and later feminist writings in the philosophy of science, epistemology, metaphysics, and ontology reiterate the originally more narrow critique. In this chapter I will attempt to trace this critique through these various fields in roughly the last fifteen years, both to illustrate the breadth and depth of the feminist tradition on which I am drawing in my own arguments, and also to use the important insights and examples provided by other feminist philosophers to support some of the specific claims I have made here.

I have already discussed Alison Jaggar's concept of abstract individualism in *Feminist Politics and Human Nature* so, rather than repeat her arguments here, I will discuss instead Robert Paul Wolff's especially clear statement of political Individualism in "There's Nobody Here But Us Persons" from the *Philosophical Forum*.³

> I conceive of human beings, insofar as they are moral or political creatures, as rational agents capable of reasoned deliberation and choice, as persons moved by reasons, bound by their contractual agreements, metaphysically free and alike in the fundamental moral condition. (p. 128)

This Individualism has the obvious political consequence that "all . . . distinctions—of age, sex, race, and the rest—should systematically be ignored in the arrangements and operations of our social, political, and economic institutions" (pp. 128–29). Wolff's concern with the issue, like Jaggar's, arises from the increasingly obvious conclusion that our attempts at such a color-, gender-, age-blind approach in fact serve to perpetuate discrimination, and seem unable to solve many of the social problems that liberalism itself sets out to solve.

The "crisis of liberalism" that Jaggar and Wolff describe can be seen as purely political: in his view, as a result of the public/private split; or, in one of Jaggar's formulations, as due to our overemphasis on rights as opposed to needs; or as a conflict between the commitment to freedom and the commitment to equality in traditional liberalism, as Onora Nell argues in the same volume.⁴ Beneath the concern about balancing between the competing claims of freedom and equality, however, feminist analysis reveals as far larger question—how much equality *or* freedom is there in a world in which we are, as Wolff says, "socially determined, quite dissimilar in [our] moral condition, essentially and not merely accidentally differentiated from one another by sex, by race, by age, by ego-formation, by culture, and by economic class?" (p. 128). Wolff's paper comes to the conclusion that we cannot even conceive of a solution to this as a political problem, so deeply are we embedded, not only in liberalism, but in the metaphysical Individualism that underlies it.

In her book, *The Radical Future of Liberal Feminism,* Zillah Eisenstein returns to the political roots of liberal feminism to support her contention that liberalism is itself a compromise or balance between the conflicting demands of patriarchy (or the rule of men as men) and capitalism (or the rule of abstract wealth). Liberalism has succeeded in this balancing act, as Wolff and many others also suggest, by making a strong distinction between the public sphere assigned to capitalism and the private sphere where patriarchy remains in control. This is the reason that liberalism tends to define an Individual as the head of a household: In the public realm only the "productive" labor of the male worker counts as part of the "political economy," and the private "reproductive" labor of the woman in the home is covertly included in this basic economic unit. On this view, Individualism is part of an ideology that covers up not only the continuing rule of patriarchy in the family, but also the fact that women's work is necessary to the economy. Liberalism "forgets" that Individuals are born and live many years as dependent children (and many more years as interdependent adults), rather than fitting the Lockean model of an isolated, independent, atomic (male) adult who participates in society only through a conscious, and in theory totally contingent, choice.

Eisenstein draws two important conclusions from this analysis. The first is that liberal feminism, as Jaggar likewise points out, is involved in an inherent contradiction between its feminist awareness that women are oppressed as a class, as women, and its commitment to liberal Individualism, which denies the relevance of group membership to political considerations (since historically members of only one group counted as Individuals in the first place). It is this contradiction that will lead, she argues, to liberal feminism's eventual radicalization. The second conclusion she considers in her analysis is that the liberal balance between capitalism and patriarchy is beginning to break down. Capitalism increasingly requires that women work in order to create a growing market, and as women work they not only gain more economic power within the family (which has been the case for most women for most of history) but also are put in a position to see more clearly that they are treated as women, that is, patriarchically, in the marketplace as well as in the family. Since capitalism requires gender inequality in wages, and so on, to maintain profits, even independently of its patriarchal underpinnings, once women see the emptiness of liberal claims of equality in the public sphere the stage is set, empirically as well as theoretically, for a more radical feminism.

Recognizing that women in the Anglo-American world are unlikely to reject Individualism outright (while we might be willing to return to the pre-industrial family-based economy, would we really want to return to the pre-Hobbesian family-based criminal system that jailed Thomas More's wife and children along with him?), Eisenstein calls for a new concept of what she calls "individuality":

> Until a conscious differentiation is made between a theory of individuality that recognizes the importance of the individual within the social collectivity and the ideology of individualism that assumes a competitive view

of the individual, there will not be a full accounting of what a feminist theory of liberation must look like for Western society. (p. 5)

Such a concept of "individuality" would take account of our existence as a social species and our social interdependence, Eisenstein argues, while acknowledging that the Western concept of adulthood is deeply tied to concepts of autonomy and responsibility.

Mary Hawkesworth makes a similar point about "individuality" and Individualism in an article on "The Affirmative Action Debate and Conflicting Conceptions of Individuality."[5] There she contrasts what she calls "atomic individualism" (i.e., Individualism) with "socialized individualism," which she describes as emphasizing "the impact of cultural norms and group practices upon the development of individual identity and the pervasive influence of internal as well as external obstacles to individual freedom" (p. 336). In the specific context of affirmative action, the difference can be found between those who say that, absent formal and overt discrimination, all applicants for social goods should be considered strictly on merit, and those who point at the obvious social inequalities that continue to exist between the genders and the races as reasons why special considerations should be given to members of under-represented groups. One of Hawkesworth's main contentions is also somewhat similar to Eisenstein's in that she claims that those who would support affirmative action are hampered in their efforts because they do not make a clear distinction between the two forms of individualism and so do not see that they are no longer functioning strictly within the liberal tradition of formal equality.

Another way in which liberal ideology works against feminist consciousness is discussed in Bell Hooks's *Feminist Theory: From Margin to Center*.[6] The same emphasis on intentional discrimination used by opponents of affirmative action, when internalized by white, middle-class feminists, leads us to ignore the extent to which we are oppressors of others, as well as the victims of male oppression. Since we do not intend to oppress poor people, people of color, children, seniors, the disabled, and so on, our own liberal Individualism tells us that we are not doing so and renders our oppressive behavior invisible to us, just as it often renders men's oppressive behavior toward us invisible to them. And this is not only a problem for white, middle-class feminists as individuals, but undermines feminism as a whole, since it causes a well-founded mistrust among women from the groups in whose oppression we participate. At the same time, Hooks suggests, to be able to see ourselves as oppressors can be paradoxically liberating, both in terms of the extent to which it allows us to re-own our power (even if it is a power we do not want) and cease to see ourselves as victims (a view of our privileged position that few poor women and women of color can share), and in terms of the ability it gives us to avoid seeing men as a group as the oppressors and therefore framing feminist issues in anti-male terms, which also alienates groups of women who feel a strong solidarity with the men who share their struggles as members of other oppressed groups. Hooks argues that such a change in the attitude of white, middle-class feminists can help us "keep in mind that the struggle to end sexual oppression is only one component of a larger struggle to transform society and establish a new social order" (p. 156).

Whether put in such revolutionary terms or not, all of these arguments represent a partial repudiation of the political legacy that comes to us from British Empiricism, on both a societal and a personal level. As has already been said with regard to Locke and Hume, the political equality and freedom explicitly given to "man" in the Anglo-American liberal tradition is meaningless in the absence of concrete social equality that guarantees the means of acting on that equality and freedom. Whether women or non-European men are explicitly and intentionally excluded from certain activities and benefits in our society is less important here than the fact that those activities, what counts as a benefit (could a woman be bribed with a prostitute?), and the society itself are defined so completely in terms of the middle-class, male, European experience of the world. Thus, it has become increasingly clear in feminist thought that the purely formal equality, whether political, epistemological, or metaphysical, that the British Empiricism political legacy grants to the (European, male) Individual, serves to conceal, mystify, and perpetuate concrete inequalities of race, class, gender, age, and so on.

Applications of Individualism

In this section, I would like to take some specific examples that have been used by feminist theorists in the critique of Individualism and demonstrate how they refer back to the roots of Individualism in the metaphysical and epistemological atomism of British Empiricism. I have chosen cases that are of some contemporary political importance, but the choice is somewhat arbitrary both in that there are many other issues of public policy that I could have considered and in that these and similar cases can be found in the writings of many other feminists. These presentations seem to me, however, to be particularly clear and effective uses of the material available. There are, of course, many other ways of analyzing these cases, and my own analysis is not always exactly the same as that of the writers to whom I refer, but I believe that the critique of Individualism plays a large part in these writers' arguments, and have chosen to emphasize, and perhaps exaggerate, that aspect of their work in order to make as effective an argument as possible about the limitations of Individualism as a political theory for feminist thought and as a basis for public policy in the concrete circumstances in which women find themselves.

The first example I would like to discuss is from Eisenstein's *The Radical Future of Liberal Feminism*. In her analysis of the inherent limitations of liberal feminism, she points out that the current abortion policy of the United States denies the "individuality," as defined above, of women by paradoxically insisting, inappropriately in some cases, on our group status as women, and hence as excluded from the rights granted to men under classical Individualism, and insisting in other cases on our status as classical Individuals to deny women's rights by ignoring our group status. The Roe v. Wade Supreme Court decision, Eisenstein argues, gives the right to choose an abortion not to the woman, but to her *doctor,* thereby perpetuating the patriarchal dependence of women on men (or those who are given the "honorary" male status of a medical degree) and denying that women have the right to make such a decision on our own—we are merely given a right to medical privacy that is strictly limited by the interests of the state, for example, in regulating second and third trimester abortions. At the same time, the Hyde Amendment prohibiting the use of federal funds for most abortions ignores the social conditions that make such a limitation in effect an illegalization of abortion for poor women by asserting, in effect, that they have the right to "medical privacy" as atomic Individuals, a right that exists independently of any concrete means of exercising it. Women, as a group, are incapable of making an abortion decision, although we have the right to privacy if a doctor will make it for us, but if poor women, as a group, cannot afford to have a doctor make such a decision for them, that is their individual problem and does not interfere with the exercise of their "rights." Eisenstein argues that the two cases together prove that no woman has any rights with regard to abortion because they simultaneously deny and insist upon our status as classical Individuals.

Taking the social welfare system itself as her subject, Nancy Fraser, in "Women, Welfare and The Politics of Need Interpretation," follows Barbara Nelson and others in finding that welfare in the United States is really a two-tier, gender-defined system that allows for a very similar analysis.[7] The male tier of welfare includes compensation programs such as unemployment insurance and workmen's disability, while the female tier consists of need-based programs such as Aid to Families with Dependent Children (AFDC), food stamps, Medicaid, and so on. The male tier uses a standardized, quasi-judicial process to meet the financial needs of individuals with direct cash payments. The female tier uses a locally variable, quasi-therapeutic process to meet the administratively defined needs of "problem" (i.e., female-headed) families, often with in-kind payments. Paradoxically, it is the individualized male tier that recognizes that many of the problems that cause people to become its clients are social problems and so these programs often carry direct or indirect sanctions for employers who lay off too many workers or have too many accidents in the workplace. In the female tier, on the other hand, the "problem" family is considered to be the result of women's individual failures (not of men abandoning their families or of low wages, underemployment, lack of health benefits, etc.) and so the woman becomes the object of a "therapeutic" intervention, which is justified both as "for her own good" and as necessary to keep welfare costs down. Again, we have here the pattern of women being de-valued and treated by the government as members of a group and *at the same time* being blamed as individuals for their membership in that group. In short, women are Individuals when it comes to responsibility, a de-valued class when it comes to benefits.

There are many other examples of cases in which the needs of women created by our de-valued status under patriarchy are treated as if they were problems of individual pathology under the misplaced Individualism of our liberal political legacy. In one section of *Science and Gender*, Ruth Bleier discusses how the medical treatment of battered women, like the treatment of women in the welfare system, redefines their needs in terms of the treatment that the bureaucracy is able to provide.[8] Beyond any casual tendency in the medical establishment to blame women and their "natural masochism" for the beatings they receive, Bleier reports that Stark et al. have shown that, as a *result* of battering, women often develop problems of self-esteem, drug abuse, suicidal tendencies, and other psychopathologies. The response of medical professionals is then to determine that the battering has been *caused by* these symptomatic responses to it, which they conveniently can "treat," for example, through medication, and shift the focus and the blame from the batterer to the victim. Women are battered (and raped) because they are women, not for their individual failings, but the doctrine of liberal Individualism assures the medical personnel involved that when they have "cured" the woman, the battering will stop, because she must be responsible as an individual for the beatings she received as a woman. (Of course, it is not a complete reversal of this pattern to blame the batterer as an individual for a behavior pattern he was taught as a member of a group, i.e., as a child in a battering family. Violence, as Bell Hooks makes clear in her book, is not an individual problem in this society.)

A similar misplaced Individualism divides feminists themselves in the two cases considered by Marjorie Weinzweig in her article on "Pregnancy Leave, Comparable Worth, and Concepts of Equality."[9] On the issue of whether a state can mandate special pregnancy leaves above and beyond normal disability leave available to all employees (recently decided by the Supreme Court in California Federal Savings v. Guerra), some feminists argue against such "protective" legislation on the grounds that it would provide employers with an additional motive for not hiring women, especially in more responsible, and hence less easily replaced, positions.[10] Other feminists argue that it is ridiculous to maintain that there could be a "gender neutral" policy on pregnancy, although that was the previous Supreme Court position. (The Court argued that pregnancy divided pregnant women on the one hand from men and all other women on the other, rather than dividing men from women.) This disagreement among feminists can be seen as a result of the limited set of alternatives our society provides us with in addressing reproductive issues. *Either* we are Individuals and hence, by definition, male (so we will always be clearly disabled or not, and will have a wife and so will never be needed at home) *or* we are women, members of a class that is, by definition, given the task of child-rearing in our society and so cannot aspire to the same level of achievement as men. That men might have an interest in the bearing or raising of children, or even more radically, that employers and our society as a whole might have such an interest, is not among the alternatives our liberal tradition provides. Thus, the Supreme Court ruling in favor of pregnancy and maternity leave is paradoxically a pro-women decision that is also pro-family (i.e., patriarchal), reinforcing women's primary attachment to the home and secondary status in the workplace.

The other case Weinzweig discusses is the issue of "comparable pay" or "pay equity," that is, paying women in traditionally female job classifications on the basis of equity with jobs that require the same training, responsibility, and so on, but are traditionally male. The call for pay equity comes from two simple facts about the contemporary workplace. First, women continue to be primarily employed in traditionally female jobs and to be paid roughly seventy cents for every dollar a man makes. Since large numbers of women are unlikely to move into male-dominated jobs, this situation will probably continue for many years, keeping women in a position of financial inferiority to men. Second, many companies and governmental units have been using for some time a variety of job evaluation systems that allow them to rate different jobs with regard to comparability, although the results have been used to adjust pay rates for some classifications only within the confines of "market" conditions, that is, how much other employers pay for the same kind of work. Since the market pays less for "women's work" than it does for men's work, these comparability scales have not been used to the advantage of women in historically female job categories. What the pay equity debate brings out is that *only* the male bias of the market could explain such anomalies as the fact that nurses are paid less than truck drivers, that is, that women are underpaid with respect to what their jobs require *because they are women*. Still, the opponents of pay equity, including some feminists, argue the cure should be an individual one, that is, that women should move into male job categories and increase their pay that way, without any governmental intervention in the "free" actions of Individuals or the "market."

To take a final, closely related issue, Rosemarie Tong's discussion of sexual harassment in *Women, Sex and the Law* not only fits the pattern followed by all of the above examples, but it also provides an additional illustration of the way in which our legal system embodies our society's commitment to Individualism to the detriment of women when they are victimized as members of a group.[11] The theoretical core of Tong's account of the various legal remedies in cases of sexual harassment is that "sexual harassment is an extremely concrete way to remind women that their subordination as a gender is intimately tied to their sexuality, in particular to their reproductive capacities and in general to their bodily contours" (p. 162). On this view, the difficulty our legal system has in confronting sexual harassment stems, in part, from the fact that sexual harassment is not something that takes place between two Individuals, as a seduction might, but is the expression of the power of men as a group over their female subordinates, a reality our legal system is ill-prepared to take into consideration.

This explains several problematic features of sexual harassment. First of all, men tend not to see it as a problem, not only because they see it in terms of Individualism, but also because the exercise of their own power is invisible to them—coercing subordinates is just what one does and the "harm" of sexual coercion seems to stem merely from the fact that it is *sexual* (hence they think that those opposed to sexual harassment would also oppose consensual sex between co-workers). Secondly, it explains why the objects of sexual harassment are often chosen for reasons quite different than one would suppose if they were the objects of a seduction, for example, for their passivity or their conformity to a type or the position they hold in the organization rather than for any particular qualities they may have as persons. The group basis for sexual harassment also explains two problems our legal system finds especially difficult. The "disparate impact" approach to trying sexual harassment cases as civil rights violations that Tong discusses makes sense only if one sees that it is not only the harassed women who are victimized by the harasser, but all women in the workplace because it is *as women* that the victims are being harassed. Finally, Tong also notes that the courts have been more reluctant to find employers liable for harassment on the job by co-workers than when the harasser is in a position of power over the victim. What this ignores, on the current analysis, is that the purpose of sexual harassment is to remind women that their identity is as reproducers rather than as producers and to inappropriately sexualize their participation in the "public" realm. Often this goal is more overt in harassment by co-workers than in other cases, and the court's refusal to see this as the basic issue in sexual harassment underscores the inappropriate Individualism of our legal system with regard to this problem.

It is important to note that one "subtext" of sexual harassment, even from men who would not participate in it, often amounts to saying "What did she expect? If she wants to work [here], she'd better learn to take it." That is, behind our society's attitude toward sexual harassment lurks the idea that any woman in the public arena becomes "fair game" sexually simply because she is outside the home. Thus a powerful structure seems to be taking shape in this set of examples: women have no rights because they "belong" in the home as attachments to the heads of households to whom rights belong; when women attempt to exercise the rights they have acquired by the generalization of men's rights, they are treated as Individuals, that is, as men, and their specific needs as women are ignored; and when women work outside the home, they continue to be seen and evaluated as women, so that they are paid less and subject to sexual harassment as a result of their unpaid work in the home and their sexual status there. This ancient and very patriarchal configuration can be found very close to the surface in the cases I have discussed, and in many others besides. The usual response to such claims is "We don't do that here, so it cannot be a problem," that is, the claim that since specific men and institutions do not fit this pattern, the pattern itself does not exist. This claim, in turn, is Empiricist through and through—if you cannot trace it back to sense experience (*my* sense experience, of course, or the sense experience of those like me), it does not exist. Thus there is an inappropriate Individualism in Empiricism itself, on a meta-level as it were, a calculated denial that women as women might see things differently than men and hence that reality might be different than "we" think it to be.

The Construction of Gender

Are we the atomic, asocial Individuals that are the subjects of traditional liberal political and moral discourse? Or, perhaps more importantly, are *some* of us such Individuals and others not? And how do atomic Individuals become enmeshed in the kind of gender-biased structure I have just described? Many feminist theorists borrow the concept of a "sex/gender system" from Gayle Rubin's early article "The Traffic in Women."[12] Rubin defines a sex/gender system as "the set of arrangements by which a society transforms biological sexuality into products of human activity, and in which these transformed sexual needs are satisfied" (p. 159). In sketching the outline of our sex/gender system, Rubin relies heavily on the work of thinkers outside of the Anglo-American tradition such as Freud, Karl Marx, and Claude Lévi-Strauss. Her work, therefore, runs counter to my intention of limiting the discussion to feminist thought more directly in the British Empiricist tradition (although Marx has been hovering in the background for quite a while now), but her concept of a sex/gender system has been so central to so much feminist thought in the United States that I feel obliged to take it out of turn, as it were, in order to clarify the groundwork for much of this chapter.

Rubin discusses our sex/gender system as one in which the Freudian account of gender development (freed of its biological determinism by the sort of Lacanian semiotic shift I will discuss later) meshes with Lévi-Strauss's account of kinship to explain not only our society's beliefs about men and women, but also how human infants come to *be* the kind of men and women our society needs in order to perpetuate itself. According to Lévi-Strauss, most, if not all, cultures, including our own, have historically relied on the exchange of women between kinship groups to form larger, stronger social units. This exchange of women entails, Rubin argues, that men have rights over women that women do not have over themselves (so there is something to give), that incest and homosexuality taboos of some sort must be enforced, and that men and women must be seen as incomplete in themselves and as necessary complements of each other (so there is some reason to take). This suggests, in turn, that a certain level of passivity in women, strong feelings about sexual object choice, and polar definitions of gender identity would help make the system work more efficiently. These features of the human psyche are, according to Rubin, exactly what the Oedipus complex provides. The male child comes to see that he cannot possess his mother, but can later come to possess another woman if he plays the male role in his society. The female child comes to see that she can never possess any woman, even herself, and so turns in resentment from her mother to her father, learning to play the role complementary to his in order to win the only kind of love (and power) available to her.

In this way, Rubin's work is similar to that of Chodorow's in using Freud to claim that power relations between men and women, and the de-valuing of women in our culture that it causes, results in boys and girls, men and women, thinking of themselves and of each other in very stereotypical and opposed ways that reflect our society's general patriarchal bias. More specifically, it also results in the kind of individualistic "cauldron logic," reliance on hierarchical dualisms, and epistemological atomism that we have been tracing in the Empiricist tradition. Rubin also goes on to suggest, as does Chodorow, that this system is unnecessary, if not dysfunctional, in postindustrial society and so can be changed, primarily by major changes in how children are raised. Part of what I have been trying to outline here is the extent to which our conceptual system (if not our economic system as well) would need to be changed before any such basic change in child-rearing practices could take place.

The significance of Rubin's work for feminist thought as a whole is that if we see gender as a social product, rather than a natural category, it becomes easier to understand how the very process by which we come to define ourselves as persons of one or the other gender can be structured in such a way that those of one gender can acquire the traits required for full moral and political personhood within a given society, while those of the other gender do not. The inherent anti-Individualism in any analysis of our sex/gender system has led many feminist thinkers to reject traditional Anglo-American political and moral thought as reflecting our culture's biased sense of personhood. This constitutes one basic criticism of Individualism that is easily translated into a criticism of the Empiricist tradition once it is realized that the political commitments of that tradition cannot be conceptually separated from its epistemological and metaphysical commitments any more that they can be separated from the concrete social, economic, and political conditions under which they were developed. What an analysis such as Rubin's does is to illustrate the depth at which this conceptual scheme is embedded in our mental world.

Even for those who would reject Rubin's reliance on Freud and Lévi-Strauss, however, there is ample evidence that our language also structures us differentially as gendered beings, despite what the ideology of Individualism would have us believe. A series of papers by Elizabeth Beardsley, for instance, traces the effects of what she calls "referential genderization" and "characterization genderization" in our language. In the paper entitled "Referential Genderization," which appeared in the *Philosophical Forum* volume cited above, Beardsley argues that our language requires us to be gender specific in referring to persons if we wish to avoid incoherence.[13] Moreover, "person" appears much less frequently in English than "man" and "woman," which means that it is much more difficult for us to form the concept of personhood than of male or female personhood (or rather of manhood and womanhood). She concludes that referential genderization "helps to insure that a person's self-image will incorporate, whatever else it includes, some reference to his or her sex" (p. 291). By extension, one person's image of another will also always incorporate some reference to that person's sex as well, a phenomenon that undermines the nominal Individualism of our society, as illustrated in the examples just discussed.

In the later paper entitled "Traits and Genderization," Beardsley determines that "characterization genderization," that is, the need in assigning character traits to make reference to a person's gender, is even more insidious—it doesn't actually exist, or at least not to the extent that one would expect.[14] Rather, there is a great deal of genderization of personality traits ("witty," "vain," "gracious"), but very little of character traits ("honest," "brave," "proud"). Beardsley draws the pessimistic conclusion from this that "The bearers of [such] traits being assumed to be males, there is . . . no need for genderization in speaking of [such] traits. Females as bearers of [such] traits have simply not been present to be observed" (p. 122).[15]

It is interesting to note here that Louise Marcil Lacoste makes a point about Hume that is very similar to this account in Beardsley. As part of her critique of Hume's moral "empiricism," in her article "The Consistency of Hume's Position Concerning Women" she also notes that when he looked for examples of certain kinds of character traits it was only natural to see them in those people (i.e., men) that his society took to be paradigmatic possessors of those traits. This analysis explains why men's virtues are often women's vices: they are conceptually linked to the idea of male personhood and so can never be "womanly." It also makes it easier to understand how Hume was able to acknowledge the existence of lust in women and still describe that emotion exclusively in terms of a female object and hence, given his heterosexism, of a male subject: our language, and the sex/gender system of our culture, tell him that women's lust, their sexuality in general, is secondary to the lust of men. This is true both because lust is "genderized" as a male trait and because it is men's lust (for women, but also often for power) that has historically controlled marriage and thereby also the expression of women's sexuality. And this is surely not unrelated to the fact that even today it is men in our society who have the power to enforce their lust, and their idea of lust, on others.

The Knowing Individual

Obviously, of course, it is more than their definition of lust that men have the power to force onto others in this culture, and the sex/gender system is correlated with more than just moral and political personhood: it can also be seen in the traditional view of knowledge as a relationship between an autonomous knowing subject and a passive object of knowledge that Harding discusses. Closely related to the problem of Individualism, therefore, is a whole group of problems in the philosophy of science, epistemology, and the philosophy of mind that have come to light in the work of many philosophers over roughly the same period as the feminist critique was developing in political and moral philosophy—a "crisis of objectivity" mirroring the "crisis of liberalism." We have already seen how many feminists use a variant of Freudian theory to undermine our idea of the autonomous knowing subject, and many of the feminist political thinkers whose work I have been discussing use variants of Marxism for similar purposes. A third common form of attack on our usual assumptions in the philosophy of science, epistemology, and the philosophy of mind lacks the clear label of these two, but arises from a dissident trend within Anglo-American philosophy, a trend that can be found in the works of Wittgenstein, Austin, W. V. O. Quine, and Thomas Kuhn. Harding and many other feminists often use a combination of these approaches in their arguments.

Since I have already discussed Harding's work in some detail, here I would like to take another example of a feminist critique of the Empiricist tradition in the philosophy of science, Evelyn Fox Keller's *Reflections on Gender and Science*. Keller would agree with Beardsley that the gendered way in which we must speak, and therefore think, of science or of any kind of knowing affects the way in which women see themselves as knowers: "In a science constructed around the naming of object (nature) as female and the parallel naming of subject (mind) as male, any scientist who happens to be a woman is confronted with an a priori contradiction in terms" (p. 174). Keller applies Rubin's concept of the sex/gender system and Chodorow's work to the traditional scientific ideal, which incorporates a radical separation between the knowing subject and the object of investigation, and a correspondingly sharp division between the subjective and objective. On this view, scientific thought has traditionally been defined in terms of a stereotypically male self in our culture. As in Harding, Keller offers a history of the confusion between men's experience of themselves as knowers and the definition of science, although with more focus on the history of the modern sciences themselves than on the parallel history of British Empricisim. Thus, she looks (as do many feminist philosophers of science) at the florid gender imagery in the work of Sir Francis Bacon rather than the more subtle gender subtext in the writings of Locke and Hume, for whom the (bourgeois) nature of science and the (male) gender of the scientist were already settled issues.

Recently, however, the sharp dichotomy between subjective and objective has come into question in the philosophy of science and, Keller argues, the emphasis on strict objectivity as traditionally defined is beginning to be more of a liability than an asset in some scientific fields as well, notably particle physics and the biological sciences. In response to this, Keller offers a new model for science, one based on the notion of order rather than the traditional concept of a law, which seems to incorporate a male-biased juridical model (if not a male-biased theological model) into our concept of science. Looking at the work of Nobel Laureate Barbara McClintock, Keller points out that "The focus on order rather than law enlarges our vision of both nature and science. It suggests a way of thinking of nature as neither bound by law nor chaotic and unruly, and of science as neither objectivist nor idiosyncratic" (p. 134). At the same time, she suggests that such a revised model for scientific investigation would undermine both a tendency toward anthropomorphic (gender) categories and concepts in science *and* a purely instrumental view of the objects of scientific investigation (which is, of course, also one aspect of the genderization of science, as clearly exhibited in Bacon and discussed in some detail by Bordo). Keller's work is especially interesting because her new definition of objectivity seems to provide a better alternative to the traditional view than the epistemological relativism, or even nihilism, found in much contemporary philosophy of science, although it also lacks a clear epistemological base—something that is not necessarily a major obstacle to innovation in scientific thought.

A similar feminist argument based on recent internal attacks on the British Empiricist tradition can be found in Naomi Scheman's work in epistemology and the philosophy of mind. In one such paper, Scheman uses a variant on Wittgenstein's "private language" argument as the basis for a feminist criticism of the traditional account of mental states in Anglo-American philosophy.[16] She describes the claim in the philosophy of mind that all mental states (i.e., all "ideas" in the Lockean and Humean sense) are identifiable, atomistic particulars as an Individualist ideology that

> is deeply useful in the maintenance of capitalist and patriarchal society and deeply embedded in our notions of liberation, freedom, and equality. It is connected with particular features of psychosexual development of males mothered by women in a patriarchal society, with the development of the ego and of ego-boundaries. (p. 226)

Thus, her work correlates directly both with the political analyses discussed above and with the work of Chodorow and others on the possible psychological basis of the atomism and Individualism of the Empiricist enterprise. Since she emphasizes that our mental states are primarily structured by our language, her work also is connected with Beardsley's contention that, for instance, certain mental states or their character trait analogs (e.g., fear and bravery) carry a gender-specific meaning in our society.

What Scheman's argument shows is how the Individualism inherited from Locke and Hume distorts our awareness that states such as beliefs or emotions are quite different from the pains or itches with which they are often conflated in traditional Empiricism. Our interesting mental states are not atomic mental givens, and they are not self-grouping, self-identifying, or self-verifying. I discover that I am in love in quite a different way than I discover that my shoes hurt, but my statements about these two situations would receive very similar analyses from both Locke and Hume (although, as I noted, the potential for a more Wittgensteinian analysis is also present in Locke). The ideology required by Individualism must disregard the way in which mental states are socially constructed, and especially the extent to which they are specifically linguistic constructs that can exist only in a public language, in order to maintain both its psychological atomism (and ultimately its inherent solipsism) and the logical priority of the Individual over the society in which "he" lives. Thus, it becomes clearer in what sense the most basic categories and conceptual schemes of the British Empiricist tradition are not only male-biased, but can also be shown to be ultimately without philosophical foundation.

Hierarchical Dualism

On a deeper level, Individualism is also correlated with a metaphysics that relies on an underlying schema that is both dualistic and hierarchical.[17] We have already traced this general schema in Locke and Hume's philosophy and clarified how their positions are structured so as to exclude women's experience of the world (which is, on this account, much less dependent on either hierarchy or dualism) from the realm of the philosophical. In "Is Gender a Variable in Conceptions of Rationality?" Harding states the problematic nature of these dualisms so clearly that I will quote her at some length:

Are "the problems of philosophy" really human problems, or do they only reflect disproportionately what appears problematic to men? Are the problems of justifying the "rules" for establishing appropriate relationships between mind and body, reason and emotions, self and external world, will and desire—relationships painfully sundered for men in their infancy—really fully human problems? Notice that in each dichotomy, the latter is perceived as threatening to overcome and control the former unless the former creates rigid separation from and rational control of the latter. The history of modern philosophy appears disproportionately obsessed with establishing rules by which mind, reason, self, and the will can legitimately control body, the emotions, the external world ("nature" and "other persons"), and desire. (p. 56)

If this analysis is even roughly correct, it is not surprising that women might find such a philosophical paradigm alien to their lives.

Nancy Hartsock, in "The Feminist Standpoint: Developing the Ground for a Specifically Feminist Historical Materialism," develops a detailed account of how women's exclusion from the hierarchical and dualistic metaphysics of our culture can prove to be an epistemological advantage, the basis for a "feminist standpoint" from which we might more clearly see the reality that capitalist patriarchy seeks to hide.[18] Hartsock argues that feminism satisfies the five basic criteria for a standpoint in the Marxist sense of the term, and that the Marxist term itself can best be understood in opposition to epistemological dualism.

The concept of a standpoint structures epistemology in a particular way. Rather than a simple dualism, it posits a duality of levels of reality, of which the deeper level or essence both includes and explains the "surface" or appearance, and indicates the logic by means of which the appearance inverts and distorts the deeper reality. (p. 285)

The five criteria are that a standpoint be based in the material activity of life, that it expose the dominant belief system to be not merely wrong but perverse, that it also make clear the ways in which that perverse ideology is made real through the power of the ruling group, that it be an achieved rather than an immediate understanding, and that it provide a basis for moving beyond current power relations. Hartsock's claim is that feminism satisfies these criteria, and, by implication, that grounding feminism in this Marxist epistemology can lead to a clearer understanding of the feminist enterprise itself.

How does feminism come to constitute a Marxist "standpoint?" First, it is grounded in the activity of women's lives, which are not only deeply intertwined with the materiality of our existence, but in fact are more materially based than the lives of all but a few men in modern industrial society. Hartsock locates this materiality not only in our labor as houseworkers, but also in our bodily experience, which allows us less opportunity than men's to ignore our biological materiality. This closer relationship to the material itself mitigates against the male dualism since, for instance, not only pregnancy but also bearing and raising children escape entirely a schema that sees the world purely in terms of pleasure *or* pain, work *or* play. Secondly, she discusses the way in which the "abstract masculinity" correlated with our basic dualisms (i.e., atomistic Individualism in the philosophical realm) perverts experience. She chooses Georges Bataille's work on the substitution of death for life as her basic example, but similar points have been made here with regard to atomism and connection, etc. We have also already seen how male power makes this perverse understanding of our pre-philosophical experience of the world more than simply wrong, because it is able to force its view on us through our education, political system, and so on. Fourthly, feminism is clearly an achieved understanding, one that all of us are working here to create. And finally, feminism provides the basis for a praxis, an analysis which tells us not only what the problem is, but also what might be done about it, although the incomplete state of the theory necessarily entails that feminist praxis is far from a settled issue. Thus, the feminist standpoint clarifies the nature of post-industrial, capitalist, patriarchal society and shows how to change that society.

Hartsock's work itself, however, leaves us wondering what might lie beyond a feminist standpoint, what metaphysics or ontology might look like, once we rid ourselves of the male ideology of hierarchical dualisms. One feminist attempt to tell us about this post-patriarchal world can be found in Caroline Whitbeck's "A Different Reality: Feminist Ontology."[19] Whitbeck engages in a basic critique of hierarchical dualism by contrasting the "self-other opposition" characteristic of male thinking in our society with a "self-other(s) relation." She believes that the latter way of looking at the world provides the basis for an alternative, feminist ontology that more accurately reflects our actual experience "because relationships, past and present, realized and sought, are constitutive of the self, and so the actions of a person reflect the more- or less-successful attempt to respond to the whole configuration of relationships" (p. 76). This focus on the self as structured through relationships with others has the double advantage of emphasizing the developing and social nature of the self, as opposed to the atomic and isolated self of British Empiricism, and of bringing the mother–child relation (among others) into the foreground of philosophy without relying on any variant of Freudian discourse.

These ontological commitments in Whitbeck's work lead to an ethics that is defined in terms of the mutual realization of people. On the model of the relationship between mother and child, this is not a process of oppositional differentiation from a fixed m/other, but a process of increasing *distinctions* between self and other(s). Much like Sara Ruddick's alternative epistemology in "Maternal Thinking," Whitbeck looks to the actual experience of mothering to suggest, for instance, that nurturing can best be understood as a *mutual* relationship between mother and child (or between two adults or between two children) rather than in hierarchical terms.[20] The goal of realization then leads to an ethics of responsibilities rather than rights, in which what matters is more that a goal be accomplished than the specific actions taken to accomplish it, again using child-rearing as a model. On this basis, Whitbeck's proposed ontology leads to a feminist political philosophy that sees society primarily as a facilitator of responsibility instead of a contractual guarantor of abstract rights. She sees the political advances embodied in the work of Hobbes, Locke, and Rousseau (i.e., liberal Individualism) as the rule of the sons, come to replace the patriarchal rule of the fathers, and not as advances in any real sense for the daughters, just as the theological shift from theism to deism in the same period might be described as the shift from a patriarchal definition of God as Father to one more in keeping with "modern" ideas but equally male-biased, in the way we have discussed. Whitbeck's work, therefore, offers the basis for a complete system of what might become "women's philosophy" outside of the usual male-dominated realm.

I have chosen to discuss the epistemological, metaphysical, and ontological feminism of Hartsock and Whitbeck here both because I believe them to be some of the most basic philosophical challenges to our current male-biased ideology and the hierarchical dualisms on which it depends, and because they represent two relatively extreme positions on the use of male models in feminist philosophy. Hartsock functions clearly within a Marxist model, and relies to some extent on other feminists' appropriation of Freud. Whitbeck, on the other hand, considers Marxism, Freudian theory, and, more seriously for our present purposes, the philosophy of Georg Wilhelm Frederick Hegel, from which both draw their basic conceptual schemes, too deeply embedded in the dualism of our culture and too strongly male-biased to be turned to any feminist purpose. This puts into doubt any possible feminist appropriation of Continental philosophy, which remains deeply Hegelian in ways that I will explain later. Therefore, Whitbeck's version of "women's philosophy" calls into question not only Hartsock's work, but many of the other analyses on which my own account is based. On the other hand, I would claim that, despite the great interest and power of Whitbeck's work, it also illustrates the problems and pitfalls women's philosophy can encounter when it tries to "reinvent the wheel." There are major problems in making some of Whitbeck's arguments clear, and they occasionally open themselves to the very charge she levels against others of merely re-creating and inverting the traditional hierarchical dualisms. Relying on women's experience of mothering, for example, may provide exciting and helpful clues to the limitations of our current way of doing philosophy, but can too easily be turned back into anti-feminist essentialism to be an entirely safe path for feminist theory.

By contrast, Hartsock's use of Marxism provides a clear vocabulary and, even for those to whom that vocabulary is alien, stating criteria and proving that a given position satisfies them is a basic philosophical gambit. Still, this appropriation of men's philosophy is open to question on at least three levels. First of all, there is the simple issue of whether anyone, feminist or not, is obliged to accept the truth of the model being used. Thus, feminists can become embroiled in debates that are peripheral to doing women's philosophy—defending Marxism is not how most of us would wish to spend our time and energy. Second, there is the question Whitbeck raises of whether male-model philosophies can really be revised thoroughly enough to serve feminist purposes without undermining them. Freudian theory, for instance, has universalizing tendencies that run counter to the feminist respect for differences between women, as well as for our commonalities. Finally, as Harding points out in her book, a position like Hartsock's not only reflects a masculine model of arguing and establishing one's claims, but also assumes that there is truth, a social reality that some theory can adequately describe. Both deconstruction and feminism seem to be committed to a sceptical attitude toward such an absolute truth that someone might, some day, in theory, own. It is for these reasons that I have tried to keep my own theoretical commitments both explicit and "hypothetical" by relying on a variety of theories to illuminate and draw out the structural patterns found in British Empiricism and in feminism, but not as the basis for specific arguments. Deconstruction tells me that all theories are distortions, so all we can do is to trace the patterns of power. Feminism tells me that some distortions are worse than others—they have the power to maim and to kill.

Notes

1. An earlier version of this chapter was presented to the Minnesota Philosophical Society in October, 1985. Several members of that audience

made helpful comments, especially Karen Warren of Macalester College and Patrice Koelsch of the Center for Arts Criticism in St. Paul.

2. *The Philosophical Forum* 5, nos. 1–2 (Fall–Winter 1973–1974).

3. Robert Paul Wolff, "There's Nobody Here But Us Persons," *The Philosophical Forum* 5, nos. 1–2 (Fall–Winter 1973–1974): 128–44.

4. Alison Jaggar, "Abortion and a Woman's Right to Decide," *The Philosophical Forum* 5, nos. 1–2 (Fall–Winter 1973–1974): 347–60; Onora Nell, "How Do We Know When Opportunities Are Equal?", *The Philosophical Forum* 5, nos. 1–2 (Fall–Winter 1973–1974): 334–46.

5. Mary E. Hawkesworth, "The Affirmative Action Debate and Conflicting Conceptions of Individuality," *Women's Studies International Forum* 7, no. 5 (1984): 335–47.

6. Bell Hooks, *Feminist Theory: From Margin to Center*.

7. Nancy Fraser, "Women, Welfare and The Politics of Need Interpretation," *Hypatia* 2, no. 1 (Winter 1987): 103–21. (Reprinted in Nancy Fraser, *Unruly Practices* (Minneapolis: University of Minnesota Press, 1989.)

8. Ruth Bleier, *Science and Gender* (New York: Pergamon Press, 1984), pp. 188–89.

9. Marjorie Weinzweig, "Pregnancy Leave, Comparable Worth, and Concepts of Equality," *Hypatia* 2, no. 1 (Winter 1987): 71–101.

10. Linda J. Krieger talks about this problem in more technical detail in her article "Through a Glass Darkly: Paradigms of Equality and the Search for a Women's Jurisprudence," *Hypatia* 2, no. 1 (Winter 1987): 45–61.

11. Rosemarie Tong, *Women, Sex, and the Law* (Totowa, N.J.: Rowman and Littlefield, 1983).

12. Gayle Rubin, "The Traffic in Women," in *Toward an Anthropology of Women,* ed. Rayna R. Reiter (New York: Monthly Review Press, 1975).

13. Elizabeth Lane Beardsley, "Referential Genderization," *The Philosophical Forum* 5, nos. 1–2 (Fall–Winter 1973–1974): 285–95.

14. Elizabeth Lane Beardsley, "Traits and Genderization," in *Feminism and Philosophy,* ed. Mary Vetterling-Braggin, Frederick A. Elliston, and Jane English (Totowa, N.J.: Littlefield, Adams, 1977).

15. On ontological Individualism in the philosophy of language, see also Merrill B. Hintikka and Jaakko Hintikka, "How Can Language Be Sexist?", in *Discovering Reality,* ed. Sandra Harding and Merrill B. Hintikka (Boston: D. Reidel, 1983).

On gender-differentiated value judgments in language, see also "Of Sissies and Spinsters: Shifts in Value of Sex-Marked Terms," a paper presented by Joan Straumanis to the Central Division of the American Philosophical Association held in Columbus, Ohio in April, 1983.

16. Naomi Scheman, "Individualism and the Objects of Psychology."

17. This is a common theme in feminist philosophy. In addition to the articles cited in this section, see also, for example, Ruth Bleier's *Science and Gender;* Evelyn Fox Keller's *Reflections on Science and Gender;* Mary Daly's

Gyn/Ecology (Boston: Beacon Press, 1978); Sheila Ruth's "Bodies and Souls/ Sex, Sin and the Senses in Patriarchy: A Study in Applied Dualism," *Hypatia* 2, no. 1 (Winter 1987): 149–63; and several of the articles in Carol Gould's *Beyond Domination* (Totowa, N.J.: Rowman and Allanheld, 1983), and Sandra Harding and Merrill B. Hintikka's *Discovering Reality* (Boston: D. Reidel, 1983).

18. Nancy C. M. Hartsock, "The Feminist Standpoint: Developing the Ground for a Specifically Feminist Historical Materialism," in *Discovering Reality*, ed. Sandra Harding and Merrill B. Hintikka (Boston: D. Reidel, 1983).

19. Caroline Whitbeck, "A Different Reality: Feminist Ontology," in *Beyond Domination,* ed. Carol C. Gould (Totowa, N.J.: Rowman and Allenheld, 1983).

20. Sara Ruddick, "Maternal Thinking," in *Mothering,* ed. Joyce Trebilcot (Totowa, N.J.: Rowman and Allanheld, 1983).

Part Two

Chapter 4

Feminism and Phenomenology

Alternatives to Individualism

What do we have if we abandon traditional Empiricist Individualism? In a certain sense, as has been suggested, such a metaphysical "paradigm shift" is almost inconceivable to us. To the extent that feminist criticism of Individualism draws on other philosophical perspectives, however, we can see glimpses of different ways of thinking. Thus Hartsock may be right in believing that there are parts of a Marxist vision that feminist philosophers could adopt and adapt, as well perhaps as parts of the vision of the more optimistic Freudians. In so doing, we must be careful, however, that the liberation of women's lives and the restructuring of thought to reflect and include women's experience are of paramount importance. Feminist appropriations of analytic philosophy, as found in Austin, Wittgenstein, Quine, and so on, where there is less metaphysical baggage, may have correspondingly less to fear, but vigilance will be necessary there as well. One also finds hints in a variety of writings by feminist philosophers of other ways of doing philosophy that might be well-suited to use by feminists, including the philosophies and religions of Asia,[1] the non-dualistic metaphysics of process philosophy,[2] and the redefined objectivism of Pragmatic radical empiricism,[3] as well as the schools of contemporary Continental philosophy generally called phenomenology, existentialism, structuralism, post-structuralism, and deconstruction.[4]

These last may have a special relationship with feminist philosophy, if only because they also borrow basic insights from Freudian and Marxist thought and sometimes even linguistic analysis. At the same time, some of their most important presuppositions are often ones that they share with much feminist thought: that philosophy must begin with our lived experience of the world; that not everything is as it seems to the rational, conscious mind; that our embodiment is a significant aspect of our existence as human; that the traditional hierarchical dualisms oversimplify reality; that there is something deeply wrong with how our culture sees the world; that solutions, rather than being global, must be adjusted to local needs. Of course, there are also dangers in these texts. Sartre's work is strongly Individualistic, as Whitbeck notes, and Heidegger's work often seems to suggest a return to pre-Individualistic patriarchy. Still, this should not blind us to the creative use that can be made, for instance, of Heidegger's critique of technology in the understanding of women's lives under industrial capitalism, as Jeffner Allen demonstrates in "Motherhood: The Annihilation of Women."[5] In any event, these dangers are no more insurmountable than those to be found in feminist appropriations of Marx or Freud.

In the following three chapters, therefore, I will try to briefly summarize those aspects of contemporary Continental thought that seem to hold the most promise for Anglo-American feminists in our rethinking of our own philosophical heritage. This chapter will focus on more or less traditional phenomenological and existential thought, as exemplified in the work of Heidegger, Merleau-Ponty, Sartre, and de Beauvoir. Thus, I will trace the interplay of self and society in the concept of Dasein, as well as the existential phenomenology, in *Being and Time,* and the more complex ontological hermeneutics of the "later Heidegger." Merleau-Ponty will then be seen both as carrying on a more traditional concept of phenomenology as the description of lived experience and as providing, through his emphasis on embodiment and his rejection of hierarchical dualism, a rare opening for women's experience in the philosophical realm. Sartre's existentialism will then be compared both to the above forms of phenomenology and to the Individualism we have found in Anglo-American thought, with some emphasis on his ties to Hegel's heavily dualistic thought and on his explicit references to sexuality and gender. Finally, the work of Simone de Beauvoir can be presented in a triple perspective: as a feminist continuation of various aspects of all of the above phenomenological approaches, as a forerunner and source of contemporary French feminist thought, and as a powerful influence on Anglo-American feminism as well. The next chapter will provide a similar cursory survey of those areas of Continental thought that are roughly called post-structuralist, and the final chapter will look at contemporary

French feminism. On this basis, I hope to at least suggest the alternatives, and the dangers, that this philosophical tradition has to offer feminist thought.

There is, however, a long list of things that I might do in this chapter but will not. Primarily, I will limit the discussion to "contemporary" Continental philosophy, by which I mean that I will make only occasional excursions into the nineteenth century and the "Modern" period in trying to clarify the issues in twentieth-century Continental thought. Thus it will be necessary, for instance, to limit discussion of Kant primarily to an aside about Merleau-Ponty's attempt to balance "Empiricism" and "Idealism"; to rely almost exclusively on de Beauvoir and Sartre's understanding of Hegel; and to omit entirely Friedrich Nietzsche's "misogyny" and the role it has played in the debate between Derrida and Heidegger over Nietzsche's role in the history of philosophy. For similar reasons of focus and complexity, I will be able to refer only briefly to the work of Edmund Husserl, the teacher of both Heidegger and Sartre. In the cases of "non-philosophers" such as Freud and de Saussure, explanations will be provided when needed, as they have been so far, but not in any systematic fashion. Finally, Marxism, which plays a fairly large role in Anglo-American feminist thought, fades more into the background in the account that follows. This seems to be for two reasons. On the one hand, some form of Marxism is assumed to be true by most contemporary Continental philosophers, so there is no longer any need to argue the issue. On the other hand, since there are several other alternatives to Individualism in the Continental tradition, there has been no need to focus on Marxism as the only way for feminists to avoid Individualism, as may have been the case in Anglo-American thought.

Finally, before beginning a discussion of phenomenological and existential philosophy, it might be helpful to offer quick, if somewhat stipulative, definitions for those two terms. In *Being and Time,* Heidegger traces the word "phenomenology" to its Greek origin as "discourse about what appears" or, more cryptically, "to let that which shows itself be seen from itself in the very way in which it shows itself from itself," which he summarizes with the Husserlian slogan "To the things themselves!"[6] Descriptive phenomenology thus begins from our lived experience of the world, but aspires to a more or less "scientific" (i.e., systematic) or ontological account of the conditions that make such an experience of the world possible. "Existence" appears in Heidegger as the way in which Dasein (that is, human being) always understands itself, which "never gets straightened out except through existing itself" (p. 33). From this follows the more traditional formulation of existentialism as based on a belief that human existence, human life as it is lived in individual cases, precedes and defines human essence, rather than the reverse. In Heidegger and the philosophers who follow, as we shall see, phenomenology becomes the method for explicating the structures within which human existence comes to define itself as human.

Heidegger's Hermeneutics of Modernity

Although, as noted above, there is some nostalgia in Heidegger for pre-Individualistic patriarchy, and some feminists have accused him of sharing in Sartre's excessive Individualism (a Continental variant on the Individualism of Anglo-American philosophy, with similar roots in the Modern period), I have also suggested that certain aspects of Heidegger's work might provide an alternative to Marxism as a basis for a non-Individualistic feminist theory.[7] The apparent contradictions here become somewhat more understandable if one looks at the internal structure of Heidegger's work over his lifetime. The usual division of this corpus is into "earlier" and "later" phases, the dividing line being called the "*Kehre*" or turning, which occurred around the time of, and possibly in conjunction with, the Third Reich in Germany. For our purposes, the "early" Heidegger will generally be considered to be the author of *Being and Time*, while the "later" Heidegger will be represented by *The Question Concerning Technology* and related texts.[8] I will also, however, make a less orthodox subdivision of the "early" period, one that divides a "hermeneutic" side of *Being and Time* from an "existential" side. My claim will be that it is Heidegger's existentialism that can be called Individualistic in the Sartrean (or Anglo-American) sense, and that both the Heideggerian hermeneutics of Dasein and his later work on the problem of technology might provide significant resources for feminist thought.

Before beginning with Heidegger, however, it might be best to clarify as much as possible some key items in his creative and very Germanic vocabulary. I have already equated the term Dasein with "human being," but that is actually an oversimplification. It is a neuter noun in German, which may not be an unintended consequence of its construction, and it is never a biological category for Heidegger. (Of course, both of these exclusions may be false generalizations of male categories, rather than a true gender neutrality, as Derrida suggests and as we have already seen in Locke and Hume.) It is also important to know what Dasein is not, and one of the things that it most definitely is not is "man," "mankind," or even "humanity": part of Heidegger's questioning of modernity is a questioning of humanism as well. (Gayatri Spivak links Heidegger's "anti-humanism" to the "anti-feminism" she finds in French feminists such as Julia Kristeva.)[9] Dasein means literally "to be here" and it is the postionality of human being, its location in time and space, that creates its unique ontological status. Unlike other beings, we know that we exist and where we exist, so that we have a perspective on the world that allows us to take it *as* a world, rather than just as a mass of stimuli. The positionality of Dasein creates a space in which the world can appear to us as meaningful, as an environment in which we can move from here to there, in which we can accomplish things and act on our projects, in the Sartrean sense of the term. Most of *Being and Time* is a hermeneutics of Dasein, an interpretation of the "world" in which Dasein lives. Therefore, it is more than a phenomenology of the world, which would only tell us what we experience, because it attempts to reveal and to clarify the meanings those experiences have for us.

Now, Dasein's world has several interesting features that are tied to its primary existence as the theatre for human projects, but the most significant feature for our purposes is that Dasein is primordially (i.e., at its most basic level) social. Dasein is always also *Mitsein* (Being-with), even, and perhaps most, when it is "factically," or empirically, alone: "The Other can be missing only in and for a Being-with" (p. 157). The Being-with of Dasein arises from the fact that all of our projects have some human good, some facet of Dasein, as their ultimate goal, and they are carried out in a physical environment that is full of Dasein, in the sense of human artifacts, even when no other humans are present. (Deconstruction would say that language was the most important of these artifacts, but that point is not fully explored in *Being and Time* and the later Heidegger's ideas on language lie far beyond the scope of the present study.) Thus, our ability to have projects and exist in a world is completely tied up in the existence of other Dasein, so that Being-with is the condition for the meaningfulness of our world. This social dimension of Dasein will also be both historically and culturally variable. Such an interpretation of Dasein seems deeply opposed to any kind of transcendental Individualism. Moreover, this dimension of Heidegger's hermeneutics remains relatively constant throughout his work, providing a possible basis for a feminist critique of both Individualism and technology as related ontological errors that confuse the existence of Dasein with the existence of the non-Dasein forms of being that we encounter in the world.

Interestingly, the imagery that Heidegger uses to describe the social existence of Dasein is uncharacteristically woman-oriented. When he introduces the term solicitude (*Fürsorge,* a very difficult term to translate—see the translators' footnote to page 157 of *Being and Time*), he uses traditional female occupations to explain it. (*Fürsorge* also means "welfare work" in German, a pun Heidegger exploits below.)

> Even "concern" with food and clothing, and the nursing of the sick body, are forms of solicitude. But we understand the expression "solicitude" in a way which corresponds to our use of "concern" as an *existentiale* [definitional characteristic of Dasein]. For example, "welfare work" [*Fürsorge*], as a factical [empirical] social arrangement, is grounded in Dasein's state of Being as Being-with. (p. 158)

This is, in fact, one of the few places in Heidegger when traditionally female activities, or anything about women as such, are offered in an explanation for any of "gender neutral" Dasein's important characteristics, and while it most likely relies more on stereotypical notions of women and solicitude than on any genuine appreciation of women's nursing or welfare work, it also opens a space within which women's experience of caring for others could become a topic within philosophy.

Moreover, the definition that Heidegger offers of "authentic" solicitude corresponds more fully with the kind of moral thought that has recently been attributed to women in our culture by Gilligan and others than with the rule-centered moral thought more typical of men.

> [T]here is also the possibility of a kind of solicitude which does not so much leap in for the Other as *leap ahead* of him . . . not in order to take away his "care" but rather to give it back to him authentically as such for the first time. This kind of solicitude pertains essentially to authentic care—that is, to the existence of the Other, not to a *"what"* with which he is concerned; it helps the Other to become transparent to himself *in* his care and to become *free for* it. (pp. 158–59)

If there are any moral dictates in *Being and Time,* this is one, and while it is full of problematic concepts ("authentic," "transparent," "free"), it also evokes the work of Sara Ruddick and others who have explored the logic and values of "maternal thinking" (a paradigm case of solicitude, one would think, but Heidegger ignores it, as he ignores children). Moreover, Ruddick ties her thought to the work of Jürgen Habermas, and so indirectly to Heidegger, just as Marjorie Weinzweig, in "Should a Feminist Choose a Marriage-Like Relationship," relies more directly on Heidegger.[10] Thus, Heidegger's concept of solicitude may reflect stereotypical notions of female care, but may also create a space in which an account that is genuinely based on women's experience of the world could become a legitimate part of the philosophical enterprise.

However, it is also necessary to look at the problematic terms in the above quotation, especially "authentic," which is closely related to Sartre's concept of good faith and introduces a strongly Individualistic element into Heidegger's thought. Heidegger claims that Dasein in "its average everydayness" exists as more or less undifferentiated, each instance of Dasein carrying out and being totally defined in terms of stereotypical, interchangeable roles in the social order. And it is here that many women may begin to feel that they are on alien territory once again. While I am willing to admit that I might be completely replaceable as a teacher or thinker, and even as a wife, daughter, and mother, my deepest insight about the birth of my first child was that she was entirely unique and utterly irreplaceable to me, both as an individual and as my child. Thus, Heidegger's most basic existential insight runs strongly against my own experience of motherhood, and possibly against "maternal thinking" in general.

The male perspective in the existential part of *Being and Time* grows more obvious as it grows more Individualistic. The first step toward authenticity for Heidegger is to recognize the truth about Dasein and acknowledge one's own replaceability. This "existential crisis" can be set off by any of a number of ways of becoming aware of our own mortality, of the inevitability of death, which will erase all our projects and all the meaning that we have given to the world. (I will ignore what feminist deconstruction would insist on here, the traditional equation between women and death.) In response to the anxiety—*Angst*—brought on by this new "transparent" consciousness, Dasein may choose either an inauthentic return to its previous stereotypical way of life or an authentic reassumption of that life in full consciousness that it is without foundation, that it has no intrinsic meaning that cannot be eradicated by one's death. The choice of authenticity or its opposite, moreover, is presented as completely "free" of one's prior existence as Dasein of a certain kind in a certain context, and so completely ignores the strong social factors that might limit the opportunity for both *Angst* and authenticity in oppressed people, and certainly would limit their freedom to act on such insights. Since there is also a moral dimension to authenticity, Heidegger's insistence that it is a viable choice regardless of one's concrete social situation may seem to add an element of "blaming the victim" to his account.

One might consider here, however, that Marilyn Frye, in her contribution to an issue of *Hypatia* that focused on the work of Simone de Beauvoir, "History and Responsibility," gives a picture of feminist assertion in the face of the social construction of the self that seems in many ways to resemble Heideggerian authenticity.[11]

> It sometimes seems to me that the call to historicity and the rule against cultural parochialism occur as a coded version of these claims: we cannot demand or expect profound redefinition of ourselves or other women, or hold ourselves or others responsible for such change, because we must respect the fact that our and others' beings are conditioned by the historical and material circumstances of time and place. . . .
>
> But being responsible can simply mean one does not passively and unconsciously submit to the winds of time and culture; it means primarily that one is living, throughout one's life, as an *agent* in the matter of who and how one is and the matrix of circumstances that conditions that; and it means recognizing and caring about the fact that who and how one is has consequences for others. (pp. 216–17)

Here, as in Heidegger, we have both an awareness of our socially conditioned and contingent existence and a strong sense of ourselves as Individualistic actors in the world. I have already noted Zillah Eisenstein's recognition that most Anglo-American feminists are not yet ready to abandon Individualism completely, and Frye's formulation seems to capture something similar to Eisenstein's idea of "individuality," our ability to act, not "freely," but in full awareness of our cultural and historical limitations.[12]

From this perspective, a direct comparison with Heidegger's discussion of the role of history in authenticity might be interesting:

> The resoluteness in which Dasein comes back to itself, discloses current factical possibilities of authentic existing, and discloses them *in terms of the heritage* which that resoluteness, as thrown, *takes over*. In one's coming back resolutely to one's thrownness, there is hidden a *handing down* to oneself of the possibilities that have come down to one, but not necessarily *as* having thus come down. (p. 435)

We may be too attached to our legacy of Individualism to accept any theory in which we merely replicate and pass along what our history and culture have given to us, but that is a problem for Western thought as a whole, not just for feminism or Heidegger. If there is some ambivalence within feminism about the relationship between the socially structured self and individual self-assertion, it might be taken as a sign that Heidegger was moving in a similar direction or dealing with a similar dilemma, that he fell into the same paradox, rather than as proof that his work cannot be incorporated into feminist theory. Moreover, it is important to add that this existential side of Heidegger's thought is one of the ideas that he rejects after the "Kehre." While maintaining his awareness of Dasein's necessarily social existence, his later work moves away from the idea of Dasein as a collection of interchangeable parts to a less alienated picture of human existence at its best (which, unfortunately, was in patriarchal ancient Greece).

It is a related aspect of Heidegger's later work, the critique of technology, which is seen most often in Anglo-American feminist theory. This critique is based on an analysis of the modern "world picture" as one in which non-Dasein being, "objects," are seen solely in terms of the manipulations of Dasein, the (male) "subjects" of science (as discussed by Harding, Keller, Bordo, and others). For Heidegger, technology is not applied science, but rather science is what is not yet technology. The key to understanding this phase of Heidegger's work in light of our previous discussion is to see that technology—and by extension, modernity as a whole—is a perversion of the way in which Dasein sees its world. Instead of seeing the world as a meaningful place in which we carry out projects, the "world view" that is based on Descartes (Heidegger typically ignores the Empiricists' role in this process) sees the world only as a resource, as a "standing reserve" for exploitation by "humanity" (as constructed in the last four hundred years of "humanism"). This reduces the world to "man's" measure and ignores the many ways in which the world is something "given" to us, but not necessarily made for us, something that will in some ways remain forever hidden and mysterious. In ignoring the true nature of this world, we run the risk not only of destroying the world materially, but also of destroying ourselves ontologically, of turning Dasein itself into only an object, a "standing reserve" for future use. This can be seen not only in fascism, but also in the South African government's treatment of its black workers literally as replaceable resources, and, according to Jeffner Allen, in our culture's definition of women exclusively as reproducers of the species. From this perspective Individualism would be only the symptom of a much greater evil.

This critique of modernity in Heidegger was one of the main tenets adopted by "critical theory" of the Frankfurt School, and I have already referred to the fact that Ruddick's adaptation of some of Habermas's work can ultimately be traced back to Heidegger. Other American feminists who use Habermas's work, such as Nancy Fraser, are often more consciously drawing on the Heideggerian critique. Heidegger also finds his way into Anglo-American feminism along different routes. When Mary Daly, for example, draws on the work of Paul Tillich in *Beyond God the Father,* it is also Heidegger that she is introducing into her analysis, and her repudiation of Tillich in *Gyn/Ecology,* which has nothing to do with his Heideggerian orientation, does not remove all of its traces in her work. In the cases I have noted here and in many others in Anglo-American feminism in which one discovers the outline of a Heideggerian analysis, although no reference is made to his work or any of the theories based on it, the adaptation of certain aspects of Heidegger's thought adds to, rather than detracts from, the power of the feminist work being done. The French (and Anglo-American) feminists who draw on the work of Lacan, Foucault, and Derrida have opened up a somewhat different space within the Heideggerian text, as we shall see, but one that is also a powerful subversion of the "phallogocentric" tradition. Heidegger's work seems to provide, therefore, a place in philosophy where women might find room to breathe a bit more freely than within the Anglo-American tradition and might be able to create a space of our own from which to develop what could become women's philosophy.

Merleau-Ponty's Phenomenology of the Body

Unlike Heidegger's hermeneutics of Dasein, Merleau-Ponty's early work is more traditionally phenomenological. *The Phenomenology of Perception* returns to our actual lived experience of the world to develop a Gestaltist theory of perception that avoids the usual (in Continental philosophy, at least) dichotomy between "pre-critical" Empiricism and the more "rigorous" Idealism of Kant or Hegel.[13] Merleau-Ponty's stated intention is to show the limitations of both of these perspectives in explaining the actual phenomena of perception, and to replace them with a highly contextual theory of embodied perception that would be more faithful to the facts. In this we can already see the outline of a convergence between his thought and feminist theory: an emphasis on holism and lived experience is already a step beyond what can be found in any aspect of the Empiricist tradition, except perhaps the "psychologism" in Hume that was noted earlier. If Merleau-Ponty's work can avoid these extremes and provide the basis for genuine connectedness and holism, it might provide fertile ground for feminist thought.

From a feminist perspective, the first thing that strikes one about Merleau-Ponty's account of our perceptual, and specifically sexual, embodiment is that it exists at all. The simple fact that discussions of the body and sexuality are regarded as appropriately philosophical signifies a major difference between the Continental tradition and Anglo-American philosophy as it is usually defined. To the extent that the body has been identified with women in the Western world, and to the extent that women themselves regard their mode of embodiment as an important part of their life experience, to exclude such disussions from the philosophical realm altogether is a move that renders women's philosophy problematical in a way that is quite different from the problems presented by limiting such discussions, as the Continental tradition largely does, to a male experience of embodiment and sexuality. There is at least a space within Merleau-Ponty's phenomenology for women's embodiment to exist as a possible realm of philosophical discourse.

Moreover, in Merleau-Ponty's phenomenology of the sexual body the emphasis on tactile experience (as against the visual orientation more common in philosophy of all kinds) and on sexuality as a general aura within which one's life is lived seem to come much closer to women's sexuality than the admitted male bias of his vocabulary might suggest:

> From the part of the body which it especially occupies, sexuality spreads forth like an odour or like a sound . . . [S]exuality, without being the object of any intended act of consciousness, can underlie and guide specified forms of my experience. Taken in this way, as an ambiguous atmosphere, sexuality is co-extensive with life. (pp. 168–69)

To a female reader, this account lacks the Individualism (note the attenuated role of consciousness, as opposed to Sartre), alienation, and exclusion found in most philosophical accounts of sexuality, even if it does not capture anything that is undeniably our own experience. It is an account of which we could at least conceive of ourselves as the subject, rather than the object, and one we might even find erotic.

Furthermore, it is important to understand that embodiment and sexuality are not merely appendices to Merleau-Ponty's work, something thrown in to make him seem appropriately "liberal." Instead, they are central to his epistemological argument as a whole. In seeking to avoid the usual dichotomy of Empiricism or Kantian Idealism, Merleau-Ponty relies on a detailed account of the role our body plays as "stage director" of our perceptions to provide the basis for an account of knowing that relocates the knower in a body and a social world.[14] He refers to the case of Schneider, a German soldier who was wounded in World War I and became the subject of studies by Steinfeld and by Gelb and Goldstein. Schneider received a head wound that left his perception more or less intact, but somehow destroyed his ability to perceive a "world" in the Heideggerian sense. Instead, he perceived isolated, unrelated data of which he was able to make only marginal sense, since they were not imbedded in any meaningful larger whole. What he could perceive were, in short, "sense data" in the Anglo-American sense and, as in Hume, those atomic data alone were not ultimately enough to build what we would recognize as a coherent perceptual world.

This is discussed in the chapter on sexuality because Schneider's sexual dysfunction followed the same pattern and, although Merleau-Ponty does not comment on it, it also reveals a strong analogy between perception as sense data and a stereotypically male view of sexuality. It actually is wrong to say that Schneider has a sexual dysfunction, since he was able to perform normally if the woman took the initiative and guided him through it. He could not, however, initiate or even desire sexual activity away from the concrete situation, because that activity was severed for him from the more complex set of meanings and behaviors in which normal human sexuality is embedded. He lacked what Merleau-Ponty calls a "sexual schema," the very concept of an erotic situation. That is, Schneider was a man who was forced to regard sex literally as only a biological activity, without any meaning beyond itself. This suggests that there might be a deeper relationship between sense data theory and a "singles bar" model of sexuality than simply the classic collection of ribald anecdotes. A world without meaningful connection, a world of stereotypically male sexuality, might also become a world with sex acts, but without any sexuality at all. And perhaps, a feminist deconstruction would suggest, that is precisely the point.

In contrast to the way in which Schneider's perceptual problems affected his sexuality, Merleau-Ponty also considers the Freudian construction of the "hysteric" (who is, by definition, female) as the reverse case of psychosexual dysfunction. Here, certain malfunctions in the hysteric's rational capabilities reduce her bodily options in the world by creating a paralysis based on an attempt not to perceive sexuality, or not to perceive sexually. That is, a desire not to know becomes a desire not to perceive, which becomes an inability to move, since perception and behavior depend on, and contribute to, the same schemata of our lived world. In neither this case nor Schneider's, Merleau-Ponty argues, can a line between the mental and the organic be clearly drawn—a fact about sexuality and embodiment that may come as no surprise to women. This rejection of dualism, based on Merleau-Ponty's desire to avoid the opposition between Empiricism and Idealism as well as that between mind and body, has implications that reach far beyond these specific dichotomies and undermine the entire philosophical tradition, as he was well aware.

In his later work, Merleau-Ponty became much more interested in language and even came to presage many of the developments in what is now considered to be "post-structuralist" thought.[15] This means that he also became more critical of the philosophical tradition, especially of the hierarchical dualisms that are so central to its structure. In the unfinished manuscript of *The Visible and the Invisible* (1959–1961), he engages in a critique of his own philosophical tradition from Descartes and Kant onwards, but also shows a clear awareness not only of Empiricist thought, but of contemporary linguistic philosophy in both its structuralist and Anglo-American forms as well. He begins with what he terms "perceptual faith," later defined as "everything that is given to the natural man [sic] in the original in an experience-source, with the force of what is inaugural and present in person, according to a view that for him is ultimate and could not conceivably be more perfect or closer" (p. 158), and considers how that faith comes undone in the Modern period. In so doing, he diagnoses "Pyrrhonianism" (i.e., the philosophical scepticism of Hume) as ultimately sharing the illusions of the naïve "man" because it ignores "the *problem of the world*" (p. 6), that is, it fails to take account of the total context of perceptual experience. In general, Merleau-Ponty's criticism of Modern philosophy amounts to a reassertion of the holism of lived experience in the face of the atomism and Individualism found in the philosophers of that era. At the same time, this holism would also dissolve such basic oppositions as that between subject and object—"The same reasons that keep us from treating perception as an object also keep us from treating it as the operation of a 'subject,' in whatever sense one takes the term" (p. 23)—and so weaken the gender-bias they represent as well.

In the contemporary period, Merleau-Ponty is especially critical of Husserl and Sartre, and his primary focus is their Individualistic, if not solipsistic, accounts of other minds. He identifies Husserl's slogan about the "thing itself" as solipsistic "imperialism" that would privilege the thing I see as the "real" thing and reduce the other's perceptual object to an appearance of it (p. 10); and argues that the body and perception undermine Sartre's analysis of the For-Itself as a pure negation in the full world of the being of the In-Itself:

> For it is quite obvious that there is pure negation only in principle and that the existent For Itself is encumbered with a body, which is not outside if it is not inside, which intervenes between the For Itself and itself. Likewise pure being is nowhere to be found, for every alleged thing soon reveals itself to be an appearance, and these alternating and antagonistic images are not comprehensible as images of one sole being. (p. 68)

Although this critique of "negativism" is also intended to apply to Heidegger, the main line of Merleau-Ponty's argument comes very close to the Heideggerian concept of "world" as a total context of human life. Moreover, Merleau-Ponty often speaks in this text about the "flesh of things," which is directly related to both his concept of "invagination" (p. 152—a word one might have thought Derrida invented) and the traditional equation between Nature and the maternal (p. 267). Finally, his work remains an "interrogation," "a question consonant with the porous being which it questions and from which it obtains not an *answer,* but a confirmation of its astonishment" (p. 102). Such a denial of philosophical mastery might be the most feminist move of all.

Toward the end of *The Visible and the Invisible,* Merleau-Ponty returns more directly to the issue of perception and begins to develop the concept of the "Chiasm." This "Ch[i]asm," which is clearly heavily laden with female imagery of both negation and invagination, initially refers to the crossing point between a body that is not as material object and a perception that is not a mental state. In this nexus of perception he finds the basis of human experience and thought, and thereby further questions the entire hierarchy of dualisms on which men's philosophy has traditionally been built. The implications of this view for the "problem" of other minds, for example, are that

> There is here no problem of the *alter ego* because it is not *I* who sees, not *he* who sees, because an anonymous visibility inhabits both of us, a vision in general, in virtue of that primordial property that belongs to the flesh, being here and now, of radiating everywhere and forever, being an individual, of being also a dimension and a universal. (p. 142)

Clearly, this total denial of duality and mastery might well provide a powerful basis for philosophy that centered on the experience of those chiasmic, fleshly, radiating, dimensional, and universal alter egos even Merleau-Ponty himself generally ignores, that is, a basis for what would be women's philosophy.[16]

Sartre's Existential Individualism

So far we have discussed the sense in which some of Heidegger's work suggests a possible opening in the realm of the philosophical through which women's philosophy might emerge, in contrast to most of the Empiricist tradition, which would rule women's philosophy out from the very beginning, but much of his thought also remains highly patriarchal, so that Heideggerian hermeneutics provides only an ambiguous paradigm for feminist philosophers. At the same time, Merleau-Ponty's phenomenology comes much closer to providing such a paradigm, but as is typical of phenomenology, gives us no obvious tools for the necessary critique of the sociopolitical status quo. The work of Sartre, while both phenomenological and critical (on a generally Marxist basis), is so deeply identified with Individualism, with a basically solipsistic response to the "problem" of other minds, as to be no paradigm at all; but it is closely tied to the only extended feminist theory in France before 1965. We will discuss Sartre's work, therefore, in comparison to Heidegger and Merleau-Ponty on the one hand and to Anglo-American Individualism on the other, before turning to de Beauvoir's *The Second Sex,* in order to come to a better understanding of how the existential tradition within Continental thought can, or cannot, be articulated with a critical feminist enterprise.

I have already referred to Caroline Whitbeck's dismissal of Hegel as the true master of hierarchical dualistic thinking, and much of Sartre's work is closely aligned with exactly that aspect of Hegel's thought, although with unusual and not necessarily helpful variations. Hegel's model of social relationships is the master/slave relation, in which the master asserts his existence by negating the existence of the slave, until such time as the slave effectively ceases to exist as an independent entity at all. This dynamic, paradoxically, gives the slave a strange power in the relationship, since "his" continued existence as slave, and thus in a sense "his" continued cooperation, are necessary to the existence of the master himself. This paradox is, moreover, tied to the basic metaphysics of Hegel's system: identity is always determined through opposition, but what is opposed is always only a different aspect or dimension of oneself. Ultimately, there is only one Self, one Mind, which is also, of course, (a) male, and (b) identical with God. Thus, underlying the dualisms and the conflicts of Hegelian thought is a strange kind of holism, a sense of the world, especially in his historical aspect, as a single process of organic growth. At the same time, Hegel's holism is achieved only through an extreme Idealism that not only ignores the myriad concrete human relationships that cannot be forced into the master/slave model (maternal relationships, for one, as Whitbeck notes[17]), but also ignores any part of the world or world history that likewise does not fit the plan.

What seems to happen in Sartre is that he takes Heidegger's concept of Dasein as an entity that lacks intrinsic meaning and defines itself in terms of its projects, and superimposes it on the Hegelian master/slave dialectic (stripped of its underlying holism) to generate a more complex, but no less frightening, concept of the self. The basic dichotomy in *Being and Nothingness* is between the In-Itself (projectless, worldless, inert natural existence, a concept that does not exist as such in Heidegger) and the For-Itself, that is, Dasein with its world and its projects.[18] Despite some recognition of the deep tie between language and the social world on the one hand, and the Self and language on the other, however, the social nature of the For-Itself comes closer to the Hegelian model than to Heidegger's "Being-with." The primary social relationship of the For-Itself is "the look," the attempt by the For-Itself to reduce the alien For-Itself in its visual field to an In-Itself, that is, to objectify it and thereby nullify its power to objectify in return. "Such is the *origin* of my concrete relations with the Other; they are wholly governed by my attitudes with respect to the object which I am for the Other" (p. 473, my emphasis—compare the quotation from Merleau-Ponty above). Among other points of note here is the obvious asymmetry between the radically "free" For-Itself, which I must be for myself, and the objectified In-Itself, which I must always be for the Other, and "he" for me: we are once again in the realm of a powerful and solipsistic Cartesian Individualism, a variant on the subject/object dichotomy Heidegger considers definitive of the modern world and that Sartre adapts from the work of Husserl.[19]

Indeed, in many ways, Heidegger's critique of the Husserlian framework from which his own thought grew can be applied directly to Sartre's own reliance on that same framework. At the same time, however, *Being and Nothingness* shares much more with the existential side of *Being and Time* than a similar title, especially with regard to the concepts of authenticity and good faith, a term that seems to be a response to the untranslatability of the former term *(Eigentlichkeit)* into French (or into English either, but that is another issue). The conflict between the two might best be presented briefly by focusing on the issue of "humanism," a title Sartre claims for his existentialism and the later Heidegger rejects.[20] We have already seen with the Empiricists how liberalism imports a partial and male-biased concept of the human into philosophical and political thought, and a parallel case could well be made for "humanism" in the same period. There is a deep connection, therefore, between Sartre's Individualism and his "humanism," both seeing the world, on roughly Freudian and Marxist grounds, as an arena within which human effort can create increased autonomy for "man" in the face of an alien and often hostile natural realm. From Heidegger's point of view, this "humanism" is a tragically hubristic species-ism, an exaltation of the human to the role previously held by God as the master of the world. Where Heidegger would accept the alien mystery of non-Dasein being as something "given" to Dasein, Sartre sees it as an Hegelian Other that defies our efforts to "synthesize" it into just another variant on the Same. Since the "natural," especially when opposed to the "human," is always also the female (since the "human" is always male), this difference between the two views is clearly significant for their relevance to what would become women's philosophy.

Just to confuse things a bit in Sartre's account of "our" relationship to the Other (as the power of the slave confuses things in Hegel), it seems that the For-Itself's deepest and most basic project is exactly to become self-identical, to become God, which Sartre calls the In-Itself-For-Itself. This is a confusing element, first, because such an aspiration can never be satisfied, but also because things that might make one an In-Itself-For-Itself are easily mistaken for things that might make one an In-Itself *tout court*, as in religious martyrdom, for instance. Or, interestingly, in sexual relationships, which on Sartre's account once again follow the master/slave paradigm. What one desires in the Other is that it should become a For-Itself that freely gives itself as an In-

Itself; what one desires for oneself is to become an In-Itself-For-Itself for the Other. Therefore, sexual relationships are necessarily self-defeating, since neither of these things can ever in fact happen. One place that there seems to be a lack of male bias in Sartre's work, however, is where he locates this dynamic—it is in the caress that this futile process primarily occurs, not in phallic sexuality. Orgasmic pleasure *(jouissance)* is not the goal of sexual activity, but "the death and the failure of desire" (p. 515).[21] Now, while one might wish for a lover with such a sensual outlook, deconstruction warns me that as a metaphysical position Sartre's account may be more deeply understood not as a desire to share women's diffuse, non-phallic sexuality, but as a desire to avoid pleasure (i.e., female *jouissance* and the anxiety it causes) at the price of a certain self-castration. This sadomasochistic exchange of pleasure and pain in a gender-laden dialectic of power would not, in any case, be entirely foreign to the Hegelian model on which Sartre draws.[22]

De Beauvoir in Context

Since de Beauvoir partially adopts this Hegelian dynamic from Sartre in *The Second Sex* and combines it with a relatively uncritical reliance on Freudian psychoanalysis and a somewhat ahistorical version of the Marxist discourse on women, it is not surprising that her work presents some problems for many Anglo-American feminists.[23] At the same time, many of those problems are analogous to the problems with Anglo-American "liberal" feminism. The analogy stems, I believe, more from the contrast between her feminism and her close relationship to an Individualistic male discourse more than from any "liberal" content. Thus, de Beauvoir's feminism leads her to reject the easy move in the Sartrean account of sexuality from the master/slave dynamic to a fixed gender distribution of the sadist/masochist roles.[24] De Beauvoir claims, rather, that masochism is an incidental feature of feminine sexuality, an adolescent phase tied to the Oedipal complex, which one generally "outgrows." For de Beauvoir, mature sexuality requires that the woman be the full equal and partner of the man, so that the dynamic that Sartre describes is a reciprocal effort at self-negating self-assertion in which gender roles are not fixed. And that is the line that her argument generally takes: women should be men's equals (hence her "liberalism"), taking on projects and asserting themselves in the world on the Sartrean model.

Her explanation of the fact that most women traditionally have not done so, however, vascillates between a variant on "blaming the victim" (our biology makes "bad faith" easier for us, so we choose to live our socially determined, trivial lives) and an equally alienating and unexistential biological determinism.[25]

Still, de Beauvoir remains not only a role model for many feminists, but also a rich source of philosphical insight. As I have done with Merleau-Ponty and Sartre, I would like to focus especially on her contribution to a feminist account of embodiment and sexuality, since it provides a strong contrast both to Sartre and to much contemporary Anglo-American feminism. As in much recent French feminism, de Beauvoir emphasizes the diffuse mode of female sexuality, which she calls "vaginal" (p. 371), distinguishing it from male, orgasm-centered sexuality. (Her discourse on sexuality finds a strange ally in Freud's discredited variation on what has always really been an opposition between the virginal, vaginal mother and the orgasmic, clitoral whore.) At the same time, this part of her account undercuts in many ways the existential "liberalism" cited above—if this is the nature of women's sexuality, it fits the model of assertion and "projects" very poorly, since it follows the "feminine" side of Sartre's account in choosing endless tactile embodiment over orgasm:

> [A]nd that i[s] why coition is never quite terminated for her: it admits of no end. . . . Feminine sex enjoyment [*jouissance*] radiates throughout the whole body; it is not always centered in the genital organs; even when it is, the vaginal contractions constitute, rather than a true orgasm, a system of waves that rhythmically arise, disappear, and reform, attain from time to time a paroxysmal condition, become vague, and sink down without ever quite dying out. (p. 371)

In such a phenomenology feminism might find a basis for rethinking our own sexuality, one that might be easily severed from both of the male-oriented discourses on which it is apparently based.

What is lacking here (and is present in many of the French feminists) is the link between this phenomenology of sexuality and the social roles that women are assigned to play in this culture, most notably those of mother and of Lesbian. In the former case, the fact that women's sexuality has this diffuse, global character is surely not unrelated to the pleasures and pains, both physical and psychological, of motherhood. Are these, then, twin features of women's greater biological imperative and the resulting choice/biological destiny to live trivial lives? The work of Julia Kristeva and others of the more psychoanalytic French feminists have clear affinities to de Beauvoir's early thought in this area. In the case of "the Lesbian," feminists as diverse as Monqiue Wittig and Claudia Card have pointed out that de Beauvoir's account, including both her political beliefs and the kind of sexual phenomenology she describes, would lead to the conclusion that Lesbianism is the best choice for women, a conclusion that de Beauvoir evades.[26] Can one freely choose the position of Lesbian? If one can, is that not the only correct choice? If one can't, what does that say about the freedom, or lack of it, in the other choices women make? And is there any important difference between such social limitations and the biological ones noted above? Such questions are easily generated by de Beauvoir's text, and others more expert in her philosophy might find good answers to them there.[27] Still, on a certain level, the contradictions between de Beauvoir's feminist consciousness and the Sartrean model her work continues to follow create a conflict very similar to the one in "liberal" feminism discussed by Eisenstein. What other feminists may find themselves engaged in would be, on this reading, the "radical future" of de Beauvoir's feminism.

The third issue of *Hypatia*, the journal of the Society for Women in Philosophy, was devoted to a discussion of de Beauvoir's work, and might well provide a vision of how a radicalized feminist existentialism would look, at least from this side of the Atlantic. Despite some attacks on the male-dominated phenomenological, and specifically existential, tradition within which de Beauvoir worked, many of the papers underscored the usefulness to women's philosophy of these philosophical approaches. Thus, in reviewing just two of several significant articles from this volume to relate de Beauvoir's work more closely to contemporary Anglo-American feminist thought, and particularly to those aspects of it discussed in the last chapter, I will also suggest that her work is in many of these respects a continuation of, rather than a break from, the entire Continental tradition of which it is a part. It is probably always a mistake, although not necessarily always a serious one, to assume that de Beauvoir read only Sartre.

Linda Singer's "Interpretation and Retrieval: Rereading Beauvoir," for instance, offers a feminist criticism of the "existentialists like Sartre (but also Nietzsche, Kierkegaard and Heidegger)" based on their excessive Individualism, which explains the fact that they are "loath to construct an ethics conceived as a general set of prescriptions for social behavior" (p. 237). De Beauvoir, Singer suggests, by relying on the subtle differences between male and female moral thought in society, is able to overcome this problem and work toward a genuine ethics that in many ways foreshadows the work of Gilligan and others. Thus de Beauvoir, according to Singer, looks to women's different relationship to connectedness and relationship itself in their childhood experiences as a basis for a contextualized and social concept of freedom, in place of the Individualistic and even solipsistic account of "existential" freedom found in Sartre. This may well be true (but see also the discussion of the "freedom" to choose to be a Lesbian above), but it is not so clear that it puts de Beauvoir's concept of freedom in opposition to Heidegger's in the same way as to Sartre's. We have already discussed the problems Heidegger's account of freedom can present for feminist readers, and there is at least some parallel between the following passage from Singer's article and the Heideggerian concept of "solicitude" cited above: ". . . Beauvoir recommends an ethic of commitment geared toward a situation in which freedom ought to be mobilized in concert with others for the purpose of creating the conditions for its further development by engaging others in the recognition and exercise of their freedom" (p. 238). Thus, a valid criticism of Sartre is not always a valid criticism of all Continental philosophy as such, even when it may be a valid criticism of all men's philosophy as such.

Along similar lines in the realm of epistemology, Charlene Haddock Siegfried's "*Second Sex:* Second Thoughts" argues that de Beauvoir's discussion of embodiment has important implications as part of the feminist rejection of the fact/value distinction. This distinction is, of course, isomorphic with all the other hierarchical dualisms already discussed as part of women's exclusion from the philosophical realm. Siegfried sees de Beauvoir's work as an important contribution to the feminist argument against these dichotomies, especially as they are currently used to structure scientific discourse as male:

> Beauvoir's characterization of the body as situation, as the expression of the complex of relationships that comprise every day reality, combined with the realization that meaning and value are assigned to events through the projects adopted, would comprise the core of such a reinterpretation [of traditional explanatory frameworks in the sciences]. (p. 227)

It does nothing to reduce de Beauvoir's contribution here, however, to note that the situatedness of our embodiment as a significant epistemological fact is likewise part of Merleau-Ponty's phenomenological enterprise, where it also serves to undermine the traditional metaphysical dualisms that serve to exclude women from philosophy (and science). The phenomenological emphasis on embodiment can thus be seen as opening a space within the tradition through which women's philosophy might become more possible, both as a more complete account of women's lived experience and as a basis for a feminist epistemology.

The remaining question then is, Why should women's philosophy care or bother to find itself a place anywhere within such a male-defined philosophical discourse? As suggested above, the main advantage to such an approach is that it spares us the problem of reinventing the wheel. Given the difficulty of any appropriation of Anglo-American philosophy, with its roots in the work of Locke and Hume, in the service of women's philosophy, the avenues and fissures that phenomenology offers, for all the risks, at least suggest the possibility of both remaining a philosopher and being able to incorporate women's experience into what one does. Simone de Beauvoir herself provides at least one clear example of just how that might be done. If feminist philosophers take a hermeneutic (i.e., a Heideggerian, interpretive) approach to social realities, a phenomenological approach to our lived experience, and a deconstructive approach to philosophical (and other) texts, as I will describe in the next chapter, it seems that we would have a firmer theoretical base from which to criticize, and change, the biases in the cultural heritage that has come down to us. In so doing, we might also find a basis for doing something that is both philosophical and still entirely our own.

Notes

1. Sandra Wawrytko's *The Undercurrent of Feminine Philosophy in Eastern and Western Thought* (Washington, D.C.: University Press of America, 1981) is, unfortunately, now out of print.

2. See, for instance, Nancy Tuana, "Re-fusing Nature/Nurture," *Women's Studies International Forum* 6, no. 6 (1983): 621–32; Mary Daly, *Beyond God the Father* (Boston: Beacon Press, 1973); and Evelyn Fox Keller, *Reflections on Science and Gender.*

3. See, for instance, Charlene Haddock Seigfried, "*Second Sex:* Second Thoughts," *Women's Studies International Forum* 8, no. 3 (1985): 219–29.

4. Feminist uses of Continental philosophy are discussed by Harding in her book, *The Science Question in Feminism,* and by Gloria Bowles in "The Uses of Hermeneutics for Feminist Scholarship," *Women's Studies International Forum* 7, no. 3 (1984): 131–33.

5. Jeffner Allen, "Motherhood: The Annihilation of Women," in *Mothering,* ed. Joyce Trebilcot (Totowa, N.J.: Rowman and Allanheld, 1983).

6. Martin Heidegger, *Being and Time,* trans. John Macquarrie and Edward Robinson (New York: Harper and Row, 1962), p. 58.

7. On the issue of Sartre's Individualism see, for instance, Linda Singer, "Interpretation and Retrieval: Re-reading Beauvoir," *Women's Studies International Forum* 8, no. 3 (1985): 231–38.

8. Martin Heidegger, *The Question Concerning Technology,* trans. William Lovitt (New York: Harper Colophon, 1977).

9. Gayatri Chakravorty Spivak, "French Feminism in an International Frame," *Yale French Studies* 62 (1981): 154–84.

10. Marjorie Weinzweig, "Should a Feminist Choose a Marriage-Like Relationship?", *Hypatia* , no. 2 (Fall 1986): 139–60.

11. Marilyn Frye, "History and Responsibility," *Women's Studies International Forum* 8, no. 3 (1985): 215–17.

12. Naomi Scheman, in her unfortunately not very available paper "The Body Politic/The Impolitic Body/Bodily Politics," in *The Materialities of Communication* (in German, trans. L. Pfeiffer), ed. H. U. Gumbracht and L. Pfeiffer, forthcoming from Suhrkamp, raises this issue in an especially clear way with regard to the "we" of feminist thought, a problem that is obviously unresolved in the present text.

13. Maurice Merleau-Ponty, *The Phenomenology of Perception,* trans. Colin Smith (New York: Routledge and Kegan Paul, 1962).

14. This wonderful line is from Maurice Merleau-Ponty, *The Visible and the Invisible,* trans. Alphonso Lingis (Evanston, Ill.: Northwestern University Press, 1968), p. 8.

15. The relationship between Merleau-Ponty's later work on the one hand and semiotics/structuralism/post-structuralism/deconstruction on the other is an interesting issue in itself, but one that lies beyond the boundaries of the current project. For one preliminary exploration, see my "Merleau-Ponty on Presence: A Derridian Reading," *Research in Phenomenology* 16 (1986): 111–20.

16. In papers presented at the October 1987 meeting of the Society for Phenomenology and Existential Philosophy, both Kate Mehuron of Vanderbilt University and Eleanor Shapiro Godway of Central Connecticut State University point out close connections between Merleau-Ponty's later work and the work of Luce Irigaray. Mehuron also referred to Merleau-Ponty's concept of the chiasm in refuting accusations that Irigaray's work relies on a feminist essentialism, as explained in chapter six.

17. Caroline Whitbeck, "A Different Reality," p. 69.

18. Jean-Paul Sartre, *Being and Nothingness,* trans. Hazel E. Barnes (New York: Pocket Books, 1966).

19. Julien S. Murphy, in her "The Look in Sartre and Rich," *Hypatia* 2, no. 2 (Summer 1987): 113–24, tries to recoup "the look" in Sartre for feminist

purposes through a comparison with the poetry of Adrienne Rich. Although the effort is quite interesting, I am unconvinced that this aspect of Sartre's work is something that we would want to incorporate into women's philosophy.

20. See Jean-Paul Sartre, *Existentialism Is a Humanism* (Paris: Nagel, 1946) and Martin Heidegger, "Letter on Humanism," trans. Frank A. Capuzzi and J. Glenn Gray, in *Basic Writings,* David Farrell Krell, ed. (New York: Harper and Row, 1977).

21. Apparently, Sartre preferred caressing the Other to the sex act itself, which reminded him too much of his own passivity and his bodily contingency. (See de Beauvoir's *Adieux: A Farewell to Sartre,* trans. Patrick O'Brian [New York: Pantheon, 1984, p. 314].)

22. At a conference on "Explorations in Feminist Ethics," held October 7–8, 1988, at the University of Minnesota, Duluth, Linda Bell presented a paper entitled "A Feminist Ethics in Sartre's Existentialism" that would disagree with this interpretation. She finds a feminism in his ethics by reading his work in a way that is much closer to the way in which I read Heidegger, particularly with regard to the role of social definitions (of ourselves and of others) in the choices we make. My analysis is limited primarily to *Being and Nothingness* and may emphasize Sartre's Hegelian side more than it should, but it also seems more congruent with the usual (mis?)understanding of Sartre's work (e.g., with Merleau-Ponty's understanding, as noted above, and that of Linda Singer's article, cited in note #7). Still, I respect Bell's expertise enough to be less certain of my conclusion now than when I originally formulated it.

23. Simone de Beauvoir, *The Second Sex,* trans. H. M. Parshley, (New York: Bantam Books, 1961).

24. It must be noted here that Hazel Barnes's translation suggests more gender stereotyping than Sartre may have intended, since she uses the pronoun "she" for the masculine *"l'autrui"* (the Other) in the discussions of sexuality in *Being and Nothingness.*

25. At least two of the articles in the recent *Yale French Studies* volume on de Beauvoir ("Simone de Beauvoir: Witness to a Century," *Yale French Studies* 72 [1987]), would take issue with both of these points in my reading of her work—Judith Butler's "Sex and Gender in Simone de Beauvoir's *Second Sex,*" *Yale French Studies* no. 72 (1987): 35–49, and Margaret A. Simons's "Beauvoir and Sartre: The Philosophical Relationship," *Yale French Studies* 72 (1987): 165–79—but they may be part of the "radical future" of de Beauvoir's thought discussed below.

26. Monique Wittig, "One is Not Born a Woman," in *Feminist Frameworks,* ed. Alison M. Jaggar and Paula S. Rothenberg (New York: McGraw-Hill, 1984); Claudia Card, "Lesbian Attitudes and *The Second Sex,*" *Women's Studies International Forum* 8, no. 3 (1985): 209–14. See also Ann Ferguson's "Lesbian Identity: Beauvoir and History," *Women's Studies International Forum* 8, no. 3 (1985): 203–08.

In her 1984 interview with de Beauvoir, Hélène V. Wenzel indicates a later, but unspecified, re-evaluation of the issue of Lesbianism by de Beauvoir (Hélène V. Wenzel, "Interview with Simone de Beauvoir," *Yale French Studies*, no. 72 (1987): 5:32).

27. Again, see *Yale French Studies* 72 and the *Hypatia* volume on de Beauvoir (Women's Studies International Forum 8, no. 3 [1985]), and on the issue of choice and gender, especially the article by Judith Butler cited in note #3 and her "Variations on Sex and Gender," in *Feminism as Critique*, ed. Seyla Benhabib and Drucilla Cornell (Minneapolis: University of Minnesota Press, 1987).

Chapter 5

Women's Philosophy After the End of Metaphysics

Semiotics and Structuralism

At this point I would like to make what amounts to a small detour. To explain what has come to be called post-structuralist thought in France, it will be helpful to give a very basic account of both structuralism and the closely related field of semiotics. This is more than a simple matter of historical filiation, because the cross-cultural denaturalization central to both semiotic and structuralist thought is a necessary step in making discourses such as Freud's and Marx's available to feminist analysis, not as factual, empirical accounts of how the world is, but as analyses of the *linguistic structures* that create the social and political world in which we live. This anti-empiricist element in contemporary French thought provides both the starkest contrast to the British Empiricist tradition and perhaps the most fertile ground for women's philosophy. This anti-empiricism also leads to the charge among Anglo-American philosophers that post-structuralism is some form of Idealism, Kantian at best, Hegelian at worst, but in any case as much beneath serious consideration as Empiricism is considered to be in France. From the present perspective, however, this response to post-structuralism may be seen, in part, as an effort to deny/defend the deeply exclusionary power structure inherent in Empiricism itself. Therefore, it may be significant that nearly all of the thinkers I will discuss in this chapter and the next belong to groups that are often excluded from philosophy: unlike most Anglo-American philosophers, they are disproportionately homosexuals, Jews, cultural and national minorities, expatriates/exiles, and women.

As noted earlier, the basic insight of semiotics is that the relation between a signifier and its signified (e.g., a letter and a sound) is entirely arbitrary. This deceptively simple fact, based on the work of de Saussure, has radical implications. Even in the case of letter and sound, it suggests, for instance, that a phonetic alphabet has no advantage over a hieroglyphic or pictographic one, even though European ethnocentrism has historically argued for the advantage of the phonetic alphabet as a more "natural" way of representing what are, *from a European point of view,* primarily relationships of sounds. When applied to the relationship between words and their referents, the arbitrariness of the sign has an even more profound effect: any sign can represent any thing, there are no symbols as such, there are no metaphors—or rather everything is a metaphor, since no sign has a privileged or "natural" relationship to any signified. Perhaps the best examples of the effects of this insight on specifically feminist issues can be seen in its application to Freud. Derrida, for instance, in discussing a Van Gogh painting of a pair of unlaced boots, notes that they can be taken indifferently as phallic *or* vaginal symbols, which opens up in some very unexpected ways the debate he is considering about whether the boots are men's or women's.[1] In general, the arbitrariness of the sign shifts the discourse of the phallus in Freud from the anatomical to the linguistic mode, leaning to such exciting feminist re-readings of the tradition as Rubin's "The Traffic in Women" (which draws on Lacan's work rather than Derrida's).

The second major insight in semiotics has similarly radicalizing effects. In phonetics itself, remember, it is not the sounds that are significant, but rather the difference between sounds. This explains how we are able to understand so many highly diverse sonic inputs as the same words: no matter how high- or low-pitched the voice or how much interference there is, the interval between an *m* and an *a* remains constant within each set of stimuli. This can once again be generalized to any system of signs. I can read the writing of hundreds of different students because, no matter how each of them writes, an *i* will always be linear relative to an *o,* after every two or three consonants I will look for a vowel, and so on. It is not the content of the signs that matters so much as the empty spaces, the differences, or "differances," between them. Thus in Freud, what ultimately is of concern is not the phallus but its lack, that is, the difference between the mother and father and between the father and the son in the Oedipal situation. On the social level, Rubin discusses the fact that what matters in the exchange of wives is not the wives but the relationship between the exchange of wives and the exchange of power, that is, the phallus—as she says, "It is where we aren't" (p. 192). Semiotics in general is involved with applying this kind of analysis to very diverse sign systems, including not only kinship but also mythologies (both classical and current), propaganda, photography, film, and popular culture in general.

Structuralism can be briefly described as the generalization of this second insight of semiotics beyond simple oppositional pairs to entire relational structures. Thus, Lévi-Strauss's classic "The Structural Study of Myth" in *Structural Anthropology* looks at the cycle of myths to which the story of Oedipus belongs as an *ordered* series of oppositional pairs, where the relationships between elements in the series and its development in a certain direction are as important as the pairs themselves.[2] He creates a schema for these myths that relates Cadmos's sowing of the dragon's seed that grow to become the Spartoi both to the autochthonous origins of the dragon and the Sphinx and to Oedipus's own difficulty with bisexual parentage. These are in turn tied to the lameness Lévi-Strauss claims is referred to in the names of Oedipus (swollen-foot?), his father Laïos (left-sided?), and his grandfather Labdacos (lame?), that is, to their difficulty in relating to the earth. In the same myth cycle, we also find three opposed pairs of themes centered on the over- or under-valuing of blood ties: Cadmos's search for Europa/the fratricide of the Spartoi; Oedipus's murder of Laïos/his marriage to Jocasta; and Eteocles's murder of Polynices/Antigone's insistence on burying him. What this schema allows us to see, for Lévi-Strauss, is not only the relationships across these pairs, but also the connection between that set and the set concerned with autochthonous origins or relations to the earth. The myth cycle as a whole, on this account, is thus concerned not only with family relationships, but even more so with the "denial of the autochthonous origin of man" (p. 215). Lévi-Strauss includes the Freudian theory of the Oedipus complex as just another variant on the same structure to make the same point.

This section is a detour because, in spite of the work of Rubin, Kristeva, and others in that direction, the potential of semiotics and structuralism as such to provide a basis for women's philosophy is severely limited. This is, first of all, because they are not themselves philosophies but rather approaches to social science at the opposite end of the spectrum from the positivistic, statistical empiricism more common in the Anglo-American context. Secondly, semiotics and structuralism are, as we have seen, even more overtly committed to hierarchical dualisms as a basic analytical category than philosophy. Lévi-Strauss's triangular analysis of kinship is no more an advance in this area than Freud's or Hegel's, since the male roles are replications of each other and the basic duality remains male/female—or rather, male/male, since the woman is in fact a "place-holder" for something else (i.e., power or the missing phallus, as Rubin suggests). What semiotics and structuralism do, however, is provide critical tools that post-structuralist thought will later use in exposing the "unnatural" power relationships that underlie our seemingly "natural" systems of representation. In this chapter, I will trace the development of post-structuralist thought and what has come to be called deconstruction from its origins, exemplified by Roland Barthes's work in semiotics, through the structuralist version of Freud found in Lacan and the transitional work of historian Michel Foucault, to the more technically philosophical (and more overtly "feminist") reading of Heidegger found in Derrida. It will then be possible to turn in the next chapter to some of the so-called French feminists and their various relationships to the male discourse of contemporary Continental philosophy, and to the discourse of Anglo-American feminism as well.

Barthes on Signs and Systems

Roland Barthes's work lies on the border where structuralism, semiotics (or semiology), and post-structuralism meet. Starting from de Saussure's structuralist understanding of the nature of language, he applies the same method to the "second-order" languages of literature and what he calls "myth," that is, the pictorial and literary representations of the ideology of our (or any) culture. In his early collection of essays, *Mythologies,* he analyzes the ways in which bourgeois visions of reality come to be seen as natural, ahistorical necessities, thereby undermining any possibility of alternatives to that reality: "We reach here the very principle of myth: it transforms history into nature."[3] Perhaps his best, and simplest, example of this is a large photo on the cover of *Paris-Match* of a colonial African saluting the French flag. Structurally, Barthes tells us, the "second-order" signifier, that is, the photo itself, makes visible a signified, the equality of French soldiers of all colors and origins, and also conveys a third meaning—concept, in Barthes's terms, of the ahistorical necessity of France's colonial empire. What this picture seeks to naturalize— French domination of African peoples—is clearer to us, because it has since become de-naturalized again as our culture adjusts to the post-colonial realities of the world. At the same time, the very contingency of this image is underscored for an American reader by the fact that, both now and thirty years ago, the meaning of a similar picture with an African-American and the United States flag would offer interesting similarities with, and significant differences from, the French use of that myth.

In the same book, Barthes discusses several "rhetorical" forms used in bourgeois mythologizing, of which I will focus on three that most clearly parallel some of the arguments (from other sources) we have already considered that explain how men's philosophy disguises itself as objective and universal. The first of these rhetorical forms is "innoculation." It involves acknowledging small problems with bourgeois reality as a way of preventing the exploration of the large problems that undermine it at its base. Barthes's examples are the "discovery" of childhood irrationality and the toleration of an artistic avant garde (to which he denies any revolutionary value, since all art in bourgeois culture is ultimately defined, either positively or negatively, by bourgeois ideology). He calls this innoculation *"liberal,"* and we find it in Anglo-American liberalism most notably in the work of John Stuart Mill, who seems to have believed that if we could just "innoculate" patriarchal, capitalistic, bourgeois culture against enough of its self-induced evils, it could become an egalitarian, socialist, bourgeois Utopia.[4] There is also a hint of it, perhaps, in Locke's epistemological admissions with regard to God and substance—well, yes, we don't really *know* those things, but it doesn't *really* interfere with doing philosophy in any major way. (Berkeley, no doubt, gives the best rejoinder to this.) In Hume we have the more extreme case of declaring Empiricism without foundation, but at the same time assuming that science can continue to function as before. For contemporary feminism, perhaps the best example would be the final incarnation of *Ms.* magazine, which seemed to have just the right balance of feminist complaints and feminist success stories (both personal and political) to forestall any seriously critical feminist thought.[5]

A second favored "rhetorical" form of bourgeois naturalization is what Barthes terms "the privation of History." This implies, first, that bourgeois capitalism is the natural end state of history, and, indeed, the only state of history, since all other states are to be understood as more or less adequate approximations of it (for example, in discussions of whether the trial of Socrates was "fair" or "legal," in the almost complete absence of any adequate knowledge of the relevant *Athenian* laws, traditions, etc.). Secondly, since this is a "natural" outcome, no one is responsible for it, or for the crimes committed on its behalf. I have already attempted to make clear exactly how Empiricism, as with all post-Cartesian philosophy, sees itself primarily as a *break* with tradition, as itself a *tabula rasa,* and hence as without a history. Unlike "Scholasticism," Modern philosophy obeys neither history nor culture, but only the atemporal, "clear and distinct" laws of pure reason itself. If the conclusions those laws lead to, based on indubitable innate or empirical premises, happen to favor the interests of the socioeconomic and gender class to which the philosopher belongs, he cannot be held responsible, because it is only the natural outcome of correct philosophical thought. (It only reinforces Barthes's larger point that naturalization is the effect of *all* cultural mythologies to realize that the same can be said of many of the philosophies of ancient Greece.) In the same way, if logic and the data lead to the conclusion that blacks tested by Army intelligence tests are naturally less intelligent than whites, or that women are insufficiently left-brain dominant to be as good engineers or mathematicians as men, no one is responsible for the prejudicial actions that may follow—they are only the results of nature and pure logic.

Finally, what has been termed so far "universalization" Barthes considers under the title of "Identification." This is the rhetorical process by which any threatened Otherness is reintegrated into bourgeois ideology as simply another case of the Same (as with the African soldier above). This *"Aufhebung"* is, of course, the Hegelian move *par excellence,* although perhaps Barthes, with a marked Marxist focus at this point in his career, would not characterize it as such. He refers instead to the way in which the homosexual is recast as only Nature "gone wrong" or the unassimilable African becomes an exotic or a clown. The difference here between the bourgeois (i.e., "liberal") and the "petit bourgeois" becomes paramount—the bourgeois will homogenize the Other into the Same, while the petit bourgeois seems more directly to eradicate the threat that Otherness represents, that is, "it produces Fascism, whereas the bourgeoisie uses it" (p. 152). In the history of British Empiricism, the stages of this process with regard to women are clearly marked. As noted above, Hobbes, perhaps feeling a greater threat from the greater rational "accountability" of women in his era, more clearly excludes them from the philosophical realm than his successors. Locke, typically, is more "liberal" (i.e., bourgeois), in that he includes women in an inferior role where it suits his purposes, but ignores them otherwise. Hume seems at times to make clowns of women, as in the discussion of "Modesty" in the *Treatise,* and at (autobiographically later) times to push them into the realm of the exotic when he finds them unassimilable, as in the "Dialogue" between the two parts of Hume's *Inquiries.* In all three cases, as we have seen, insofar as women "really" count in philosophy, they are just the same as men and, insofar as they are not just the same, they do not count at all.

Similar parallels could easily be found between Barthes's other four "rhetorical" figures and discussions now current among a wide range of feminist thinkers, but these three examples should be sufficient to underscore the contribution his thought can make to a feminist analysis. What I would like to do at this point instead of reiterating examples is to turn to a paradigmatic case of Barthes's later, more complete readings of bourgeois mythology, *S/Z*.[6] This "essay" uses a semiotic system of oppositions and an elaborate structural schema in a very detailed reading of Balzac's *Sarrasine. S/Z* establishes almost purely by demonstration, with little discursive argument, that the story primarily serves to "naturalize" bourgeois gender categories and relationships. The horror with which Balzac's text considers the "gender bending" of the Italian *castrati* and the structural necessity of its tragic outcome powerfully reinforce traditional gender roles, much more so than any message that might be sent by the manifest content of the story. At the same time, those roles are defined in a way that reaffirms the inferiority of women and perpetuates the entire set of hierarchical dualisms that underlie men's philosophy. This is clearly a case in which careful reading of a text can provide the basis for a more thorough and political feminist analysis of culture as a whole.

Starting with a declaration of the nonexistence of the masterful, unified self—"This 'I' which approaches the text is already itself a plurality of other texts, of codes which are infinite or, more precisely, lost (whose origin is lost)" (p. 10)—Barthes divides the entire text of *Sarrasine* into five codes and traces the development of each code through the story. Since the story concerns a *castrati,* the first important realization is that Balzac replaces the polarity male/female with the polarity castrated/uncastrated, which cannot be mapped directly onto it. Thus, there are castrated men other than the literal *castrati* (including all the central men in the story) and uncastrated women, who are figured (of course) as castrating, although not necessarily of the same castrated men. (The literal castrator in the story is a minor male character whose only sign of castration is his homosexuality.) The castrating effect of the tale extends beyond the narrated story of

Sarrasine himself to the framing story in that the horror the story instills in the object of the narrator's intended seduction frustrates the seduction. Ultimately, the very existence of the *castrati* is presented as the grounds for a total collapse of value because it prohibits a simple adherence to the usual (dualistic, hierarchical) gender polatiry. ". . . [I]n a word, it is no longer possible to *represent,* to make things *representative,* individuated, separate, assigned; *Sarrasine* represents the very confusion of representation, the unbridled (pandemic) circulation of signs, of sexes, of fortunes" (p. 216). If, due to castration, one is unable, as Sarrasine is, to tell a woman from a man, (bourgeois) culture itself is in serious jeopardy—a thought all feminists might well take to heart.

At the same time, *S/Z,* as with much of Barthes's work, is a metacritique of the text itself, so that he regards the careful braiding of his five codes in the text as an example of the Freudian belief that women invented weaving and braiding to hide their castration. Balzac's carefully constructed edifice/artifice of "realism" is thus also a fetish designed to cover over the castration it cannot help but reveal. Barthes says of what he calls the "readerly" (i.e., the traditional/bourgeois) text in general that it also is obsessed both with being determinate or at least determinable (i.e., among other things, clearly male or female), and with creating a fullness, a plenum, a complete world "as if the *readerly* abhors a vacuum" (p. 105)—or a castration. In its representation of fullness, this readerly writing both creates and satisfies the expectations of its readers, a device clearly exposed by the many ways in which Balzac (sadistically?) manipulates our expectations, and those of the object of the intended seduction, in both the framing story and the main narration of his tale. As was noted with regard to Mill above, if just enough filling in can somehow be done, bourgeois reality might still be saved from the dire threat presented by revolutionary criticism, by the contingencies of history, by the Other, by castration, in short, by women, or rather, by Woman as bourgeois culture has always already defined her.[7] What Barthes can provide for the feminist project, then, is some of the tools necessary for excavating this primordial manoeuvre in all its various forms.

Lacan on Freud on Women

As with Barthes, the work of Jacques Lacan spans the dividing line between structuralist and post-structuralist thought. Drawing on de

Saussure's work in linguistics, Lacan argues that the unconscious, since it is accessible only through language, must itself be structured as a language. He regards the linguistic approach to psychoanalysis as an extension of Freud's own writings, especially his conceptualization of the dream as a rebus and his reliance on double entendres in *The Psychopathology of Everyday Life*. This linguistic orientation, moreover, implies that since the analytic process itself is a dialogue, the unconscious that is revealed in the analysis is in fact a transpersonal one, a product of both analyst and analysand, even if the former most often remains silent. Thus, in one paper reprinted in *Feminine Sexuality,* Lacan attributes the problem in the Dora case to Freud's failure to integrate Dora's Lesbian attachment sufficiently into the dialogue.[8] Furthermore, this linguistic reinterpretation of psychoanalysis reiterates Barthes's definition of the reader of literature, which undermines the very concept of a unified and masterful Self that underlies so much men's philosophy:

> This passion of the signifier then becomes a new dimension of the human condition, in that it is not only man who speaks, but in man and through man that it *[ça]* speaks, that his nature is woven by effects in which we can find the structure of language, whose material he becomes, and that consequently there resounds in him, beyond anything ever conceived of by the psychology of ideas, the relation of speech. (p. 78)

In *The Language of the Self,* Lacan uses this linguistic approach in a reformulation of the Oedipal conflict in which the role that the Father (who is not necessarily the father) plays in the Oedipal stage is one of forcing the child's entry into the "Symbolic" (i.e., linguistic) order, and so reducing its access to the world to the limits provided by language, that is, to the realm of the "Real."[9] "It is in the *name of the father* that we must recognize the support of the Symbolic function which, from the dawn of history, has identified his person with the figure of the law" (p. 41). (That the law depends on the Symbolic/linguistic order is shown by Lévi-Strauss's observation—now a poststructuralist cliché—that the basis of all laws, incest, exists not because of kinship, but because of kinship *naming* systems, which measure in various ways the lineages by which incest is defined.) The introduction into the Symbolic functions as a castration in the "Imaginary" of the child, that is, in its fantasy as revealed in the psychoanalytic dialogue, because it causes a rupture in the child's relationship to the inchoate, polymorphous pleasures of the pre-verbal mother/child bond without providing any substitute (although in the case of the male child there is an implicit—and false—promise of one in the future). The acquisition of language also has an "Oedipal" effect in that it undermines the child's attachment to its mother, both because it forces the recognition of their separation and hence of the mother's desire outside the mother/child dyad (i.e., her desire for the Father/phallus—cf. Freud's *"Fort/Da"* in *Beyond the Pleasure Principle,* another post-structuralist cliché) and because it is the mother who enforces law/language on the child in the name of an always absent Father (this is the negative, socializing side of Ruddick's "maternal thinking").

It is important to realize that, for Lacan and many of those who follow, the Symbolic order, on the Saussurean model, is completely arbitrary and hence bears no necessary relationship to any "empirical" reality. "The Symbolic function presents itself as a double movement within the subject: man makes an object of his action, but only in order to restore to this action in due time its place as a grounding" (p. 48). That is, we objectify ourselves in language and then use that language as the basis of the Real, the world of empirical "facts" that in turn becomes the referent of our language and our science. In true post-structuralist fashion, there are no "facts" in Lacan except linguistic ones. "Here the opposition which is traced between the exact sciences and those for which there is no reason to decline the appellation of 'conjectural' seems no longer an admissable one—for lack of any grounds of that opposition" (p. 49). Thus the Symbolic and the Real are no less "imaginary" for Lacan than the Imaginary, although they may have a broader socio-linguistic basis, and the Imaginary is never strictly private, arising as it does only in the dialogue between analyst and analysand. Nor is Lacan's view any more comforting on the personal level, since the relationship of the subject to the Symbolic, while necessary if one is to avoid madness and live as fully human, is always one of alienation and frustration: "I identify myself in Language, but only by losing myself in it like an object" (p. 63). I can only become a Self in the Real through the Symbolic, but in so doing I alienate, and hence necessarily frustrate, the (Imaginary) desire that was the original impetus for communication. Thus, Lacan has radically de-centered the structure of psychoanalysis and so even more completely undermined the autonomy of the speaking subject then Freud himself.

At the same time, however, Lacan's critics, including Derrida and Luce Irigaray, consider this an incomplete deconstruction of Freud's text. Most notably from a feminist point of view, Lacan seems to follow Freud in identifying all libido/desire as male, so that women can exist only as the object of male (infantile) desire. This leaves us only the choice between playing the role of the masculine woman or the maternal one, that is, we are always defined in terms of whether we frustrate or satisfy men's needs. Since the Symbolic is a paternal/ patriarchal function, that is, since language is male-defined, we are necessarily, as women, silent, and once again it is clear that the description of women's "necessary" silence can function as a prescription that we *be* silent as well. Worse yet, since the mother exists only as part of the (male) Imaginary, ultimately, Lacan carries this silence to its logical conclusion by saying that, as women, we really do not exist at all. (We have already discussed several texts that either enact or label this shift from the "Oedipus complex" to the Orestean matricide that it seeks to cover up.)

Feminist Lacanians, on the other hand, would deny that Lacan, in describing the phenomena our culture provides for him to interpret, is endorsing them as well. There is no place in the "Real" of our culture for female desire as such, and so Lacan is not to blame for his failure to discuss it, but rather reflects the fact that it does not exist in any meaningful (i.e., linguistically formulable) sense of the term. As a descriptive claim, this argument can be both supported and refuted by the efforts of Irigaray, Cixous, Wittig, and others, to capture female desire, since their success is always, and necessarily, only partial. As a political claim, however, the argument seems to fail for a reason that also throws into question the gender neutrality of British Empiricism: There is a very fine, possibly nonexistent, line between describing a cultural reality and endorsing it. Simply to restate the basic Freudian schema in contemporary society, no matter how much it is reinterpreted as a linguistic matter, without an explicit rethinking of gender issues *is* to take a political position in an inescapable and inescapably male-dominated material "reality." The de-centering of social structures that defines post-structuralism in general is itself political, and to deny its political weight is only another form of politics. In reading Lacan, one always feels that he knows who *really* has the phallus.

In this regard, it is important to remember that the title of the collection of papers edited by Juliet Mitchell and Jacqueline Rose is *Feminine Sexuality,* that is, that it focuses on the sexuality our culture defines as feminine, not necessarily the sexuality of those of us who happen to be female. Thus, Lacan's contributions to this volume not only exclude women from the male-defined realm of language, but also echo, without obvious irony, the most classically misogynistic Freudian doctrines: vaginal orgasm, the secret of which women either *choose* to keep slient about or are themselves ignorant of; frigidity, apparently with all of its traditional connotations; and female masochism—"Even given what masochistic perversion owes to masculine invention, is it safe to conclude that masochism of the woman is a fantasy of the desire of man?" (p. 92). (One would hope that by now it would be "safe" not only to conclude this, but to assert it as a basic tenet of the criticism of traditional psychoanalytical thought in which Lacan purports to be engaged.) Even Lacan's account of the role of female *jouissance* (a supposedly untranslatable word that simply means orgasm but that male post-structuralists tend to use as a term for *excessive* pleasure, especially when referring to women, as if any orgasm in women would be too much) ends by equating it with (male) mysticism, relating it to a God, and so returning it to male ownership. Similarly, Lesbianism is described as reactive to male homosexuality, and hence also under male ownership, in a way that does not simply repeat the Freudian account.

It is also important to note that, while all of these apparently minor issues might seem to function purely on the level of cultural definitions and so have little to do with the material oppression of women, which one is reluctant to claim Lacan would endorse, real women and men do creep into his text in strange places and ways. On a single page, for instance, Lacan explains that frigidity is "relatively well tolerated in women" (well tolerated by whom?) and that one effect of the exchange of the phallus in love relations is that men have "a persistent divergence towards 'another woman' [as if there were only one other woman—which, of course, from this perspective, there is] who can signify this phallus under various guises, whether as a virgin or a prostitute" (p. 84). Here, description clearly merges into prescription: if these two claims are true, and Lacan gives no hint that he does not intend us to take them as such, it follows that men need not feel guilt or take responsibility for their wives' "frigidity," since it is both the wife's problem (the core meaning of the concept of frigidity) and a "relatively" tolerable outcome of inviolable psychic processes; and that women *should* feel guilty if they are bothered by their husbands' "persistent divergence," over which the poor men apparently have no control. These and similar cases indicate that it may take very little cross-cultural or historical (or even anatomical) awareness to suspect that at least parts of Lacan's text serve, perhaps against his explicit intentions, precisely the function of bourgeois naturalization of the sexual status quo that Barthes so carefully exposes. Perhaps, in its own way, this text serves in part to innoculate us against a genuinely feminist psychoanalytic critique or, as in Balzac, merely weaves new clothes for the Emperor-Phallus.

Foucault and the Post-Structuralist Opening

Post-structuralist thought is identified as such because it maintains structuralism's schematic and semiotic orientation, but radically decenters the structures that result, opening them to the "free play" of signifiers across the whole range of schematic possibilities. It literally deconstructs the structures that semiotic and structuralist analyses uncover to show that they lack any fixed center, any foundational point of reference, but are in fact, as with language itself, arbitrarily arranged configurations of interchangeable elements. The privileged example here is once again that of Freud. Psychoanalytic discourse opens the possibility of a restructuring of gender when Freud refers to the bi-sexuality of the infant, but closer readings by French feminists such as Irigaray and Sarah Kofman have revealed that this supposedly bisexual infant is in fact always male. That opening, however, allows us to consider how Freud's basically deconstructive insight was reincorporated into the dominant discourse on gender precisely as its inverse, as a way in which women may be coerced into more rigidly sterotypical behavior to avoid the accusation of "penis envy." That psychoanalytic discourse might be restructured around issues of female desire, non-sexual desire, polymorphous pre-Oedipal desire, or even an unrestricted sexual economy provides a frequent topic of deconstructive texts, as do other issues that this kind of reading of Freud suggests. As was noted above, Lacan is one of the key figures in this transition between structuralism and post-structuralism, both because of his structuralist method and because of his repetition of Freud's repetition of the basic dynamic of male dominance.

Although his early work might also be counted in the structuralist camp, Michel Foucault's *The Order of Things* is perhaps one of the first post-structuralist texts.[10] The "reading" of Velázquez's "Las Meninas" that opens the book, for instance, presents the painting as a foreshadowing of the replacement of the kingly, Godlike center of the sixteenth-century world view with the more diffuse but still centralizing concept of "man" that develops in the seventeenth-century "world picture." To take just two elements of the painting that suggest this "humanistic" turn in the transition from the pre-Modern to the Modern, the mirror at the focal point of the painting, which should reflect what the painter sees as he looks around his canvas, that is, the person looking at the picture, shows instead the King and Queen whose portrait Velázquez represents himself as painting. This identification of the spectator and the kingly is reinforced by the figure immediately to the right of the mirror, a servant in a doorway, who can also represent the ascendent power of "the common (i.e., bourgeois) man." This analysis is in many ways a literalization of Heidegger's "The Age of the World Picture," which traces the decline of European thought since Descartes into a "world view" in which the world exists only for exploitation by "man."[11] Foucault's reaction to this story is quite different, however: rather than seeing it as a decadent development in the carefully structured history of the West, Foucault regards the dawning of the Modern period as just another in a series of fairly arbitrary variants in the intellectual structure of European thought. Foucault does not decry this "humanism" as Heidegger does, but considers it transitory: "As the archaeology of our thought easily shows, man is an invention of recent date. And one perhaps nearing its end" (p. 387).

Foucault terms each of the successive variant structures he finds in European thought an "episteme," a basic organizing principle or schema for an epoch that "defines the conditions of possibility of all knowledge, whether expressed in a theory or silently invested in a practice" (p. 168). Thus, the "episteme" of the sixteenth century centered on language as symbolic and assumed a meaningful relationship between signs and what they signified based on natural resemblance. In the seventeenth and eighteenth centuries, however, the relationship between signifiers and signified became simply one of direct and transparent representation. This move should be obvious in Descartes and, far more than his methodology, marks his work as Modern in a way that Bacon's is not. In this argument, Foucault makes relatively frequent reference to the linguistic work of the British Empiricists, and even summarizes the transition between epistemes by saying that "The knowledge that divined, *at random,* signs that were absolute and older than itself has been replaced by a network of signs built up step by step in accordance with a knowledge of what is probable. Hume has become possible" (p. 60). That is, for Foucault the history of the Modern era can be traced in the disintegration of language understood as pure representation, and the pivotal figures marking the transition at the end of the epoch will be the Marquis de Sade, who gives us the bare representational word in all its power, and

Kant, who, in a certain sense, does much the same.[12] In the new episteme, "The very being of that which is represented is now going to fall outside representation itself" (p. 240), so that two of the key figures of the nineteenth century will be Marx and Freud, and the key question will be the place of the subject—"Who speaks?"

The above account, in which Marx and Freud occupy somewhat parallel places, suggests to a certain extent why Foucault, as with Lacan and post-structuralism in general, is regarded as "apolitical," and therefore patriarchal and conservative, in many feminist circles. Unlike Lacan, however, Foucault's work as it develops deals more and more with the political, and most often with where the "personal" and the political overlap, which might explain the relatively lively interest his work sparks in some Anglo-American feminists. Foucault is concerned with power and the historical structures through which it is created and transmitted in our culture. Thus, he is "apolitical" in the sense that he is not automatically in favor of some kinds of power and against others. Rather, he is concerned with a decentralization of power that is opposed as much to the power of the left as of the right. Still, since his historical deconstructions of central aspects of our modernity (the medical establishment, mental "health," prisons, the human sciences, sexuality) expose how arbitrary they are and the extent to which they are structured so as to increase the power of centralized institutions across the whole political spectrum, his work is radically political, and politically radical. Nancy Fraser's work, referred to in Chapter Three, is just one example of the potential value of his analysis for feminist thought, and it could also easily be applied to the problem of liberal feminism as an attempt to simply increase the power of women, without regard to what effect that would have on the economy of power as such in our society. (Is what we want, or need, just *more* female CEOs?)

Most Anglo-American feminist discussions of Foucault's work, however, focus less on his general analysis of power than on his work on sexuality, especially Volume I of *The History of Sexuality*.[13] The "shock value" of that title when it first appeared suggests at least some of the power of the bourgeois "naturalization" of sexuality, which had always seemed, even to some degree within feminist discourse, as an ahistorical given within the confines of which feminist thought had to work, rather than an historically (and culturally) contingent construct that could be rethought from its very foundation. Thus feminists, such as Judith Butler, who are deeply concerned with the structures and interrelationships of sex and gender in our culture find a basis in Foucault's analysis to evaluate the relative "biologism" of earlier feminists, most notably in Butler's case Simone de Beauvoir. Furthermore, as noted above, the possibility of thinking our sexuality differently is a constant subtext in post-structuralist thought and, combined with the contingent and very limited history of "man" that Foucault outlines, it can open up several new ways to approach the development of what would become women's philosophy.

The first volume of *The History of Sexuality* traces the construction of sexuality in the Modern period which, Foucault claims, has not been a matter of *repression* that might be combatted by sexual "liberation," but rather of *confession,* a moving of sexuality into the forefront of cultural discourse that reconsolidates the power of the State and is only increased by calls for more "liberation." The new possible constructions of the Self that come into existence during this period include the homosexual man (as distinguished from homosexual acts) and the hysterical woman. With regard to the latter, Foucault notes that the increase of power centered on sexuality was not applied in the first case to the lower classes, but rather to the women of the dominant class itself: "The primary concern was not repression of the sex of the classes to be exploited but rather the body, vigor, longevity, progeniture, and descent of the classes that 'ruled' " (p. 123). Thus, on this analysis, there is a distinction between political or economic liberation and sexual liberation in the case of men, while a feminist reading of the same history might find important reasons why its own women became the first victims of the new bourgeois power over sexuality.[14] Moreover, Foucault describes the relationship between the construction of sexuality and the creation of "man" as the center of philosophical discourse in the same era as one of parallel developments in the service of power—"An immense labor to which the West has submitted generations in order to produce . . . men's subjection: their constitution as subjects in both senses of the word" (p. 60). At the same time, it often seems that Foucault's text continues the traditon of constituting *women* as subjects in only one sense of the word.

This can perhaps be seen more clearly in the second volume of his *History, The Uses of Pleasure.*[15] The index for this book contains more than the single listing of "women's bodies, hysterization of" found in Volume One, but all of the listings under "women"—and "wives"— are concerned solely with women's place in the male sexual economy. Of course, Foucault is not necessarily responsible for the index to the English translation of his book. More importantly, the lack of concern with women or their pleasure in many ways reflects the reality of the

Greek world he is describing. Still, it seems strange to read such a skillful post-modern test that is so unself-conscious about the gender subtext of the discourse it analyzes. The very lack of comment by Foucault on gender issues makes the conclusion women might derive from his reading all the more obvious: the rules that govern the behavior of young men in the Greek homosexual romance are not simply similar, but *identical,* to the rules for women's sexual behavior in the modern world. The construction of women's sexuality, whatever changes it may have undergone over the centuries, has always been deeply determined by a sexual economy that will allow no sexual difference more significant than that between a young man and an older one.[16] As Lacan already told us, women do not exist, but not only because they are defined as the impossible objects of (male) infantile desire—they are also the horrific objects of (male) infantile castration fears and, as such, cannot be allowed to enter as living beings into the sexual consciousness of Western man/men, much less into their political world or their philosophy. In many ways Foucault's work both illuminates and repeats this ancient eroticism of the Same, which would always substitute a young male body for the reality of women's desire and women's pleasure.

Derrida, Women, and Politics

I have already discussed Derrida's deconstructive methods in the Introduction, and hope to have just illustrated them in my readings of Lacan and Foucault, but here I would like to discuss at more length the philosophical suspicions that underlie those methods, and how they can be articulated with a feminist "deconstruction" of our culture's discourse on gender. Derrida places the de-centering of the structure and of the subject that defines post-structuralism explicitly in the context of Heidegger's critique of our modernity to focus on the lack of foundations in all modern philosophical thought. From the current perspective, the argument can be summarized by saying that rationalism cannot provide foundations for philosophy and science without innate ideas, which Locke proved to be untenable, and that Berkeley and Hume's radicalization of Locke similarly prove the untenability of the Empiricist alternative. Since philosophy lacks a foundation on which to build an epistemology, all the specific sciences, except insofar as they concern themselves with discourse, are without philosophical basis (no matter how useful they may be in fact). The structures of our modernity, therefore, are linguistic houses of cards, ordered piles of discourse without any necessary or orderly connection to the supposed material would they claim to represent. Metaphysics, in the Heideggerian sense of an attempt to provide an account for the Being of beings independently of the Being of Dasein, can go no further. Still, the full effect of the end of metaphysics, of the lack of foundation for our "world picture," is only now slowly being absorbed into our culture in the phenomenon known as "post-modernism."

It is especially important for feminists in the Anglo-American tradition to see the deeply significant distinction between Derrida's account of the end of metaphysics and the positivist rejection of metaphysics as "meaningless" because it lacks empirical referents. One of the points I have tried to make in my discussions of Locke and Hume is the metaphysical commitments that underlie, and make possible, such a dismissal of "metaphysics." Empiricism is not an epistemology without any metaphysics, but rather a metaphysical system based on specific, and debatable, epistemological premises. We do not know that Idealism is wrong because we know that all meaningful statements must be translatable into sense data statements, but rather we believe that language can be traced to pre-linguistic sensory givens because we have accepted an atomistic and materialistic metaphysics and reject the Idealist alternative. I have also tried to demonstrate how this particular form of the rejection of metaphysics obscures the gender (and race and class and cultural) bias built into its tacit metaphysical commitments. The doctrine of the end of metaphysics in Derrida, on the other hand, opens up the structure of philosophy, rather than hiding it, to make clear the interests and powers that have shaped it in the Modern period and how it functions as a structural whole to perpetuate those forces. Earlier I referred to the major figures in semiotics, structuralism, and post-structuralism as members of traditionally excluded groups. Since that is not true of many of those who "do" deconstruction in the Anglo-American context, it is important to note again that these are at base minority discourses, and as such provide by their very existence a critical stand on all metaphysical traditions that is very different from all but the most radical thought in the Empiricist tradition.

One way to look at Derrida's radicalism would be to focus on the "debate" between Derrida and Heidegger. This debate can be summarized (and oversimplified) by saying that Heidegger believes that there is an alternative to metaphysics, although it is only a remote possibility (*"Nur noch ein Gott kann uns retten"*—"Only a god can save us"), and that the clue to this alternative can be found, as has been noted, in the language and culture of ancient Greece, which Derrida, and most feminists, find a dubious model for a non-patriarchal, non-hierarchical discourse. As in Foucault, Derrida believes that we cannot evade post-modernism and that there is no transhistorical standard by which we can even decide whether it is a good thing or not. Therefore, he often sees Heidegger's work, his "nostalgia," as a modification, rather than a denial, of traditional (male, Christian, European) metaphysics.

This argument provides some of the clearest examples of Derrida's use of "feminism." Two recent papers on Heidegger called *"Geschlect"* (which means race, people, sex/gender, species, and generally denotes the difference between "our" kind and "others") take issue with the supposed gender neutrality of Dasein.[17] The dangers of this neutrality and the near absence of women in *Being and Time* have already been noted, but Derrida draws on the Marburg lectures of 1928 to trace a link between the denial of gender specificity and a more general denial of duality, of any hint of *Geschlecht,* in the concept of Dasein. He says at one point that Heidegger "has silenced sex," denying it any ontological significance, so that the difference between men and women would be "only" ethical or anthropological.[18] At the same time, Derrida points out that Heidegger stresses the fact that the apparent negativity of Dasein's gender neutrality is in fact a positive source of power and richness, while sexual duality is negative. A familiar pattern should be emerging here: if Dasein is neutral and its neutrality is a positive source of power, then perhaps Dasein is in fact being conceived of as male for Heidegger, since power is masculine in our culture. As with the Freudian libido, if Dasein is covertly male, then much of its "power" would come from the implicit exclusion of the female threat to male power. With the appearance of sexual difference, on the other hand, comes negativity, absence, and, Derrida claims, even "a certain 'impotence'" (p. 72).

Derrida argues that this problem seems to haunt Heidegger more than his dismissal of it might indicate, suggesting that he is not so sure, after all, that Dasein is not always already sexed, that is, that he might himself suspect that the "neutrality" of Dasein in fact means that it is defined as male. Therefore, the independence of Heidegger's thought from "the most traditional philosophemes" (p. 79), on this issue at least, seems not nearly so clear as Heidegger would perhaps wish it to be, and *"Geschlecht II"* traces a less overtly feminist path to much the same point.[19] There the distinction between the human and animal or the "monstrous" is determined by the human hand (with its etymological relationship to technology). Derrida notes that it is always a question of *the* hand in Heidegger, so that "man" is also a one-handed "monster," another denial of duality, sexuality, and desire, since a caress or love-making requires two hands (p. 182)—unless, of course, one thinks (as Derrida suggested when I heard him read this paper) of masturbation as desire for the Same, and/or of women as the "monstrous." This often torturous argument concludes that "as every [hierarchial] opposition does," the distinction between the human and the animal (or, by implication, between "races" or between men and women) "effaces the differences and leads back, following the most resistant metaphysico-dialectic tradition, to the homogeneous," that is, to more of the Same (p. 174). At the same time, however, Derrida repeatedly notes the extent to which his own thought is not simply critical of Heidegger, but rather relies on his work as the basis of Derrida's own criticism: "His text could not be homogeneous and is written with two hands, at least" (p. 189).

This apparently self-defeating, or at least self-deconstructing, assertion marks one source of the many criticisms of Derrida's work. He is often accused not only of contradicting himself, but even worse, of not taking himself seriously, or of taking himself too seriously and his audience not seriously enough. More substantially, Derrida is often condemned for doing only critical readings. On his account, however, that is all that we can do, since the full form of post-modern existence is hidden from us by our continuing attachment to the metaphysical illusion. There is as yet no basis for what philosophy would be beyond metaphysics, and the only paradigm he takes seriously, Heidegger's, is clearly dangerous. Another criticism of Derrida is that his deconstructions have become repetitive, resembling a Freudian hysteric in constantly reworking the same "material." This repetition, however, has two bases. One is the redundancy of the "material" itself: the structures of patriarchy and power are much the same everywhere, in Husserl or Freud, apartheid or rape. The second is that deconstruction, on the model of psychoanalysis, is an infinite project, not a cure but a process in which one's own metaphysical "nostalgia," one's own "transference," is most to be feared.

In this context, however, the most significant criticisms of Derrida are clearly those leveled against him by feminist theorists. While two of these criticisms from outside the philosophical realm were discussed in the Introduction, a third significant difference between deconstruction and feminist thought remains to be considered. Naomi Scheman, in a paper entitled "The Body Politic/The Impolitic Body/Bodily Politics," and Daryl McGowan Tress, in "Modernism, Postmodernism, and Feminist Ethics," stress the contrast between the denial of an essential Self in deconstructive or post-modern philosophy and the apparent need within feminist thought for an appeal to some essential reality about women as the basis, in Scheman, for our ability to speak of a feminist "we" and/or as the basis, in Tress, for moral claims about our right to develop as "authentic" human selves.[20] The implicit argument in both cases is that, if we use deconstruction as a "tool" in feminist thought, we may be undermining our own ability to make many of the sociopolitical and moral claims that are central to modern feminism. In terms of practice, this argument has considerable merit, but it also seems to rely in part on a "modernism" that Scheman and Tress would agree is no longer tenable. In a paper entitled "How Can Ethics be Feminist?" Alison Jaggar seems to undercut this argument by denying that feminism requires essentialism, at least as it is usually defined.[21] Instead, she suggests that a uniquely feminist ethics must be based on a (moral) epistemology that avoids both "naïve" realism and subjectivism. Such a questioning of essence and realism, of the feminist "we" and of the goals of feminist (moral) thought, might prove, in the long run, to be a link between feminism and deconstruction, rather than an objection that one might raise against the other.

Indeed, in one of his few explicit comments on feminism, an interview with Christie McDonald called "Choreographies," Derrida deals precisely with this issue.[22] He argues, as do some of the "French feminists," that any feminist essentialism would simply reverse the values of the traditional male dualisms, and so remain strictly metaphysical:

> The specular reversal of masculine "subjectivity," even in its most self-critical form—that is, where it is nervously jealous both of itself and of its "proper" objects—probably represents only one necessary phase. Yet it still belongs to the same program, a program whose exhaustion we were just talking about. (p. 67)

On the other hand, since the structure of patriarchy is, if not monolithic, at least highly uniform for the Western world in the Modern period, it can and must be attacked in ways that directly address the evils it creates. The material conditions of women's lives require that they deal with their oppression, not by withdrawing from (male) metaphysics, but by confronting it head-on, often in its own terms.

> [T]he *real* conditions in which women's struggles develop on all fronts (economic, ideological, political) . . . often require the preservation (within longer or shorter phases) or metaphysical presuppositions that one must (and knows already that one must) question in a later phase—or an other place—because they belong to the dominant system that one is deconstructing on a *practical level*. (p. 70)

A call for consistency of the sort that Scheman, Tress, and others who share their reservations would like to have may simply be a sign of our own entrapment in a (male) metaphysics designed to immobilize us.

If almost everything I have said about Derrida here and elsewhere sounds familiar, it is doubtlessly due at least in part to the strong influence his work has had on my own understanding, not only of the dilemmas of our modernity, but also of the authors I have been discussing. At the same time, I allow Derrida to have this central role in my understanding of the world precisely *because* he provides so compatible an intellectual framework for my own feminist thinking. That the demand for consistency is one of many tools that men's philosophy uses to exclude or discount women's thought is not something I had to learn from Derrida, nor did I need Heidegger to show me the evils of "man" making "him-self" the center of the universe. What I did need was a theoretical framework that would not only explain how the (male) subject of modern discourse was coming undone, but also how the disintegration of that subject *at the same time* threw into questions such seemingly settled issues as how many sexes, much less how many persons, were present in a couple.[23] Men's philosophy wants, more or less literally, some-*thing* to hold on to, and abhors or excludes whatever represents absence in the male experience of the world. What deconstruction proves to me is that this obsession with foundations and possession and certainty and control (which predates by far the Modern world but takes a unique form since the sixteenth century and a very specific form in British Empiricism) is not merely harmful to women—it is also a demonstrable philosophical error. This, in turn, allows me to see more easily how I can be both a philosopher and a woman.

Notes

1. See Derrida's "Restitutions," in *The Truth in Painting*, trans. Geoff Bennington and Ian McLoed (Chicago: University of Chicago Press, 1987).

This is one of the most interesting of Derrida's deconstructions for feminist purposes, although it requires some background in Heidegger. For a preliminary account of the role that gender plays in the Derrida/Heidegger "debate," see my "Heidegger and Derrida Redux: A Close Reading," in *Hermeneutics and Deconstruction,* ed. Hugh J. Silverman and Don Ihde (Albany: State University of New York Press, 1985) and the discussion of Derrida below.

2. Claude Lévi-Strauss, *Structural Anthropology,* trans. Claire Jacobson and Brooke Grundfest Schoepf (New York: Basic Books, 1963).

3. Roland Barthes, *Mythologies,* trans. Annette Lavers (New York: Hill and Wang, 1972), p. 129.

4. See John Stuart Mill, *Utilitarianism,* George Sher, ed. (Indianapolis: Hackett, 1979).

5. This example, and the reminder about this aspect of Barthe's work, is due to my colleague in the English department at Hamline University, Karyn Sproles.

6. Roland Barthes, *S/Z,* trans. Richard Miller (New York: Hill and Wang, 1974).

7. Barthes draws a much more complete parallel between the desire for fullness and castration anxiety in the fascinating *Sade/Fourier/Loyola,* trans. Richard Miller (New York: Hill and Wang, 1976).

8. Jacques Lacan, *Feminine Sexuality,* ed. Juliet Mitchell and Jacqueline Rose, trans. Jacqueline Rose (New York: Norton, 1982).

9. Jacques Lacan, *The Language of the Self,* trans. Anthony Wilden (New York: Delta Books, 1968).

10. Michel Foucault, *The Order of Things,* translation unattributed (New York: Vintage Books, 1973).

11. See "The Age of the World Picture," in Heidegger's *The Question Concerning Technology.* John Berger, in chapter three of his *Ways of Seeing* (New York: Viking Penguin, 1977), illustrates very clearly the specific form this "world view" takes when the object being contemplated is a woman.

12. Luce Irigaray makes a similar point in *Speculum of the Other Woman,* trans. Gillian C. Gill (Ithaca, N.Y.: Cornell University Press, 1985), p. 212.

13. Michel Foucault, *The History of Sexuality, Volume I: Introduction,* trans. Robert Hurley (New York: Pantheon Books, 1978).

14. For an interesting view about some of the possible results of this particular deployment of sexuality, see Marilyn Frye's *The Politics of Reality,* especially the paper "In and Out of Harm's Way." At the very least, this class differential in the construction of women's sexuality has served in the long run to make significant divisions between women of different classes and races a permanent part of feminist discourse on sexuality and reproduction.

15. Michel Foucault, *The Use of Pleasure: The History of Sexuality, Volume II,* trans. Robert Hurley (New York: Pantheon Books, 1985).

16. This insight has, of course, been part of feminist discourse at least since Germaine Greer's *The Female Eunuch* (New York: McGraw-Hill, 1971), which

considers some of the same classical texts, but Foucault situates it in a more complex theoretical matrix.

17. For another version of this "debate," see my "Heidegger and Derrida Redux."

18. Jacques Derrida, "Geschlecht: sexual difference, ontological difference," trans. John Sallis, *Research in Phenomenology* 13 (1983): 67.

19. Jacques Derrida, "Geschlecht II: Heidegger's Hand," trans. John P. Leavey, Jr., in *Deconstruction and Philosophy,* ed. John Sallis (Chicago: University of Chicago Press, 1987). Needless to say, issues of race, anti-Semitism, and Heidegger's association with the National Socialist party lie very close to the surface in both "Geschlecht" papers, but a full account of that aspect of the "debate" is far beyond the scope of the present work.

20. Tress's paper was presented at a conference on "Explorations in Feminist Ethics: Theory and Practice," sponsored by the University of Minnesota at Duluth and held October 7 and 8, 1988.

21. Jaggar's paper was also presented at the conference on "Explorations in Feminist Ethics: Theory and Practice," held in Duluth October 7 and 8, 1988.

22. Jacques Derrida, "Choreographies," interview with Christie V. McDonald, *Diacritics* 12 (Summer 1982): 20–31.

23. See "Choreographies," p. 76, but also "Restitutions."

Chapter 6

Feminine Writing/The Writing of Women

The "French Feminists" in Context

The importance of post-structuralism/deconstruction for feminist thought is not, however, merely a personal judgment of my own. The so-called French feminists are largely women who have moved on from work with Lévi-Strauss, Barthes, Lacan, Derrida, and others, to apply many of the same ideas and "methods" to the problem of women's writing, what some of them call *"l'écriture feminine."* Their work, therefore, provides an additional bridge between the phenomenological tradition in which they were trained and a set of interests and preoccupations that are very similar to, where they are not identical with, those of many Anglo-American feminists. At the same time, of course, there are significant differences in the way the French and Americans see themselves as women, as scholars, and as feminists. As I have noted, many or even most of the "French feminists" would even reject the title "feminist," as the term has a narrower meaning in the French context, referring most often to a bourgeois or "liberal" feminism that is seen as primarily interested in achieving a larger share of male power as traditionally defined. This approach to women's problems, moreover, seems to be considered by the French to be the predominant source of feminist activity in the United States. On the other hand, French feminism has been called an "anti-feminism" by some feminists in the Anglo-American tradition, presumably because of its resemblance to a feminine "essentialism" that most Americans would reject.[1]

To illustrate briefly this combination of similarity and difference in the meeting of French and American feminisms, a recent article by Luce Irigaray that has appeared twice in American journals should provide a few basic points of comparison.[2] Beyond the initial incomprehensibility of the style and vocabulary of "Is the Subject of Science Sexed?" Irigaray's very idea of what counts as a science and of what a science is seems deeply alien to our own thought about such issues. Having ruled out the "human [i.e., social] sciences" at the beginning of the paper, Irigaray proceeds to talk about the "science" of psychoanalysis (her quotation marks, however), and the sciences of economics and linguistics, as well as biology, mathematics, logic (!) and physics. Moreover, her focus in this discussion is not on the content or ideology of science, but on the language of science, on how scientists can speak to one another when the subject of science, that is, the subjective in science, does not exist. It is just here, however, that one can see connections between Irigaray's point and the discussion of subjectivity and objectivity in Keller's book or in other feminist philosophy of science. And many of the questions she asks are familiar questions: What desire lurks at the heart of scientific investigation? Are male and female brains organized differently? What does it mean to ask such a question? What is the significance of the answer? How are we to make sense of the phenomenon of the female scientist? And so on.

On the other hand, even the title, "Is the Subject of Science Sexed?" introduces a deconstructive ambiguity into Irigaray's discussion. Anglo-American feminists may question whether *science* is gendered as male or whether the *scientist* is defined as male, but to ask both questions at once, as well as the question of whether there is any place *outside* of science in our society from which we can question science at all, puts both the questions and any possible answers to them in a very different light. In her blending of these questions, however, Irigaray draws upon two threads in contemporary philosophy that make her arguments at least somewhat less mysterious. First, she more or less explicitly refers to the Heideggerian critique of technology discussed previously. Thus she emphasizes the fact that science is constituted as a placing of the world as an object in front of us onto which we project our models of the world as something radically different from ourselves that we have the right, if not the duty, to exploit to our own ends. (This is a near paraphrase and yet should strongly evoke the work of Harding, Keller, and the "eco-feminists.") Secondly, Irigaray relies on logic and linguistics (i.e., the philosophy of language) to make part of her point. The very process of symbolization, she argues, de-subjectivizes science and forces the data into the (male) mold of the signs used, which means, (a) that in science there is no "difference . . . reciprocity . . . exchange . . . permeability . . . or fluidity," since signs for these "feminine" values do not exist in the scientific lexicon, and (b) that scientific language is dominated by identity, intolerance for ambiguity, and hierarchical dualisms (p. 74). That the article ends with a discussion of Freudian orthodoxy only underscores the combination of the alien and the familiar here.

In addition to this play of sameness and difference, another difficulty for Anglo-American feminists in reading the French feminists is the combination of theory and avant garde literary creation that has become the hallmark of *"l'écriture feminine"* in writers such as Monique Wittig and Hélène Cixous. Needless to say, translation does not make this already complex writing any more accessible to the uninitiated reader. Moreover, the splits and factions among the French feminists often seem deeper and more serious than our own, and also tend to follow the complicated lines of schism between the male theorists with whom they have been allied (very roughly, Derrida for Cixous, Lacan for Irigaray, more diverse influences in the case of Kristeva). Again, it seems that in their differences from us, such as their more linguistic, but also more orthodox, interpretations of Marx and Freud, and looser attachment to strict logic and "argument," the French feminists are more like each other, and in their similarities to us, for example, differences of opinion influenced at least in part by sexual preference and institutional affiliation (i.e., academic philosophy vs. psychoanalytic practice), they are more different from each other. Without tracing in any detail either the history or the ideology of any of these schisms, what I hope to do in this chapter is to clarify the work of the four French feminists who seem most central to the American understanding of their common enterprise, and to place it in the context of both American feminism and the Continental philosophical tradition from which it arose.

The next section, therefore, will briefly discuss the highly literary work of Monique Wittig, whose theoretical starting point will be taken to be the quotation from Simone de Beauvoir's *The Second Sex* that "One is not born, but rather becomes, a woman" (p. 249). Then I will turn to the more traditionally academic work of Julia Kristeva, whose interests and expertise range from linguistics to psychoanalysis to the role of Mary in the doctrine of the Catholic Church. The following section will return to a more literary figure, Hélène Cixous, although it will, as in the discussion of Wittig, focus primarily on her theoretical writing and its relationship to her literary practice. Finally, I will return at greater length to the major work of Luce Irigaray and attempt to trace more carefully its specific roots in Lacanian psychoanalysis and Derridian deconstruction. At that point, it should be possible for the reader to see more clearly how others, in this case women who are more familiar with the European theorists I have been discussing so far, if less so with Anglo-American feminist concerns, might illustrate, as well as agree or disagree with, my belief in the usefulness of Continental philosophy, especially post-structuralism and deconstruction, as a tool for feminist thought.

Wittig and the Female Body

Above I referred to the Marxism in French feminist thought, but it is important to understand that the post-structuralist Marx has been re-interpreted on a linguistic level, as has been done with the post-structuralist Freud. When Monique Wittig, therefore, refers to "Materialism" in "One is Not Born a Woman," she is referring not to the theoretical complement of "Idealism" per se but rather both to the actual material reality of women's bodies and women's lives, and to the chain of signifiers that both "Materialism" and "Idealism" cannot help but introduce into any contemporary discourse. This Materialism, then, if taken rigorously enough, indicates that the very existence of Lesbians, that is, women who do not define themselves in terms of their relationship to men, proves that the class of women is not a natural class but a political one created historically for the oppression of its members. The supposed bodily basis of this classification, the "deformed" bodies (and minds) of women oppressed as a class, are the result, not the cause, of their oppression. That is, the existence of women, Lesbians, who deny the hierarchical opposition between men and women and whose very existence negates its eternal, universal, immutable applicability, proves that this opposition, and by extension all of its many analogs, is a socially constructed instrument of men's oppression of women. The Lesbian is not a woman, in the sense this hierarchy requires, but neither can she be a man (although many male thinkers, especially in the psychoanalytic tradition, try to make her one), which clearly shows that the duality itself fails to adequately capture the reality of human life in all its complex diversity.

In this early paper, however, Wittig is concerned less with the biologism of male thinkers than with the resurgent biologism she saw in feminist thought itself. Thus, she clearly places herself outside of the sphere of feminist "essentialism" where others have attempted to place some of the French feminists. In line with a redefined Marxism, she denies that women have any fixed biology, but rather asserts the primacy of social structure and the mutability of the human mind and body. Although many of the writers to whom her work seems opposed are themselves Lesbians, she argues that claims of a superior female biology, because they so often refer back to women's role as mothers, are "heterosexist," that is, assume a natural and primary heterosexuality in both women and men. This argument provides a "material" reason for refusing merely to reverse the traditional valuation of the male/female duality, in addition to the theoretical basis for such a refusal. "Matriarchies are no less heterosexual than patriarchies: it's only the sex of the oppressor that changes" (p. 149). What happens in feminist biologism is that it continues the bourgeois naturalization of our current sex/gender categories and in many ways reinforces it, so that its very Lesbian orientation (when it has one) obscures the most radical implications of Lesbian existence. She compares the current status of the hierarchical opposition between men and women to the similar one between the "black" and "white" races, which she quotes French sociologist Colette Guillaumin as attributing not to any classification that preceded the advent of African slavery, but rather as a result of that historical event and of the need to find an ideological justification for it. Similarly, "men" and "women" are not immediate, natural categories, but rather oppressive socio-historical creations.

Wittig also points out that when other oppressed classes finally rise up in revolt, it is not for the perpetuation of themselves as a class, that is, it is not an assertion of their class identity, but a battle to cease to be a class, to be regarded simply as persons. (The balance of this argument might weigh somewhat differently in an American context of "Black Pride," but the ultimate outcome seems to be largely the same.) Why then, she asks, would women want to assert their class status as women, appeal to their own biological uniqueness, in an effort to end their oppression? Borrowing more than a title from de Beauvoir, she chooses to emphasize individual existential commitment over biological "necessity," but without falling into de Beauvoir's tendency to identify this ability to transcend with an overly Individualistic and masculine sense of self. For Wittig, the goal of feminism is the destruction of the class "man," which by eliminating the slaveholders will also destroy the slave class "woman." For very different reasons than Lacan's, Wittig is also led to conclude that "woman" does not exist, but is rather a universalizing classification created by the oppressors to naturalize and hence more effectively manipulate this supposedly natural category. The nonexistence of "woman" is not, on this account, simply the logical result of men's linguistic hegemony, not simply a linguistic or a psychological fact, although it is certainly also that, but is instead part of a socially and purposefully determined structure of domination.

Thus the text of *The Lesbian Body* is riddled by the rupture of the J/e (I) in French, by the division of the Lesbian self who seeks to insert herself in a language that is not naturally, but in fact, the language of men alone.[3] Unlike male homosexuals, she says in the "Note" to the English translation of this very rich and unsettling text, Lesbianism has no language, no literature, no past. "The lesbians for their part, are silent—just as all women are as women at all levels" (p. 9). Thus the male distinctions between the fictional, symbolic, and actual, with all the divisions, exclusions, and value judgments they imply, fail to capture the reality of women's writing. (This translation was done before the current wave of interest in post-structuralist thought, so it is difficult to determine whether the reference here to "fictional, symbolic, and actual" is intended to refer to the Lacanian concepts of the Imaginary, the Symbolic, and the Real, which do function, both in Lacan and in our culture, as Wittig describes.) For this reason, Wittig's "fictions" cannot be delineated from the "actuality" that a more theoretical approach to the same questions might try, perhaps in vain, to reflect. At the same time, the violence done to the language by the eruption of the J/e and similar attacks upon traditional discourse in Wittig's avant garde "fictional" texts only reflect the violence inflicted on the Lesbian J/e who would dare to insert herself as such into a language that was designed to exclude her.

What I find unsettling about Wittig's "fictions," however, is the ("symbolic"?) violence of women toward women. If at least one American feminist would reject Derrida, if not deconstruction, as a model for feminist discourse because he uses the French "hyman" as "a feminine metaphor, written across the fragmented female body," one wonders what to make of a Lesbian/feminist writing that details and seems to glorify wounds, dismemberment, kidnapping, and (Lesbian) seduction that borders on rape.[4] Again, this merely reflects the violence that women's experience must undergo in order to enter into language, but it is at the same time difficult to take Wittig's picture of an Amazon "utopia" as an entirely positive image of feminist/Lesbian life. In "One is Not Born a Woman," Wittig notes a feminist tendency to "call our passivity 'non-violence' " (p. 150), but to an American who remains (perhaps too) attached to this illusion, the image of interpersonal violence might merit more subtlety than is found in parts of *The Lesbian Body:*

> But you know that not one will be able to bear seeing you with eyes turned up lids cut off your yellow smoking intestines spread in the hollow of your hand your tongue spat from your mouth, . . . not one will be able to bear your low frenetic insistent laughter. (p. 15)

The standards for the theoretical uses of (consensual?) sadistic acts against women might arguably be different for male and female writers, but the opportunities that Wittig provides for a voyeuristic male pornographization of her work might in the long run prove more of a threat to feminism than, for example, Ruddick's perhaps too biological/heterosexist concept of "Maternal Thinking." Wittig's clear defense, of course, is that she is avowedly "careless of male approval" (p. 9).

Kristeva and the Freudian Mother

If Wittig is, perhaps, too careless of male opinion, many feminists on both sides of the Atlantic seem to believe that Julia Kristeva is too careful of it, too "male-identified." A close look at her text that is most available in English, "Women's Time," serves to illustrate both this aspect of her work and how her work follows the pattern of the alien and the familiar that seems to be true of French feminism in general.[5] Thus, she borrows the distinction between "linear history" and "monumental time" from Nietzsche (p. 189) as a basis for drawing a strong distinction between the time recognized and valued by our culture and "women's time" in a way that can easily seem "essentialist" to an American reader. She then attributes to a first generation of feminists a continued attachment to the former and to a second generation (post-1968) a new awareness of the symbolic richness of the latter in a way that seems to echo Alison Jaggar's distinction between "liberal" and "radical" feminism. She finally calls for a third form of thought that would transcend all such hierarchical dualisms, "an attitude of retreat from sexism (male as well as female)," but then goes on to ask "What discourse, if not that of a religion, would be able to support this adventure?" (p. 210). While many American feminists might also phrase this question in religious terms, many would not, and in any case, the issue would most likely be seen in terms that are quite different from Kristeva's, as we shall see.

Other ideas of Kristeva's, while not necessarily central to Anglo-American feminism, bear strong analogies to points already made in the present argument. From the relatively banal observation that a major distinction between European and American feminism lies in the central role played by both Feudian psychoanalysis and Marxism (she uses the term "socialism") in Continental thought of all kinds, to her complex analysis of the process whereby gender "neutrality" becomes an erasure of the specificity of women's experience, her (far more profound) background in semiotics, structuralism, and post-structuralist thought leads to many of the same conclusions that I have attempted to defend here. Interestingly, it also leads her to reject many of the ideas associated with other French feminists, such as the special status given to *"l'écriture feminine"* as a counter-hegemonic discourse. (In "Women's Time," Kristeva classifies the effect of such writing with marginal discourse per se, with no gender-specific virtues—elsewhere in *The Kristeva Reader* she calls it "hysterical" [p. 228].) This means that she seems to disagree with Wittig on almost every point, rejecting a Lesbian utopia based on violence and the "scapegoating" of men as a mere reversal of the traditional sexist hierarchies with no revolutionary value. At the same time, and somewhat paradoxically, I think, she attributes a feminist tendency toward terrorism to the "myth of the archaic mother" (p. 205) while taking a renewed concern with maternity as a paradigm of creativity in the third generation feminism she would advocate. At the very least, it is hard to understand how a new vision can be modeled on the experience of pregnancy and motherhood without excluding men (if not necessarily scapegoating them), not to mention women who, through choice or necessity, remain childless.[6]

It remains to me now, however, to trace out each of these themes in more detail in Kristeva's work as a whole. Her critical, yet close, relationship with several of the male theorists whose work I have already discussed is clear. The most obvious and predominant influence in her early work is that of her teacher, Roland Barthes, from whom she develops a very complex linguistic concept of semiotics (not to be confused with her later psychoanalytic concept of the semiotic, which refers to pre-Oedipal experience). She considers the major discovery of this "science" to be "the fact that there is a general social law, that this law is the symbolic dimension which is given in language and that every social practice offers a specific expression of that law" (p. 25). (This insight can also be seen in the work of Foucault, in a somewhat different form.) Later, the influence of thinkers associated with Derrida comes more to the forefront of her thought, as in her rejection of the traditional priority given to the spoken word in linguistic theory, although she retains a critical stance to deconstruction and a special attachment to the materiality of the female body in the face of the idealizing tendencies of Derrida's opposition to the bodily voice. Finally, her psychoanalytic writings seem in constant critical dialogue with Lacan, applauding his shift from the literal to the linguistic in readings of Freud and agreeing that women per se are excluded from language, while attacking, for instance, "his scandalous sentence 'There is no such thing as Woman' " (p. 205). However, some of her psychoanalytic claims may still seem too Freudian in the Anglo-American context, especially her apparent attachment to the vaginal orgasm and its implications in her analysis of Lesbianism.

Given our exclusion from the linguistic, Kristeva sees feminist thought as having two options: we may either speak, use language and hence come under the control of the law of the Father, or we may be true to our experience as women and achieve only silence or hysterical incoherence, which in one guise she sees as mere rebellion (the basis of her opposition to *"l'écriture feminine"*) and in another guise as a quasi-mystical expression of our maternity. Kristeva would incorporate the last into her third generation feminism, neither a "liberal" feminism that would perpetuate the power status quo nor a "radical" feminism that would only replicate it in reverse:

> let us reject the development of a "homologous" woman, who is finally capable and virile; and let us rather act on the socio-politico-historical stage as her negative: that is, act first with all those who refuse and "swim against the tide"—all who rebel against the existing relations of production and reproduction. But let us not take the role of Revolutionary either, whether male or female: let us on the contrary refuse all roles to summon this "truth" situated outside time, a truth that is neither true nor false, that cannot be fitted into the order of speech and social symbolism, that is an echo of our *jouissance,* of our mad words, of our pregnancies. (p. 156)

The fine line Kristeva seems to want to draw here between "hysterical," "radical" (Lesbian?) feminism and "mystical," "maternal" (Christian?) feminism is perhaps one of the most disturbing aspects of her work for Anglo-American feminists. What can be gained, according to Kristeva, by denying transcendental truth in the name of "our pregnancies" and the *"jouissance"* she believes is specific to them?

In her analysis of Bellini in *Desire in Language,* Kristeva argues that maternity represents for women both their exclusion from the (male) linguistic realm and a return to/identity with the pre-Odepial mother.[7] "Male" logic has no place for the becoming-two that pregnancy represents, and that doubly: no place for becoming, at least since Parmenides and his Platonic followers gained the upper hand in Athens, and no place for two that cannot be resolved, phenomenologically or otherwise, into one.[8] Thus, pregnancy (and female orgasm or *jouissance*) puts women in a privileged position with regard to language, and hence to the male hegemony of power. For that reason, while she agrees with the Freudian account of the desire for pregnancy as a desire to have a child by one's own father, she also sees it as a relation to the mother in a way that is deeply subversive. For men, she suggests, the same experience can only be had in artistic expression, although the male desire for/attachment to the penis is always a desire to return to the mother, for which the penis (or the paint brush) would be only an instrument. However, this desire to return to the pre-Oedipal mother is accompanied (for men, at least) by a fear of her phallic power. The object of this fear is characterized in *The Kristeva Reader* as the "abject," the pre-objective "locus of needs, of attraction and repulsion, from which an object of forbidden desire arises" and which can also "be understood in the sense of the horrible and fascinating abomination which is connoted in all cultures by the feminine" (p. 317). It is ultimately this deeply ambivalent relationship to the mother, or more accurately for Kristeva, to the maternal body, that is the source of men's need to control and dominate women by excluding them from language and all that it represents.

When this Freudian vision of the abstract pre-Oedipal or Phallic Mother is combined with Kristeva's attachment to Christian doctrine, it becomes clearer why some feminists closer to the Anglo-American context have been led to accuse her of "Mariolatry."[9] Kristeva's Christian orientation, while not uncritical of the Church and its historical role in the oppression of women, is clear throughout much of her work. In a discussion of homosexuality and fascism, for instance, she says that "The feminist movements are equally capable of a similar perverse denial of biblical teaching. We must recognize this and be on our guard" (p. 145). However, within a page of this she acknowledges that the primary roles for women in the Church have been as virgin or whore, and (as noted in discussing Locke) that "Between these two extremes, the mother participates in the community of the Christian Word not by giving birth to her children, but merely by preparing them for baptism" (p. 146). At a minimum, Anglo-American (and secular) feminists might ask, as with Freud, how far Kristeva accepts the Christian doctrines she describes, and partially "deconstructs," in papers such as "Stabat Mater." How, for example, are we to take her claim that" the virginal maternal is a way (not among the less effective ones) of dealing with feminine paranoia" (p. 180)? For whom is it "effective" and who has defined this "paranoia," which includes "the repudiation of the other woman (which doubtless amounts basically to a repudiation of the woman's mother) by suggesting the image of A Unique Woman," a "longing for uniqueness" (and who would deny us our uniqueness?) that can be achieved only by "an exacerbated masochism" (p. 181). The parallel text in "Stabat Mater"—a quasi-mystical account of her own experience of motherhood—does little to ease any of these concerns.

Thus, while many of Kristeva's ideas, even when they are not familiar to us, may be attractive to feminists of all kinds, they are often mixed with more equivocal ideas that can be more confusing than helpful in evaluating their usefulness. For instance, she says that

> real female innovation (in whatever social field) will only come about when maternity, female creation and the link between them are better understood. But for that to happen we must stop making feminism into a new religion, undertaking or sect and begin the work of specific and detailed analysis which will take us beyond romantic melodrama and beyond complacency (p. 298).

This call for detailed analysis and the rejection of the (radical?) romantic and the (liberal?) complacent, as well as the concern with female creation, could easily be incorporated into several versions of Anglo-American feminism, but the pivotal role that maternity seems to play in this passage, even without any Christian subtext, could quickly lead to serious questions in many of those same contexts. To determine whether it would *necessarily* constitute either an insidious female essentialism or a divisive heterosexism would require a more authoritative and detailed analysis of Kristeva's work than is possible here, but the contrast with Wittig and with the mainstream of Anglo-American feminist thought could hardly be more clear. This ambiguity and this contrast seem to mark the paradox that Kristeva's work, and French feminism in general, presents for us.

Cixous's Middle Path

While Hélène Cixous would assert with Wittig, as against Kristeva, the necessity of a specifically women's writing, in so doing she seems to avoid some, if not all, of the essentialism that an American reader might find in many of the other French feminists. In her earlier work such as "The Laugh of the Medusa," Cixous even offers reasons for preferring *"l'écriture feminine"* over standard discourse, although in her most recent work she tends more to enact than to argue for a new self-definition of women through writing.[10] For her, women's writing is "a *new insurgent* writing which, when the moment of her liberation has come, will allow her to carry out the indispensable ruptures and transformations in her history," both at an individual level of reawakening to our own bodies and strength, and at a political level of grasping language away from men and transforming it to our own uses (p. 250). As in Kristeva, this argument is based on the Freudian/Lacanian premise that language as presently constituted is masculine, just as reason, that is, philosophy, is also always male. At the same time, for Cixous, *"l'écriture feminine"* is a matter of social definition, independent of bodily gender, allowing her to feature in her discourse homosexual male writers such as Jean Genet.[11] Similarly, her references to the maternal and motherhood are explicitly figurative: "The mother, too, is a metaphor. It is necessary and sufficient that the best of herself be given to woman by another woman for her to be able to love herself and return in love the body that was 'born' to her" (p. 252). What is privileged in both cases, it seems, is a relationship to discourse and to the other, not biology or any immutable, metaphysical essence.

For Cixous, *"l'écriture feminine"* is neither an end in itself nor a romantic fantasy, but a step on the way toward what would be bisexual writing—"a multiple and inexhaustible course with millions of encounters and transformations of the same into the other and into the in-between, from which woman takes her form (and man, in his turn, but that's his other history)" (p. 254). In "Castration or Decapitation?" she contrasts this with male writing based on a preoccupation with the penis and fear of castration.[12] The resulting need for control is, she argues, a fear of women's uncontrolled and diffuse sexual pleasure, (not their maternity) which cannot be accounted for in the economy of male exchange. Thus, Freud is wrong—it is woman's *lack* of castration, our full sexuality, rather than our castration, that men fear, leading them to "decapitate" and silence us by taking our minds, and language, from us by force. Cixous shares the post-structuralist concern with language as a primary locus for this basic dynamic of oppression, and also ties it to the traditional hierarchical dualisms currently under attack by both deconstruction and Anglo-American feminism. On this view, these oppositional structures are actually monolithic in that any true alterity is excluded and, on the Hegelian model, Otherness always returns to more of the Same. This means, Cixous argues in *The Newly Born Woman,* that the silencing or beheading of women is a murder, specifically a matricide: in the Hegelian family there is no mother but only the replication of the Father in the Son. Thus, "Philosophy is constructed on the premise of women's abasement" (p. 65) because it is only by domination and control of woman's "excessive" sexuality (the chaotic "matrix") that Orestian (male) reason can (re)create (the masculine) order and so come to know it(self).

In the same section of *The Newly Born Woman,* "Sorties," Cixous also refers to her own feminist odyssey, one that parallels in somewhat starker form the history of many feminists of her generation worldwide. Her first understanding of the Hegelian dynamics described above came not with regard to gender, she reports, but rather with regard to her status as a colonial Algerian and her experiences in the Algerian War. It was only later that she began to see herself as doubly playing the slave in the master/slave dialectic, subjected to erasure by the men she had taken to be her partners in the struggle as they were all subjected to the erasure of European colonialism. It is this experience, perhaps, that leads her to a more inclusive view of the feminist project than is evident in either Wittig or Kristeva. More inclusive of men, and not only of homosexual men, but of all men, whose "loss in phallocentrism is different from but as serious as women's" (p. 83). More inclusive, certainly, of a variety of life choices for women, rejecting both literal motherhood as a basic category of major importance *and* the demand that all women refuse in the present the real bodily *"jouissance"* of motherhood because of what it has meant in the past. For Cixous, as for Wittig, gender is always a mutable social definition, not an essential or biological fact, and her vision of a future reality is always one in which bisexuality plays a central role. The privilege that women currently have in this process, she argues, falls not from any innate advantage, but merely from the fact that, as things now stand, *"woman is bisexual,"* men merely monosexual (p. 85).

Thus, Cixous appears to some extent to avoid both the extremes that Wittig and Kristeva may be taken to represent in an Anglo-

American context, or at least it seems that way to someone already convinced by the Derridian discourse from which much of Cixous's own work is drawn. She sounds "reasonable" to us (or to me) without being co-opted by masculine discourse, and her autobiography, in parallel with her theory, may well be only a more extreme case of our (or my) own. She is also closer, on my reading, to our desire for a pluralistic feminism—in the "Exchange" with Catherine Clément in *The Newly Born Woman,* Cixous rejects masculine logic not because it is masculine, but because it is monolithic, whereas she believes "There will not be *one* feminine discourse" (p. 137). Perhaps more importantly, she is careful neither to re-create nor simply to reverse the hierarchical oppositions that so much of my own argument has regarded as central to male reason, and so serves as a model for a feminism that would genuinely be something new, something "third," beyond what now is considered to be metaphysics. "It is not a question of appropriating their instruments, their concepts, their places for oneself or of wishing oneself in their position of mastery" (p. 96). It is a question, one could say, of creating something, at last, that is truly Other.

In reading Cixous's more recent, more literary work, however, the lineage of *"l'écriture feminine"* that links it to Wittig is quite clear. It is non-linear, evocative, bodily, sensual, open to a pornographization at the hands of male voyeurs that is clearly far from Cixous's intent, open also to a literalization of its emphasis on the maternal that she has explicitly denied. It does not so much argue with male discourse as present it in its own "truth." Her play based on the "Dora" case, for example, demonstrates the perversity of Freud's version of the story simply by re-telling what in fact happened to his patient, from Dora's point of view.[13] In general, her claims in *The Newly Born Woman* about women's writing echo both her more traditional arguments and what is manifest in her own most recent work:

> At the present time, *defining* a feminine practice of writing is impossible with an impossibility that will continue; for this practice will never be able to be *theorized,* enclosed, coded, which does not mean it does not exist. But it will always exceed the discourse governing the phallocentric system....
>
> In a way, feminine writing never stops reverberating from the wrench that the acquisition of speech, speaking out loud, is for her . . . Really she makes what she thinks materialize carnally, she conveys meaning with her body. She *inscribes* what she is saying because she does not

deny unconscious drives the unmanageable part they play in speech. (p. 92)

"L'écriture feminine" as inscribed/inscription on a body that is bisexual, maternal, sensual, *jouissant,* becomes in Cixous, perhaps more clearly than elsewhere in the Continental tradition, a vision for a future world that many, if not all, feminists might share.

Irigaray and Language

As was noted earlier, the relative familiarity of Luce Irigaray's work for Anglo-American feminists undoubtedly arises in part from her interest in science and language, although in very different forms than what we would call the philosophy of science or of language. One of her basic concerns is with the extent to which science is structured as a male enterprise, centered on men's experience of the world and used (implicitly or explicitly) to foster male domination. Her purpose in *Speculum of the Other Woman,* she says in *Ce Sexe qui N'en Est Pas Un,* was to upset "this linearity of a project, this teleology of discourse, in which no place is possible for the 'feminine' except the traditional one of the repressed, the censured."[14] Her specific case, in both works, is the Freudian/Lacanian account of femininity, which she criticizes for ignoring, to cite only a partial list of the errors she notes, the plurality of female "sex organs" (vagina and clitoris, but also breasts, vulva, labia, uterus, cervix); the possibility of female autoeroticism without agency, and hence without any dichotomy between the active and the passive; the specificity of female homosexuality, which is not simply the inverse of male homosexuality; the possible role in female sexuality of puberty, sexual initiation, marriage, pregnancy, or motherhood, all of which are central to our cultural definition of femininity and all of which occur after the early childhood phase on which Freud and Lacan focus; the relationship between motherhood and eroticism in women's experience; and all of the historical and cultural variations on female sexuality that run counter to the norm of femininity in our culture that Freud and Lacan accept as necessary.

Irigaray's argument is that desire, including epistemological desire, has been defined as both monolithic and male, excluding the specificity as well as the plurality of desire and pleasure as experienced by women. "Woman's desire most likely does not speak the same language as man's desire, and it probably has been covered over by the logic that has dominated the West since the Greeks'' (p. 25).[15] This last claim is supported not only by her reading of Freud and Lacan, but also by readings of the classical Greeks, including Plato, and modern science. In the former case, for instance, she asks in *Speculum* what has been forgotten in the Greek *a-letheia* (truth as the negation of forgetting), a word in which "*Forgetting what we have forgotten* is sealed over at the dawning of the photological metaphor-system of the West.''[16] (This question might well be applied to the emphasis on that very term in much of the later Heidegger.) As for science, one section of *Ce Sexe* questions its focus on the physics and mathematics of solids rather than fluids, of closed rather than open space, and in general on aspects of the physical world that are isomorphic with the male. These questions lead her, in *Speculum*, to two conclusions that should be familiar: that male discourse centers on an eroticism of repetition, of the Same, and is ultimately "hom(m)osexual"—" 'Sexual difference' is a derivation of the problematics of sameness . . .'' (p. 26)—and that this attempt to deny the female determines the structure of the hierarchical dualisms created by male discourse to support and justify its own hegemony: "Out of this difference will be lifted one of the two terms—but determined in relation of what?—and this one term will be constituted as 'origin,' as that by whose differentiation the other may be engendered and brought to light'' (p. 21).

At the same time, Irigaray, as is the case with most of the other French feminists, accepts the Lacanian prescription that women are outside of language, and hence shares Wittig and Cixous's attachment to *"l'écriture feminine."* In *Ce Sexe*, she offers one explanation of what this term is meant, in her case at least, to convey:

> One must listen to her differently in order to hear an *"other meaning"* which is constantly in the process of weaving itself, at the same time ceaselessly embracing words and yet casting them off to avoid becoming fixed, immobilized. For when "she" says something, it is already no longer identical to what she means. Moreover, her statements are never identical to anything. Their distinguishing feature is one of continguity. They touch *(upon)*. And when they wander too far from this nearness, she stops and begins again from "zero": her body-sex organ. (p. 28).

However, she also criticizes the mixture of descriptive and prescriptive elements in both Freud and Lacan's account of the silencing of women, our exclusion from the law/language of the Logos. She says of Lacan, for instance, "This exclusion is *internal* to an order from which nothing escapes: that of his discourse. To the objection that it may not be all, the response will be that it is [women] who are 'not [at] all' " (p. 86). By the same token, the exclusion of women from language allows us to function as de-stabilizing, free-floating signifiers in the (male) linguistic system. "She is neither *one nor two*. . . . She renders any definition inadequate. Moreover, she has no 'proper' name [of her own]. And her sex [organ], which is not *a* sex [organ], is counted as *no* sex [organ]" (p. 26).[18]

This exclusion from the linguistic, paradoxically, is again what gives women a privileged position with regard to any deconstructive effort to undermine the metaphysical tradition that assumes the transcendence, universality, and objectivity of what is clearly a local, partial, and ideological system with no foundation outside of itself. However, this implies that male theorists who approach the problem in much the same way can easily end up sounding, especially to themselves, as if they were women, taking on "Woman's" voice in a way that is problematized in Alice Jardine's *Gynesis*. Most clearly with regard to Lacan in *Speculum,* but arguably in other cases as well, Irigaray shares Jardine's reservations about this phenomenon, seeing it as potentially just another repetition of the Same, a feigned homo/bi/transsexuality that would only cover over again the underlying structures of male discourse and male dominance.

> The "subject" plays at multiplying himself, even deforming himself, in this process. He is father, mother, and child(ren). And the relationships between them. He is masculine and feminine, and the relationship between them. What mockery of generation, parody of copulation and genealogy, drawing its *strength* from the same model, from the same model of the same: the subject. (p. 136)

The question that seems to remain after this analysis, for both Jardine and Irigaray, would seem to be whether the risk of such co-optation is worth the benefits to be gained from recognizing the validity and usefulness of deconstructive discourse, even in some cases that of Lacan, in feminist readings. It is a question that is not easily resolved, as Jardine makes clear.

In any case, it is because our speech would escape and disrupt the male hom(m)osexual linguistic system that women must be silenced and relegated to the role of commodities or merchandise to be traded among men—as Rubin says, relegated to being instead of having the phallus/penis. On this basis, Irigaray is able to incorporate intriguing, if familiar, Marxist elements into *Speculum,* asking "what *economic infrastructure governs Freud's conception of the role of woman?*" (p. 121) and answering that it clearly reflects and perpetuates a capitalist vision of woman as confined (by nature) to the so-called private sphere and so also as uninterested in "justice" or other aspects of the public realm. Her positive feminist vision, therefore, relies on what is said by "The Merchandise Among Themselves." While the exact form of this feminist vision is (necessarily?) not entirely clear, in *Ce Sexe* she underscores the need for detailed historical and political analyses in feminist thought, and argues for sexual pluralism since, again, a mere reversal of the existing monolithic male order would be, as always, more of the Same—"But if women are to preserve their auto-eroticism, their homosexuality, and let it flourish, would not the renunciation of heterosexual pleasure simply be another form of this amputation of power that is traditionally associated with women?" (p. 31).[19] Still, Irigaray seems somewhat sceptical of the possibility of women's politics on this basis, for reasons that should be familiar. Male discourse always speaks of "Woman" and so would deny that more than one woman exists. Therefore, there would never be *another* woman with whom one might speak as a woman. That is, as soon as a woman speaks, she must speak as, and hence become, a man, the castrated male homosexual that Freud, and male discourse in general, has always considered her to be.

Kate Mehuron has argued that this limitation on women's speech is what leads to Irigaray's *apparent* female essentialism, which Mehuron sees as a form of "ironic mimesis."[20] This interpretation is suggested by Irigaray herself in *Ce Sexe*: "To play at imitating is therefore, for a woman, to try to locate the site of her exploitation by discourse, without allowing herself simply to be reduced to it" (p. 74). As in Cixous's "Medusa," laughter allows women to communicate among ourselves without necessarily being re-inscribed in the male linguistic system. Such a reading of Irigaray serves to some extent to reconcile the seeming contradiction in *Speculum* between what is ultimately a strong emphasis on female anatomy—"The/a woman cannot be collected into *one* volume, for in that way she risks surrendering her own *jouissance,* which demands that she remain open to nothing utterable but which assures that her edges not close, her lips not be sewn shut" (p. 240)—and an almost "liberal," that is, almost American, understanding of what women need to do politically in order to bring an end to our own oppression—"Nonetheless, women have to advance to those same privileges (and to sameness, perhaps) before any consideration can be given to the differences they might give rise to" (p. 119). In *Ce Sexe* this political side of Irigaray's thought carries with it a message that all feminists might do well to keep in mind: while she recognizes the need for pluralism in what she calls movement*s* of liberation, Irigaray also notes (as does Derrida) the structural similarities of all forms of male domination *qua* male domination: "The first strategy of movements of liberation is a consciousness in each woman that what she undergoes in her personal experience is a condition shared by all women, which allows this *experience to become politicized*" (p. 159).

Here again the familiar importance of combining the personal and the political is embedded in an apparently arcane, possibly essentialist, seemingly "structuralist," arguably ironic discourse that can only remain, in many ways, deeply alien to most Anglo-American feminists. In this chapter, or indeed, in this book, I cannot pretend to have cleared away all the veils that seem to fall between the perhaps too rigid insistence on "masculine" logic and clarity in most of "our" versions of feminist thought, and what cannot help but seem at times to be the elitism and purposeful obscurantism of the French feminists. At the same time, I would insist neither that Anglo-American feminists must understand, much less accept, French feminism nor that we should copy it in our own work. Rather, I would suggest that we might "translate" it, with all the baggage that word carries within deconstructive discourse, that is, that we might rewrite it, not in different words that refer to the same, universal, fixed referent beyond language, but in words that both shape and describe our unique experience of feminist consciousness in the contemporary world. How we might begin to do that, and how the work of the French feminists and other Continental thinkers might be helpful in so doing, is the next phase of my work.

Notes

1. For instance, see Alice Jardine's "Introduction to Julia Kristeva's 'Women's Time,' " *Signs* 7, no. 1 (Autumn 1981): 5–12; or Gayatri Chakravorty Spivak's "French Feminism in an International Frame." It is perhaps worth noting that both comments are several years old and both refer most directly to Kristeva.

2. Iragaray's "Is the Subject of Science Sexed?" appeared in *Cultural Critique* (trans. Edith Oberle, *Cultural Critique* 1 (Fall 1985): 73–88) and in

Hypatia (trans. Carol Mastrangelo Bové, in *Hypatia* 2, no. 3 (Fall 1987): 65–87). My references will be to the *Hypatia* version because there the original French text is printed in parallel with the translation.

3. Monique Wittig, *The Lesbian Body,* trans. David Le Vay (Boston: Beacon Press, 1986).

4. Frances Bartkowski, "Feminism and Deconstruction: 'a union forever deferred,' " *enclitic* 4, no. 2 (Fall 1980): 72.

5. In addition to being reprinted in *The Kristeva Reader,* "Women's Time," (translated by Alice Jardine and Harry Blake) also appeared in *Feminist Theory,* ed. Nannerl. O. Keohane, Michelle Z. Rosaldo, and Barbara C. Gelpi (Chicago: University of Chicago Press, 1982). Page references are to *The Kristeva Reader.*

6. This point is made by Drucilla Cornell and Adam Thurschwell in their "Feminism, Negativity, Subjectivity," in *Feminism as Critique,* ed. Seyla Benhabib and Drucilla Cornell (Minneapolis: University of Minnesota Press, 1987).

7. Julia Kristeva, *Desire in Language,* ed. Leon S. Roudiez, trans. Alice Jardine, Thomas A. Gora, and Leon S. Roudiez (New York: Columbia University Press, 1980), pp. 237–70.

8. For a similar point made in the Anglo-American context, see Iris Young's "Pregnant Embodiment: Subjectivity and Alienation."

9. By Gayatri Spivak in her "Critical Response," *Critical Inquiry* 9, no. 1 (September 1982): 270.

10. While "The Laugh of the Medusa" was written originally as an independent piece for *L'Arc,* many of the passages I refer to here also appear in Hélène Cixous and Catherine Clément's *The Newly Born Woman.* References in the text are to the translation of "The Laugh of the Medusa" by Keith Cohen and Paula Cohen found in *New French Feminisms,* ed. Elaine Marks and Isabelle de Courtivron (Amherst: University of Massachusetts Press, 1980).

11. This point bears comparison with Eve Sedgwick's *Between Men: English Literature and Male Homosocial Desire* (New York: Columbia University Press, 1985).

12. Hélène Cixous, "Castration or Decapitation?", trans. Annette Kuhn, *Signs* 7, no. 1 (Autumn 1981): 41–55.

13. Hélène Cixous, "Portrait of Dora," trans. Sarah Burd, *Diacritics* 13 (Spring 1983): 2–32. My understanding of Cixous's play on the Dora case has benefited from Martha Noel Evans's "Portrait of Dora: Freud's Case History as Reviewed by Hélène Cixous," *SubStance* 11, no. 3 (1982): 64–71.

14. Luce Irigaray, *Ce Sexe Qui N'en Est Pas Un* (Paris: Editions de Minuit, 1977), p. 67. Excerpts, translated by Claudia Reeder, are included in *New French Feminisms,* and a full translation by Gillian C. Gill is now available from Cornell University Press.

15. This translation is from p. 101 of "Ce Sexe Qui N'en Est Pas Un" in *New French Feminisms.*

16. Luce Irigaray, *Speculum of the Other Woman*, p. 345.
17. This translation is from p. 103 of "Ce Sexe Qui N'en Est Pas Un" in *New French Feminisms*.
18. This translation is adapted from p. 101 of "Ce Sexe Qui N'en Est Pas Un" in *New French Feminisms*.
19. This translation is from p. 106 of "Ce Sexe Qui N'en Est Pas Un" in *New French Feminisms*.
20. The reference is to a paper Kate Mehuron, of Vanderbuilt University, presented as part of a panel on "Phenomenology and French Feminism" at the Society for Phenomenology and Existential Philosophy meeting held in October, 1987. As already noted, the same paper draws connections between Irigaray's work and the later Merleau-Ponty's, especially on this point.

Chapter 7

Conclusion

A Recommendation

At this point I would like to make a general recommendation, offer two brief examples of how following that recommendation might benefit the development of women's philosophy, and summarize the argument of this book. As already suggested, my recommendation is that feminists consider a three-dimensional approach to doing women's philosophy. The first dimension, the historical, would involve a systematic deconstruction of the dominant discourse of our culture along gender lines. The second or internal dimension would be the development of a detailed and global phenomenology of the lived experience of all kinds of women in a wide variety of life situations from all over the world. The third and final dimension, what might be called the horizontal, would be a call for women from these diverse realms to undertake the hermeneutic or interpretation of their own phenomenologies in light of the critical, deconstructive reading of their histories to locate and celebrate the possibility of creating a women's philosophy. At the same time, these three projects might provide the basis for a social and political practice that could foster the genuine liberation of women from their traditional status in human life. I have tried to argue here, however, that the first phase of this enterprise for many of us would be to recognize that Anglo-American philosophy gives us no basis for doing this philosophical work because its analytical tools are deeply embedded in a specifically and powerfully male experience of the world.

Thus, in a way, the first two chapters of this book can serve as an example of the first dimension of the project. By seeking to re-read classical philosophical texts in ways that illuminate both their intrinsic gender bias and the relationship between that bias and their strictly philosophical failures, feminist philosophers can continue to read and draw on the work of philosophers in what will always be our historical context, but at the same time maintain a consistent and powerfully critical feminist stance in the face of what are often very seductive, and very male-biased, texts. Annette Baier's work on Hume's moral theory might be one example in which a deconstructive ear for the subtext in Hume could sharpen an already incisive analysis. In the phase of the project, we also have the advantage of being able to take existing deconstructive texts, by male or female writers, as a starting point in a more specifically feminist re-reading of the tradition. I have already referred to Gary Shapiro's work on the British Empiricists as opening up the possiblity of a gender-oriented reading of those texts that he himself does not engage in, and many deconstructions of both literary and philosophical texts are similarly suggestive. This is, in fact, one of the ways in which contemporary French feminism has developed, as a deep and powerful feminist criticism that has its roots in the (often sexist) readings of Barthes, Lacan, Derrida, and others. Many examples of a similar approach in Anglo-American feminist theory have already been discussed, although they are generally less systematic, and occasionally less concious of thier origins, than in France.

What a phenomenology of women's lived experience would consist in will be less immediately clear from this particular study, although the examples that follow may help to clarify the concept. As is often the case in feminist thought, it is easier to say how it would be different from traditional male-oriented phenomenology that to say how it would actually be done. In *Being and Time,* Heidegger defines "phenomenology" as the careful study of our lived experience, not as an "objective" scientific investigation, but in the hermeneutic sense of a search for the interpretative meaning that can be found there. As opposed to the Husserlian or Satrean model, which both Heidegger and Merleau-Ponty still follow to some extent, women's phenomenology will be more concerned with the body and less concerned with "conciousness" and its objects; it will focus more on the senses of taste, smell, and touch, and less on visual and auditory experience than is typical in men's phenomenology (although arguably not in men's lives); it will be more concerned with sexuality and especially the issue of female desire in a male-dominated world, as well as with child-bearing and "maternal thinking"; it will be concerned with what Kristeva calls "women's time," the multidimensional time in which we live that underlies and undermines the linear time that has proved so perplexing to male phenomenology (and to male philosophy as a whole); and above all, it will not assume that phenomenology is a "science," since the very concept of science is part of the men's philosophy we seek to re-think.

Husserlian phenomenology draws together its apparently disparate objects and results through what is called an "eidetic reduction" which ultimately is exactly what it sounds like, a return to the Idea in the Platonic sense. Given Husserl's solipsistic Individualism, that is the only way in which phenomenology can escape the "subjectivity" of its origins. In Heidegger, however, phenomenology has a different link to ontology that also allows it to become a general theory of human life (Dasein): since Dasein is intrinsically social, and socially formed to a large extent, it follows that the phenomenology of Dasein can be generalized in this world through the simple expedient of communication. *Being and Time* (and to some extent *Being and Nothingness* as well) has a vague air of "isn't it that way for you, too?" that is almost reminiscent of consciouness-raising in the feminist movement, and certainly had a similar effect on young intellectuals in the postwar years. (Merleau–Ponty, on the other hand, replaces Idealism with psychology, using the empirical Gestalt psychology as the basis for his own "hermeneutics," but that method has more limitations from a feminist point of view and was abandoned for a more linguistic focus in Merleau-Ponty's own later work.) Women's hermeneutics, then, or the hermeneutics of women's experience, would build upon as broad a basis as possible of women's own accounts of their lives in an attempt to make sense of them in terms that would be available to all. That is, we must look for and systematize our commonalities, discover and celebrate our differences, and work to give all of us the life we would like to have in terms of our own experience of it. And then, we might wish to see how this hermeneutics might articulate with the traditional male-biased accounts of the nature of "human" life.

In the following sections I will suggest how a deconstructive/phenomenological/hermeneutic approach to women's philosophy might be applied to two key issues of modern moral life. I do not intend these to be definitive accounts, but rather mere outlines of possible first steps in a women-centered analysis of these problems. Nor do I mean to imply that these problems are more important for women's philosophy than a wide variety of others might be. These are simply two topics on which I have already written, using the kind of approach I have just outlined, and which provide an especially sharp contrast between what traditional Anglo-American philosophers have suggested as "solutions" to the problems posed and what many feminists would regard as an adequate account of the basic issues they present. They are, moreover, topics on which my own thinking has been instigated, commented on, and enriched by the work of other feminist philosophers, so that these accounts are already the kind of collaborative work that seems needed in doing women's philosophy.

The Problem of Abortion

Abortion is a traditional "women's issue," and one that it is becoming increasingly obvious cannot be resolved in the terms provided by traditional Anglo-American philosophy.[1] A detailed deconstruction of the dominant discourse in the Western world on the issue of abortion would be a fascinating enterprise, especially if it traced the relationships between this discourse and those of both religious orthodoxy and pro-natalistic national policies over the course of at least the last two hundred years. Much demographic evidence exists, for example, to suggest that (maternal) infanticide has been a common and accepted phenomenon throughout history, at least among the poorer classes, and it would be interesting to correlate this data with contemporary cross-cultural data on the frequency and motivation for legalized abortions. Here I will be forced, however, to limit my feminist deconstruction to a mere suggestion of the state of things in the Anglo-American philosophical discourse on abortion in the last twenty years, and its roots in the work of the British Empiricists.

The approaches usually taken to the abortion issue in this tradition are either legal or moral. In the first case, the concern becomes the rights of the woman and of the fetus and, secondarily, whether the fetus is even a person who can have rights. Thus, these versions of the debate tend to bog down in the kind of Lockean "rights talk" that Gilligan and others regard as more relevant to men's experience of the world (and, Mailyn Frye suggests, it is the fetus that men identify with, not the woman, so "rights talk" tends to become "fetus talk"[2]). Needless to say, few women experience an abortion primarily as a matter of "rights," unless they are denied one by the legal system under which they live. While Gilligan's work suggests that women do seem to see abortion as a moral dilemma, however, the terms in which our tradition casts that dilemma are often as alien to women's lives as is "rights talk." Kantian accounts, in the Anglo-American context at least, run parallel to the political approach, seeing the woman's concrete situation as merely one instance of a more general rule (again, a male way of doing morality) or bogging down in issues of personhood. Similarly, a Humean or utilitarian approach to the issue, if taken superficially, sounds much too similar to simple expediency to be entirely comfortable for most of us, and if taken more seriously opens up a whole range of "slippery slope" arguments that are often ultimately irrelevant to the question at hand. Utilitarianism seems to concern too few people, those directly involved, or too many, the whole society, and so runs counter to the woman's experience of herself as neither an isolated individual nor a mere exemplar of some more general, abstract social good (both of which, of course, once again reflect a stereotypically male experience of the world).

If we start with the woman's experience, however, it becomes clear that thinking about abortion—which is precisely the termination of a pregnancy—needs to start with thinking about pregnancy itself.[3] What is the relationship between a woman and a fetus, that is, what is the phenomenology of pregnancy? I have already cited Iris Young's phenomenological study of pregnancy, and while she and I disagree to some extent about the exact nature of the phenomenon (especially the extent to which a woman experiences the movement of the fetus as part of her own body), the general outlines in both cases suggest that, from the woman's point of view, the personhood of the fetus, and hence the nature of the relationship between them, is something that develops over the course of the pregnancy and can be widely variable across time (and possibly across different pregnancies). This would follow the phenomenological structure of the existence of infants and very young children—one watches them becomes human, become Dasein, over a period that finally ends with the acquisition of language, which is only the completion of a process that requires a far greater level of socialization than simple speech. Thus, phenomenologically, the fetus is an I-not-I which shares the physical confines of my body without being part of my own intentional activity, and which also gradually becomes for me an independent existence exhibiting what I at least take to be its own intentional activity (e.g., trying to get more comfortable in its cramped quarters). It follows that there is no fixed relationship between the woman and the fetus; that there is no definitive point at which, even for the woman herself, the fetus becomes a person, a part of the woman's Being-with; but also that it does at some time before birth usually come to be for her another person independent of herself.

One can already draw the conclusion from this phenomenology that any attempt to fix this highly mutuable relationship will necessarily violate the woman's experience of her own pregnancy. Thus, it will be equally questionable to tell a woman who suffers an early miscarriage that she has not really had a baby die as to tell a woman for whom the fetus is only a barrier and a threat that at some given point in time she must regard it as a person with the same legal rights as herself. What a hermeneutic approach adds to this is a discourse in which these phenomenological considerations can be clearly related to more general considerations of relationship and personhood. In Heidegger, the existence of Dasein as Dasein, that is, the "personhood" of Dasein, has the same interpersonal structure as the relationship between the woman and the fetus. On at least one reading of Heidegger, what makes an instance of Dasein Dasein is not its internal states, but rather its relationships to other Dasein, its Being-with. As noted before, the Being-with of Dasein means that it exists for others as an ultimate referent in the world of their own projects and roles. This "social" definition of Dasein is, however, entirely congruent with what seems to be phenomenologically the case in pregnancy: the fetus becomes Dasein as it becomes more and more a part of the world created by the woman's projects. Thus, setting the personhood of the fetus in the context of Heidegger's concept of Dasein, rather than in the context of atomistic Individualism, makes it possible to theorize more adequately about the relationships that are central to the abortion issue. In so doing, moreover, it also becomes possible to follow more closely women's own experience of abortion and to place the legal and moral discourse on the subject in terms that remain meaningful to them.

This is only, of course, the briefest possible sketch of what might be the account of abortion in a complete women's philosophy. It does, however, make clearer the role that each of the three dimensions I am recommending could play in such an account, and how the three can be related to each other, and to traditional discourse on the topic, so that they are both mutually supportive and effectively critical of the alternative. It is important to note in this case also that a central feature of both the problem and the proposed path to a "solution" is the social nature of Dasein, that is, the denial of atomistic Individualism. Humans, Dasein, can only exist as such in a social context and thus it is that context that creates them as human in anything more than a purely biological sense. Thus, while it is cross-culturally true that women will abort or kill a child to increase their own well-being or to improve the lot of other, already existing children, it is also true that such a choice indicates that they live in a society that creates that dilemma for them, that is, that they live in a world that either does not allow them to choose whether they will become pregnant, or that fails to provide enough goods for everyone, *or both*. Abortion is the product of coercion and scarcity, natural or man-made. Given this understanding of the social nature of the abortion problem, it becomes increasingly clear that to debate the "rights" or the personhood of the fetus is a sadly inadequate response that avoids, rather than serves, women's most basic human needs.

The Wrong of Nuclear War

The second "example" that I will discuss here is not one that is usually seen as a "women's" issue. The threat of nuclear war does, however, open up the possibility of a woman-centered analysis, if only because, as in the case of abortion, the existing discourse on the subject seems increasingly inadequate. Unlike the case of abortion, the literature on this topic available for deconstruction is all very recent and relatively limited in volume. Moreover, it is almost entirely political in nature and so subject to a powerful deconstruction on that basis alone. (One need not be a careful reader to find what Casper Weinberger has to say about nuclear war both frightening and ultimately without foundation.) If one takes that discourse as a species of Anglo-American philosophy (of sorts) with its roots in the British Empiricist tradition, however, more complicated lines of deconstruction begin to emerge. The nuclear threat exists because it can, because we have the ability to create more and more destructive nuclear weapons. It is a scientific (Heidegger would say a technological) inevitability, and once the possibility has been created, going back to a non-nuclear world is a mere pipe-dream. Thus, the confines of the discourse are set by the "objective," scientific facts of the case and everything else is simply cleaning up the messy details. Who has how many of what pointed at whom or who has the power to push which button when is then subjected either to strictly Utilitarian—or worse yet, utilitarian—calculations, or to more-or-less unrealistic Kantian "just war" analyses. Politically, we have no "right" not to be annihilated by a nuclear war or mishap, only "managed" risks of "excess deaths."[4]

The women's movement in the United States in the 1960s grew in part out of an increasing awareness among left-wing women that war (in this case, the war in Vietnam) was not just a men's issue on which we could be relegated to servile, and preferably supine, silence. War, any war, deeply affects women's lives. It affects us as women in a war-driven economy and a war-oriented society; as colleagues, friends, lovers, wives, sisters, daughters, and mothers of the men who fight or flee or die or are destroyed in the process and sent home; as fellow-women with the victims of rape in the war zone and prostitution and illegitimate pregnancy behind the lines; and as ourselves the victims of the male victims of the war when they are sent home trained in violence but with little else to show for their ordeal. To this litany nuclear war would add the twist that all places would be the war zone, that there would be no safe haven behind any border or across any sea. In a nuclear war we would be all of the above all at once. And as women we would have before us also the image of the children for whom we had cared but whom we could longer either nurture or protect, and whose survival might depend on our teaching them that utterly ruthless self-preservation was their only chance to live. Our "maternal thinking" would be limited to the choice of raising them to be what we could not want them to become or teaching them to die nobly for our vision of what they might have been. As a mother, dying in a nuclear war frightens me much less than the idea of my children surviving unprotected in the chaos that would inevitably follow.

What this preliminary phenomenology of the threat of nuclear war, and the fact of present and past wars, reveals is the lines of connection between different women's experience of motherhood when society has broken down or been completely destroyed. This account suggests, for instance, a deep affinity between the threat of a nuclear holocaust and the actuality of the holocaust of World War II. At the same time, it makes a distinction between the way in which "maternal thinking" must be modified when women are without *any* power to protect their children from *any* threat, as in the concentration camps, and the more "normal," equally deadly decisions that women must make in orderly but seriously distorted social contexts, such as famine or non-nuclear war. Thus, it seems that the nuclear threat raises fears that would echo those of mothers under slavery, at least in its American form, but not those of Stalin's Ukrainian "holocaust," where civil order survived despite the massive loss of life.

The question remains, however, of what we think will be lost in our children should they be forced to live in a post-nuclear era, in a time when there is no social order to protect them, and not even enough mentally and physically healthy survivors to provide the basis for one.

A consideration of the critique of technology in the later Heidegger provides one possible clue to this loss. Heidegger regarded nuclear war as the logical outcome of a technological age that gives us a degenerate understanding of the meaning of Being and represents Dasein in a way that would ultimately reduce it to the status of a "standing-reserve," as it does with everything else. That is, technology turns human being into a material, mechanical existence, denying the ability to transcend, or project beyond, the merely present that is definitive of Dasein. For Heidegger, technology will lead to the eventual end of human existence whether or not it does so through nuclear annihilation. Such a pessimistic interpretation of the dangers of the nuclear threat fits well with at least parts of the phenomenology I tried to sketch out above. Beyond fears about physical harms to my children in a post-nuclear world, what I fear is an existence so grim and so minimal that the hope, even the memory, of anything else is erased from their minds. I do not want my children to cease to be Dasein, to be so deprived that they can no longer project a future on the world as they encounter it, to be so concerned with their survival that they cease to exist in a "with-world" in which they can encounter other human beings *as such*. As Paula Smithka says in "Heidegger and Nuclear Weapons," "Through nuclear weapons we see the possibility for the loss of meaning in and of the world—the loss of self-conscious awareness of being."[5]

Again, this is only the suggestion of an analysis of the problem, but it indicates the general direction that women's philosophy might take and also connects that potential analysis with existing feminist thought and with the failure of the dominant philosophical discourse to deal adequately with the problem. As Derrida points out in his discussion of nuclear war, it is something "unheard of" in the Western world, "unheimlich" in Heidegger's terms, "uncanny" in English translations of both Heidegger and Freud. The same could be said of the relationship between a woman and a fetus who will at some point become her unborn child. For Freud, the most primordial experience of the uncanny is the (male) child's experience of "his" mother's "castration," but perhaps here we see that the category of the uncanny is a category of those things that men's philosophy has been unable to assimilate to their usual hierarchical dualisms, that is, to their own experience of the world, and hence they have always already equated it with women, the other great unknown. If this is the case, we must be wary of turning any of these unresolved issues into reaffirmations of the uncanniness of women, as too much emphasis on a maternal analysis might (including the ones I myself suggested). Most "women's" issues are really "human" issues, and their solutions must also be "human" solutions. At the same time, given that all philosophy is men's philosophy, in order to come to "human" solutions, what is most needed is precisely a woman-centered analysis of what has been excluded and covered in the dominant discourse. As has been noted before, the fine line between a women-centered analysis of human problems and a reaffirmation of our concern "merely" with "women's" issues is one that we are forced to tread in the process of creating what would be women's philosophy.

Although my presentation in this book may not fit the model of argument generally recognized in Anglo-American philosophy, I believe that I have demonstrated, if not proven, several important claims. The first is that Locke and Hume did men's philosophy, that is, their philosophy reflects a specifically (European) male experience of the world and then takes that experience to be definitive of human experience as a whole. The second is that this male bias in British Empiricism is deeply connected to the failure of philosophy in that tradition to solve certain philosophical problems, even in its own terms. The third is that the feminist analysis of traditional Anglo-American philosophy provides one powerful method for exposing this problem in the Empiricist tradition. The fourth point I would claim to have made is that in order to develop more powerful critiques of the tradition and to begin to think about what women's philosophy might be, we should look to the hermeneutics, phenomenology, and deconstruction found in contemporary Continental philosophy. This would, perhaps, protect us from the dangers of beginning philosophy all over again without introducing an undue risk of having our work co-opted into what would only be more men's philosophy. Finally, I have suggested what direction women's philosophy might take on two issues, if it followed this paradigm. Thus, the answer to the question "Is women's philosophy possible?" seems to be yes, no, and maybe. Yes, it is possible, and exists, as a critique of the philosophical tradition. No, it may not be possible strictly within the confines of traditional Anglo-American philosophy. And maybe, someday, something that would be women's philosophy will be possible, but that will come about only in a world that is very different from, and perhaps better than, anything we can presently imagine.

Notes

1. See, for instance, Kathryn Payne Addelson's "Moral Revolution," in *Women and Values,* ed. Marilyn Pearsall (Belmont, Calif.: Wadsworth, 1986) or Janet Farrell Smith's "Rights-Conflict, Pregnancy and Abortion," in *Beyond Domination,* ed. Carol C. Gould (Totowa, N.J.: Rowman and Allanheld, 1983).

2. This discussion is in Marilyn Frye's *The Politics of Reality,* pp. 100–01.

3. This analysis is a very abbreviated version of a paper that I presented at the Central Division meeting of the American Philosophical Association in April, 1985. In addition to Iris Young, my thinking on these issues has benefited from the comments of my respondent, Terry Winant of the University of Wisconsin at Madison, my colleague at Hamline, Joseph Uemura, the students in a Philosophical Psychology class I taught at Hamline in the Spring term of 1984, and Bert Dreyfus of the University of California at Berkeley (none of whom, by the way, would entirely agree with what I say here).

4. This analysis is very loosely based on part of a paper on Derrida's "No Apocalypse, Not Now (full speed ahead, seven missiles, seven missives)," trans. Catherine Porter and Philip Lewis, *Diacritics* 20 (Summer 1984): 20–31, that I presented at the International Association for Philosophy and Literature meeting in May, 1986. The paper has also benefited from discussion of the war issue with Duane Cady, my other Hamline colleague. (The issue of Apocalypse in Derrida, and its relationship to gender, is one of many topics I cannot go into here.)

5. Paula J. Smithka, "Heidegger and Nuclear Weapons," *Concerned Philosophers for Peace Newsletter* 7, no. 1 (April 1987): 9.

References

Addelson, Kathryn Payne. "Moral Revolution." In *Women and Values,* edited by Marilyn Pearsall. Belmont, Calif.: Wadsworth, 1986.

Allen, Jeffner. "Motherhood: The Annihilation of Women." In *Mothering,* edited by Joyce Trebilcot. Totowa, N.J.: Rowman and Allanheld, 1983.

Arthur, Marilyn. " 'Liberated' Women: The Classical Era." In *Becoming Visible: Women in European History,* edited by Renate Bridenthal and Claudia Koonz. Boston: Houghton Mifflin, 1977.

Ayer, A. J. *Language, Truth, and Logic.* New York: Dover, 1952.

Baier, Annette. "Hume, the Women's Moral Theorist?" In *Women and Moral Theory,* edited by Eva Feder Kittay and Diana T. Meyers. Totowa, N.J.: Rowman and Littlefield, 1987.

Barthes, Roland. *Mythologies.* Translated by Annette Lavers. New York: Hill and Wang, 1972.

———. *Sade/Fourier/Loyola.* Translated by Richard Miller. New York: Hill and Wang, 1976.

———. *S/Z.* Translated by Richard Miller. New York: Hill and Wang, 1974.

Bartkowski, Frances. "Feminism and Deconstruction: 'a union forever deferred.' " *enclitic* 4, no. 2 (Fall 1980): 70–77.

Beardsley, Elizabeth Lane. "Referential Genderization." *The Philosophical Forum* 5, nos. 1–2 (Fall–Winter 1973–1974): 285–95.

———. "Traits and Genderization." In *Feminism and Philosophy,* edited by Mary Vetterling-Braggin, Frederick A. Elliston, and Jane English. Totowa, N.J.: Littlefield, Adams, 1977.

Bell, Linda. "A Feminist Ethics in Sartre's Existentialism." Paper presented at a conference on "Explorations in Feminist Ethics," University of Minnesota, Deluth, October 1988.

Benhabib, Seyla, "The Generalized and the Concrete Other." In *Feminism as*

Critique, edited by Seyla Benhabib and Drucilla Cornell. Minneapolis: University of Minnesota Press, 1987. (Also in *Women and Moral Theory,* edited by Eva Feder Kittay and Diana T. Meyers. Totowa, N.J.: Rowman and Littlefield, 1987).

Benhabib, Seyla, and Drucilla Cornell, eds. *Feminism as Critique.* Minneapolis: University of Minnesota Press, 1987.

Berger, John. *Ways of Seeing.* New York: Viking Penguin, 1977,.

Berkeley, George. *Three Dialogues Between Hylas and Philonous.* Edited by Robert M. Adams. Indianapolis: Hackett, 1979.

Bleier, Ruth. *Science and Gender.* New York: Pergamon Press, 1984.

Bordo, Susan R. *The Flight to Objectivity.* Albany: State University of New York Press, 1987.

Bowles, Gloria. "The Uses of Hermeneutics for Feminist Scholarship." *Women's Studies International Forum* 7, no. 3 (1984): 131–33.

Brewer, María. "A Loosening of Tongues: From Narrative Economy to Women Writing." *Modern Language Notes* 99, no. 5 (December 1984): 1141–61.

Burns, Steven. "The Humean Female." *Dialogue* 15, no. 3 (1976): 415–24.

Butler, Judith. "Sex and Gender in Simone de Beauvoir's *Second Sex.*" *Yale French Studies* no. 72 (1987): 35–49

———. "Variations on Sex and Gender." In *Feminism as Critique,* edited by Seyla Benhabib and Drucilla Cornell. Minneapolis: University of Minnesota Press, 1987.

Butler, Melissa. "Early Liberal Roots of Feminism: John Locke and the Attack on Patriarchy." *American Political Science Review* 72, no. 1 (March 1978): 135–50.

Card, Claudia. "Lesbian Attitudes and *The Second Sex.*" *Women's Studies International Forum* 8, no. 3 (1985): 209–14.

Chodorow, Nancy. *The Reproduction of Mothering.* Berkeley: University of California Press, 1978.

Cixous, Hélène. "Arrive le chapitre-qui vient." Translated by Stan Theis. *enclitic* 4, no. 2 (Fall 1980): 45–58.

———. "Castration or Decapitation?" Translated by Annette Kuhn. *Signs* 7, no. 1 (Autumn 1981): 41–55.

———. "The Laugh of the Medusa." Translated by Keith Cohen and Paula Cohen. In *New French Feminisms,* edited by Elaine Marks and Isabelle de Courtivron. Amherst: University of Massachusetts Press, 1980.

———. "Portrait of Dora." Translated by Sarah Burd. *Diacritics* 13 (Spring 1983): 2–32.

Cixous, Hélène, and Catherine Clément. *The Newly Born Woman.* Translated by Betsy Wing. Minneapolis: University of Minnesota Press, 1986.

Cornell, Drucilla, and Adam Thurschwell. "Feminism, Negativity, Subjectivity." In *Feminism as Critique,* edited by Seyla Benhabib and Drucilla Cornell. Minneapolis: University of Minnesota Press, 1987.

Daly, Mary. *Beyond God the Father.* Boston: Beacon Press, 1973.

———. *Gyn/Ecology.* Boston: Beacon Press, 1978.

de Beauvoir, Simone. *Adieux: A Farewell to Sartre.* Translated by Patrick O'Brian. New York: Pantheon, 1984.

———. *The Second Sex.* Translated by H. M. Parshley. New York: Bantam Books, 1961.

Deleuze, Gilles. *Empirisme et Subjectivité.* Paris: Presses Universitaires de France, 1953.

Derrida, Jacques. "Choreographies." Interview with Christie V. McDonald. *Diacritics* 12 (Summer 1982): 20–31.

———. *Dissemination.* Translated by Barbara Johnson. Chicago: University of Chicago Press, 1981.

———. "Geschlecht: sexual difference, ontological difference." Translated by John Sallis. *Research in Phenomenology* 13 (1983): 65–83.

———. "Geschlecht II: Heidegger's Hand." Translated by John P. Leavey, Jr. In *Deconstruction and Philosophy,* edited by John Sallis. Chicago: University of Chicago Press, 1987.

———. *Margins of Philosophy.* Translated by Alan Bass. Chicago: University of Chicago Press, 1982.

———. *Memoires.* Translated by Cecile Lindsay, Jonathan Culler, and Eduardo Cavada. New York: Columbia University Press, 1986.

———. "No Apocalypse, Not Now (full speed ahead, seven missiles, seven missives)." Translated by Catherine Porter and Philip Lewis. *Diacritics* 20 (Summer 1984): 20–31.

———. "The Question of Style." Translated by Ruben Berezdivin. In *The New Nietzsche,* edited by David B. Allison. Cambridge, Mass.: M.I.T. Press, 1985.

———. *Speech and Phenomena.* Translated by David B. Allison. Evanston, Ill.: Northwestern University Press, 1973.

———. *The Truth in Painting.* Translated by Geoff Bennington and Ian McLoed. Chicago: University of Chicago Press, 1987.

de Saussure, Ferdinand. *Course on General Linguistics.* Translated by Wade Baskin. New York: Philosophical Library, 1959.

Descartes, René. *The Philosophical Works of Descartes.* Translated by Elizabeth S. Haldane and G. R. T. Ross. Cambridge: Cambridge University Press, 1976 (in two volumes).

Di Stefano, Christine. "Masculinity as Ideology in Political Theory: Hobbesian Man Considered." *Women's Studies International Forum* 6, no. 6 (1983) 633–644.

Eisenstein, Zillah. *The Radical Future of Liberal Feminism.* Boston: Northeastern University Press, 1981.

Evans, Martha Noel. "Portrait of Dora: Freud's Case History as Reviewed by Hélène Cixous." *SubStance* 11, no. 3 (1982): 64–71.

Flax, Jane. "Political Philosophy and the Patriarchal Unconscious: A Psychoanalytic Perspective on Epistemology and Metaphysics." In *Discovering Reality,* edited by Sandra Harding and Merrill B. Hintikka. Boston: D. Reidel, 1983.

Foucault, Michel. *The History of Sexuality, Volume I: Introduction.* Translated by Robert Hurley. New York: Pantheon Books, 1978.

———. *The Order of Things.* Translation unattributed. New York: Vintage Books, 1973.

———. *The Use of Pleasure: The History of Sexuality, Volume II.* Translated by Robert Hurley. New York: Pantheon Books, 1985.

Frankel, Lois. "Lady Marsham." In *A History of Women Philosophers, Volume III/1600–1900,* edited by Mary Ellen Waithe. Forthcoming from Martinus Nijhoff.

Fraser, Nancy. "Women, Welfare and The Politics of Need Interpretation." *Hypatia* 2, no. 1 (Winter 1987): 103–21. (Also in her *Unruly Practices,* Minneapolis: University of Minnesota Press, 1989.)

Fraser, Nancy, and Linda Nicholson. "Social Criticism Without Philosophy: An Encounter Between Feminism and Postmodernism." In *Universal Abandon? The Politics of Postmodernism,* edited by Andrew Ross. Minneapolis: University of Minnesota Press, 1988. (Also in *The Institution of Philosophy,* edited by Avner Cohen and Marcelo Dascal, forthcoming from Rowman and Littlefield.)

Freud, Sigmund. *Beyond the Pleasure Principle. The Standard Edition of the Complete Psychological Works of Sigmund Freud,* vol. 18. Translated and edited by James Strachey. London: The Hogarth Press, 1953.

———. "Fragment of an Analysis of a Case of Hysteria." *The Standard Edition of the Complete Psychological Works of Sigmund Freud,* vol. 7. Translated and edited by James Strachey. London: The Hogarth Press, 1953.

———. *Moses and Monotheism.* Translated by Katherine Jones. New York: Vintage Books, 1939.

———. *The Psychopathology of Everyday Life. The Standard Edition of the*

Complete Psychological Works of Sigmund Freud, vol. 6. Translated and edited by James Strachey. London: The Hogarth Press, 1953.

Frye, Marilyn. "History and Responsibility." *Women's Studies International Forum* 8, no. 3 (1985): 215–17.

———. *The Politics of Reality*. Trumanburg, N.Y.: The Crossing Press, 1983.

Genova, Judith, ed. *Power, Gender, Values*. Edmonton, Alberta: Academic Printing and Publishing, 1987.

Gilligan, Carol. *In a Different Voice*. Cambridge, Mass.: Harvard University Press, 1982.

Gould, Carol C., ed. *Beyond Domination*. Totowa, N.J.: Rowman and Allanheld, 1983.

Greer, Germaine. *The Female Eunuch*. New York: McGraw-Hill, 1971.

Harding, Sandra. "Is Gender a Variable in Conceptions of Rationality? A Survey of Issues." In *Beyond Domination*, edited by Carol C. Gould. Totowa, N.J.: Rowman and Allanheld, 1983.

———. *The Science Question in Feminism*. Ithaca, N.Y.: Cornell University Press, 1986.

———. "The Social Function of the Empiricist Conception of Mind." *Metaphilosophy* 10, no. 1 (January 1979): 38–47.

Harding, Sandra, and Merrill B. Hintikka, eds. *Discovering Reality*. Boston: D. Reidel, 1983.

Harré, Rom. *Personal Being*. Cambridge, Mass.: Harvard University Press, 1984.

Hartsock, Nancy C. M. "The Feminist Standpoint: Developing the Ground for a Specifically Feminist Historical Materialism." In *Discovering Reality*, edited by Sandra Harding and Merrill B. Hintikka. Boston: D. Reidel, 1983.

Hawkesworth, Mary E. "The Affirmative Action Debate and Conflicting Conceptions of Individuality." *Women's Studies International Forum* 7, no. 5 (1984) 335–47.

Heidegger, Martin. *Basic Writings*. Edited by David Farrell Krell. New York: Harper and Row, 1977.

———. *Being and Time*. Translated by John Macquarrie and Edward Robinson. New York: Harper and Row, 1962.

———. *The Question Concerning Technology*. Translated by William Lovitt. New York: Harper Colophon, 1977.

Hintikka, Merrill B., and Jaakko Hintikka. "How Can Language Be Sexist?" In *Discovering Reality*, edited by Sandra Harding and Merrill B. Hintikka. Boston: D. Reidel, 1983.

Hobbes, Thomas *Leviathan*, Parts I and II. Edited by Herbert W. Schneider. New York: Bobbs-Merrill Library of Liberal Arts, 1958.

Holland, Nancy. "Heidegger and Derrida Redux: A Close Reading." In *Hermeneutics and Deconstruction,* edited by Hugh J. Silverman and Don Ihde. Albany: State University of New York Press, 1985.

———. "Merleau-Ponty on Presence: A Derridian Reading." *Research in Phenomenology* 16 (1986): 111–20.

———. "The Treble Clef/t: Jacques Derrida and the Female Voice." In *Philosophy and Culture: Proceedings of the XVIIth World Congress of Philosophy,* Volume 2 (microfiche), Editions de Montmorency, 1988.

Hooks, Bell. *Feminist Theory: From Margin to Center.* Boston: South End Press, 1984.

Hume, David. *Dialogues Concerning Natural Religion.* Edited by Richard H. Popkin. Indianapolis: Hackett, 1983.

———. *Hume's Enquiries.* Edited by L. A. Selby-Bigge. New York: Oxford University Press, 1975.

———. *A Treatise of Human Nature.* Edited by L. A. Selby-Bigge. New York: Oxford University Press, 1975.

Husserl, Edmund. *Cartesian Meditations.* Translated by Dorion Cairns. The Hague: Martinus Nijhoff, 1973.

Irigaray, Luce. *Ce Sexe Qui N'en Est Pas Un.* Paris: Editions de Minuit, 1977. (Excerpts, translated by Claudia Reeder, included in *New French Feminisms,* edited by Elaine Marks and Isabelle de Courtivron. Amherst: University of Massachusetts Press, 1980. A full translation by Gillian C. Gill is now available from Cornell University Press.)

———. "Is the Subject of Science Sexed?" Translated by Carol Mastrangelo Bové. *Hypatia* 2, no. 3 (Fall 1987): 65–87. (Also, translated by Edith Oberle in *Cultural Critique* 1 (Fall 1985): 73–88.)

———. *Speculum of the Other Woman.* Translated by Gillian C. Gill. Ithaca, N.Y.: Cornell University Press, 1985.

Jaggar, Alison. "Abortion and a Woman's Right to Decide." *The Philosophical Forum* 5, nos. 1–2 (Fall–Winter 1973–1974): 347–360.

———. *Feminist Politics and Human Nature.* Totowa, N.J.: Rowman and Allanheld, 1983.

Jardine, Alice. *Gynesis.* Ithaca, N.Y.: Cornell University Press, 1985.

———. "Introduction to Julia Kristeva's 'Women's Time.' " *Signs* 7, no. 1 (Autumn 1981): 5–12.

Johnson, Barbara. *A World of Difference.* Baltimore: Johns Hopkins University Press, 1987.

Kant, Immanuel. *Prolegomena to Any Future Metaphysics.* Translated by James W. Ellington (from Carus). Indianapolis: Hackett, 1977.

Keller, Evelyn Fox. *Reflections on Gender and Science*. New Haven, Conn.: Yale University Press, 1985.

Keohane, Nannerl O., Michelle Z. Rosaldo, and Barbara C. Gelpi, eds. *Feminist Theory*. Chicago: The University of Chicago Press, 1982.

Kittay, Eva Feder, and Diana T. Meyers, eds. *Women and Moral Theory*. Totowa, N.J.: Rowman and Littlefield, 1987.

Kofman, Sarah. *The Enigma of Woman*. Translated by Catherine Porter. Ithaca, N.Y.: Cornell University Press, 1985.

———. "Rousseau's Phallocratic Ends." Translated by Mara Dukats. *Hypatia* 3, no. 3 (Fall 1988): 123–36.

Krieger, Linda J. "Through a Glass Darkly: Paradigms of Equality and the Search for a Women's Jurisprudence." *Hypatia* 2, no. 1 (Winter 1987): 45–61.

Kristeva, Julia. *Desire in Language*. Edited by Leon S. Roudiez. Translated by Alice Jardine, Thomas A. Gora, and Leon S. Roudiez. New York: Columbia University Press, 1980.

———. *The Kristeva Reader*. Edited by Toril Moi. New York: Columbia University Press, 1986.

Kuhn, Thomas. *The Structure of Scientific Revolutions*. Chicago: University of Chicago Press, 1970.

Kuykendall, Eleanor H. "Toward an Ethic of Nurturance: Luce Irigaray on Mothering and Power." In *Mothering*, edited by Joyce Trebilcot. Totowa, N.J.: Rowman and Allanheld, 1983.

Lacan, Jacques. *Feminine Sexuality*. Edited by Juliet Mitchell and Jacqueline Rose. Translated by Jacqueline Rose. New York: Norton, 1982.

———. *The Language of the Self*. Translated by Anthony Wilden. New York: Delta Books, 1968.

Lacoste, Louise Marcil. "The Consistency of Hume's Position Concerning Women." *Dialogue* 15, no. 3 (1976): 425–40.

Lévi-Strauss, Claude. *Structural Anthropology*. Translated by Claire Jacobson and Brooke Grundfest Schoepf. New York: Basic Books, 1963.

Locke, John. *An Essay Concerning Human Understanding*. 2 vols. Edited by John W. Yolton. New York: Everyman's Library, 1974.

———. *Second Treatise on Government*. Edited by C. B. Macpherson. Indianapolis: Hackett, 1980.

Longino, Helen E. "Rethinking Philosophy." In *Women's Place in the Academy*. Edited by Marilyn R. Schuster and Susan R. Van Dyne. Totowa, N.J.: Rowman and Allanheld, 1985.

Lugones, Maria C., and Elizabeth V. Spelman. "Have We Got a Theory for You." *Women's Studies International Forum* 6, no. 6 (1983): 573–81.

MacKinnon, Catherine. "Feminism, Marxism, Method, and the State." In *Feminist Theory*, edited by Nannerl O. Keohane, Michelle Z. Rosaldo, and Barbara C. Gelpi. Chicago: University of Chicago Press, 1982.

Marks, Elaine, and Isabelle de Courtivron, eds. *New French Feminisms*. Amherst: University of Massachusetts Press, 1980.

Mehuron, Kate. "Dionysian Mimesis." Unpublished paper presented to the Society for Phenomenology and Existential Philosophy meeting held April 15–17, 1987 at the University of Notre Dame.

Merleau-Ponty, Maurice. *The Phenomenology of Perception*. Translated by Colin Smith. New York: Routledge and Kegan Paul, 1962.

———. *The Visible and the Invisible*. Translated by Alphonso Lingis. Evanston, Ill.: Northwestern University Press, 1968.

Mill, John Stuart. *Utilitarianism*. Edited by George Sher. Indianapolis: Hackett, 1979.

Murphy, Julien S. "The Look in Sartre and Rich." *Hypatia* 2, no. 2 (Summer 1987): 113–24.

Nell, Onora. "How Do We Know When Opportunities Are Equal?" *The Philosophical Forum* 5, nos. 1–2 (Fall–Winter 1973–1974): 334–46.

Pateman, Carole. "The Disorder of Women." *Ethics* 91 (October, 1980): 20–34.

———. "Sublimation and Reification: Locke, Wolin, and the Liberal Democratic Conception of the Political." *Politics and Society* 4 (1975): 441–67.

Quine, Willard Van Orman. *From a Logical Point of View*. Cambridge, Mass.: Harvard University Press, 1953.

Rawls, John. *A Theory of Justice*. Cambridge, Mass.: Harvard University Press, 1971.

Rubin, Gayle. "The Traffic in Women." In *Toward an Anthropology of Women*, edited by Rayna R. Reiter. New York: Monthly Review Press, 1975.

Ruddick, Sara. "Maternal Thinking." In *Mothering*, edited by Joyce Trebilcot. Totowa, N.J.: Rowman and Allanheld, 1983.

Ruth, Sheila. "Bodies and Souls/Sex, Sin and the Sense in Patriarchy: A Study in Applied Dualism." *Hypatia* 2, no. 1 (Winter 1987): 149–63.

Ryle, Gilbert. *The Concept of Mind*. New York: Barnes & Noble, 1949.

Sartre, Jean-Paul. *Being and Nothingness*. Translated by Hazel E. Barnes. New York: Pocket Books, 1966.

———. *Existentialism Is a Humanism*. Paris: Nagel, 1946.

Scheman, Naomi. "The Body Politic/The Impolitic Body/Bodily Politics." In *The Materialities of Communication* (in German, translated by L. Pfeiffer), edited by H. U. Gumbracht and L. Pfeiffer, forthcoming from Suhrkamp.

———. "Individualism and the Objects of Psychology." In *Discovering Reality*, edited by Sandra Harding and Merrill B. Hintikka. Boston: D. Reidel, 1983.

———. "Othello's Doubt/Desdemona's Death: The Engendering of Scepticism." In *Power, Gender, Value*, edited by Judith Genova. Edmonton, Alberta: Academic Printing and Publishing, 1987.

Sedgwick, Eve Kosofsky. *Between Men: English Literature and Male Homosocial Desire*. New York: Columbia University Press, 1985.

Seigfried, Charlene Haddock. "*Second Sex:* Second Thoughts." *Women's Studies International Forum* 8, no. 3 (1985): 219–29.

Shapiro, Gary. "British Hermeneutics and the Genesis of Empiricism." *Phenomenological Inquiry* (October 1985): 29–44.

———. "The Man of Letters and the Author of Nature: Hume on Philosophical Discourse." *The Eighteenth Century: Theory and Interpretation* (1985): 115–37.

"Simone de Beauvoir: Witness to a Century." *Yale French Studies* 72 (1987).

Simons, Margaret A. "Beauvoir and Sartre: The Philosophical Relationship." *Yale French Studies* 72 (1987): 165–79.

Singer, Linda. "Interpretation and Retrieval: Re-reading Beauvoir." *Women's Studies International Forum* 8, no. 3 (1985): *Hypatia:* 231–38.

Smith, Janet Farrell. "Rights-Conflict, Pregnancy, and Abortion." In *Beyond Domination*, edited by Carol C. Gould. Totowa, N.J.: Rowman and Allanheld, 1983.

Smithka, Paula J. "Heidegger and Nuclear Weapons." *Concerned Philosophers for Peace Newsletter* 7, no. 1 (April 1987): 8–10.

Spivak, Gayatri Chakravorty. "Critical Response." *Critical Inquiry* 9, no. 1 (September 1982): 259–78.

———. "French Feminism in an International Frame." *Yale French Studies* 62 (1981): 154–84.

Straumanis, Joan. "Of Sissies and Spinsters: Shifts in Value of Sex-Marked Terms." Paper presented at a meeting of the Central Division of the American Philosophical Association, Columbus, April 1983.

Stroud, Barry. *Hume*. London: Routledge and Kegan Paul, 1977.

Tong, Rosemarie. *Women, Sex, and the Law*. Totowa, N.J.: Rowman and Littlefield, 1983.

Trebilcot, Joyce, ed. *Mothering*. Totowa, N.J.: Rowman and Allanheld, 1983.

Tuana, Nancy. "Re-fusing Nature/Nurture." *Women's Studies International Forum* 6, no. 6 (1983): *Hypatia:* 621–32.

Vetterling-Braggin, Mary, Frederick Elliston, and Jane English, eds. *Feminism and Philosophy*. Totowa, N.J.: Littlefield, Adams, 1977.

Waithe, Mary Ellen, ed. *A History of Women Philosophers,* vol. 1 (600 B.C.–500 A.D.). Dordrecht, The Netherlands: Martinus Nijhoff, 1987.

Wawrytko, Sandra. *The Undercurrent of Feminine Philosophy in Eastern and Western Thought.* Washington, D.C.: University Press of America, 1981.

Weinzweig, Marjorie. "Pregnancy Leave, Comparable Worth, and Concepts of Equality." *Hypatia* 2, no. 1 (Winter 1987): 71–101.

———. "Should a Feminist Choose a Marriage-Like Relationship?" *Hypatia* 1, no. 2 (Fall 1986): 139–60.

Wenzel, Hélène V. "Interview with Simone de Beauvoir." *Yale French Studies,* no 72 (1987): pp. 5–32.

Whitbeck, Caroline. "A Different Reality: Feminist Ontology." In *Beyond Domination,* edited by Carol C. Gould. Totowa, N.J.: Rowman and Allenheld, 1983.

———. "Love, Knowledge, and Transformation." *Women's Studies International Forum* 7, no. 5 (1984) *Hypatia:* 393–405.

Wittgenstein, Ludwig. *Philosophical Investigations.* Translated by G. E. M. Anscombe. New York: MacMillan, 1968.

Wittig, Monique. *The Lesbian Body.* Translated by David Le Vay. Boston: Beacon Press, 1986.

———. "One is Not Born a Woman." In *Feminist Frameworks,* edited by Alison M. Jaggar and Paula S. Rothenberg. New York: McGraw-Hill, 1984.

Wolff, Robert Paul. "There's Nobody Here But Us Persons." *The Philosophical Forum* 5, nos. 1–2 (Fall–Winter 1973–1974): 128–44.

Wolgast, Elizabeth. "Wrong Rights." *Hypatia* 2, no. 1 (Winter 1987): 25–43.

Young, Iris. "The Ideal of Community and the Politics of Difference." *Social Theory and Practice* 12, no. 1 (Spring 1986): 1–26.

———. "Impartiality and the Civic Public: Some Implications of Feminist Critiques of Moral and Political Theory." *Praxis International* 5, no. 4 (January, 1986): 381–401. (Reprinted in Seyla Benhabib and Drucilla Cornell, eds. *Feminism as Critique.* Minneapolis: University of Minnesota Press, 1987.)

———. "Pregnant Embodiment: Subjectivity and Alienation." *The Journal of Medicine and Philosophy* 9 (1984): 45–62.

Index

Abortion 69, 74, 170ff
Addelson, Kathryn Payne 177n
Affirmative action 39, 72
Allen, Jeffner 96, 103, 117n
Anglo-American philosophy 2ff, 15, 19, 22n, 28, 34–35, 54, 62ff, 69, 79, 81, 83–84, 105, 116, 121, 167, 170, 173, 176
Aristotle 38
Arthur, Marilyn 45n
Atomism 16, 21n, 22n, 30, 32ff, 37, 42ff, 47ff, 57ff, 71–72, 80, 84, 106–7, 138, 172
Austin, J.L. 9, 31, 67n, 83, 95
Authenticity 100–1, 111, 141. *See also* Bad faith
Ayer, A.J. 2, 15, 21n, 34, 45n, 62

Bacon, Sir Francis 17–18, 83–84, 134
Bad faith 113. *See also* Authenticity
Baier, Annette 62–63, 65n, 168
Barnes, Hazel 118n
Barthes, Roland 20, 124ff, 132, 143n, 145, 152, 168
Bartkowski, Frances 164n
Beardsley, Elizabeth 81ff, 84, 90n
de Beauvoir, Simone 20, 96–97, 102, 109, 112ff, 118n, 119n, 136, 147, 149

Bell, Linda 118n
Benhabib, Seyla 53, 66n
Berger, John 143n
Berkeley, George 28, 31, 34–35, 45n, 49, 59, 125, 137
Biologism 113–14, 136, 148, 151, 156–57
Bleier, Ruth 75, 90n
Bordo, Susan 16, 22n, 53, 66n, 84, 103
Bourgeois 32, 37, 53, 124ff, 132, 134, 136, 145, 149
Bowles, Gloria 116n
Brewer, María 66n
British Empiricism 2ff, 11, 15ff, 21n, 29–31, 33ff, 38, 40, 42ff, 45n, 46n, 48ff, 73, 79ff, 83–85, 87, 95, 97, 103ff, 111, 121, 125–26, 131, 134, 137–38, 142, 168, 170, 173, 176. *See also* Empiricism
Burns, Steven 65n
Butler, Judith 118n, 119n, 135
Butler, Melissa 45n

Capitalism 18, 23n, 32, 37, 70–71, 84, 86–87, 96, 125, 162
Card, Claudia 42, 46n, 114, 118n
Castration 112, 127–28, 137, 143n, 156–57, 162, 175

189

Cauldron dream logic 12–13, 80
Causality 30, 49ff, 54ff
Chodorow, Nancy 52–53, 66n, 80, 83–84
Cixous, Hélène 20, 131, 147, 156ff, 160, 162, 164n
Continental philosphy 7, 9, 16–20, 21n, 88, 95ff, 105, 124, 147–48, 159, 163, 176
Cornell, Drucilla 164n

Daly, Mary 90n, 104, 116n
Dasein 96ff, 110, 138–39, 169, 171ff, 175
Deconstruction 5, 9ff, 19–20, 31–33, 35, 45n, 55, 62, 89, 95, 99, 101, 106, 112, 116, 117n, 124, 133, 137ff, 145ff, 153, 155, 157, 161, 163, 167ff, 173
Deism 59ff, 88
Deleuze, Gilles 21n
Denaturalization 121, 132, 135, 149
Derrida, Jacques 5, 9ff, 20, 21n, 22n, 66n, 97, 104, 108, 122ff, 130, 137ff, 142n, 143n, 144n, 145, 147, 150, 153, 158, 163, 168, 175–76, 177n
Descartes, René 8, 16, 18, 28–30, 37, 50–51, 53–54, 57ff, 107, 110, 125, 134
Desire 112, 131–32, 137, 140, 146, 154, 159, 168
Dialogues Concerning Natural Religion 51, 60–61, 65n
Differance 11–13, 33, 122
DiStefano, Christine 53, 66n
Dualism 64, 88, 95, 107ff, 110, 127, 139ff

l'écriture féminine 145, 147, 152–53, 156, 158, 160
Eisenstein, Zillah 18, 23n, 70–72, 74, 102, 114
Embodiment 96–97, 104ff, 113, 115

Empiricism 7–8, 17, 28, 37, 63, 95, 121, 123, 126, 130. *See also* British Empiricism
Epistemology 8, 17, 28, 31–33, 42–44, 45n, 49–50, 54ff, 63, 69, 73, 81ff, 106, 137–38, 141
Essay Concerning Human Understanding 27ff, 50, 59
Essentialism 29, 37–38, 89, 117n, 141, 145, 149, 151, 155ff, 162–63
Ethics 40–43, 61ff, 69, 87, 100, 102, 114–15, 141, 168ff. *See also* Moral reasoning
Evans, Martha Noel 164n
Existentialism 20, 95ff, 109ff

Father 88, 129–30, 153
Feminism 13–14, 16ff, 30n, 65n, 69ff, 79, 86ff, 97–98, 102ff, 117n, 121–22, 124ff, 130, 133, 135, 139ff, 143n, 145, 148, 150, 153ff, 157, 163, 167, 169–70, 175–76. *See also* Feminist philosophy
Feminist philosophy 5ff, 13, 19, 36, 51ff, 60, 65, 69ff, 82, 84, 90n, 95, 168. *See also* Feminism
Ferguson, Ann 118n
Ferguson, Kathy 22n
Flax, Jane 53, 66n
For-Itself 108, 110
Foucault, Michel 20, 22n, 46n, 104, 124, 133n, 139, 143n, 144n, 153
Fraser, Nancy 22n, 75, 90n, 104, 135
French feminism 20, 96ff, 113ff, 124, 141, 145ff, 148, 155–56, 160, 163, 168
Freud, Sigmund 11–12, 22n, 66n, 79ff, 88–89, 95–97, 106, 111ff, 121ff, 128ff, 133, 135, 139–40, 147–48, 152ff, 156, 158–59, 162, 175
Frye, Marilyn 39, 45n, 102, 117n, 143n, 170, 177n

Index

Gender Neutrality 28, 139, 152
Gilligan, Carol 41–42, 46n, 51, 62, 100, 115, 170
God 34, 49, 52–53, 59–61, 88, 110–11, 125, 132, 133, 138
God's existence 30, 40, 59–60
Godway, Eleanor Shapiro 117n
Grant, Judith 13–14
Greer, Germaine 143n

Habermas, Jürgen 101, 104
Hampton, Jean 44n, 46n
Harding, Sandra 7–9, 18, 21n, 36, 45n, 60–61, 82–83, 85–86, 89, 103, 116n, 146
Harré, Rom 38–39, 45n
Hartsock, Nancy 86ff, 91n, 95
Hawkesworth, Mary 72, 90n
Hegel, George W.F. 5, 88, 96–97, 104, 109ff, 118n, 121, 124, 126, 157
Heidegger, Martin 19, 96ff, 106, 108, 110–11, 114ff, 117n, 118n, 124, 134, 137ff, 143n, 144n, 146, 160, 168–69, 172, 173ff
Hermeneutics 19, 96–98, 116, 167ff, 172, 176
Heterosexism 48, 82, 127, 149, 155
Hierarchical dualisms 4, 8–9, 13, 22n, 30, 36, 51, 62–63, 66n, 80, 85ff, 96, 107ff, 115, 124, 127–28, 140, 147ff, 151, 157–58, 160, 175
Hintikka, Jaakko 90n
Hintikka, Merrill B. 90n
Hobbes, Thomas 3, 17, 21n, 29, 32, 46n, 53, 71, 88, 126
Holism 104–5, 107, 110
Holland, Nancy J. 66n, 117n, 143n, 144n
Homosexuality 80, 121, 126–27, 132, 136–37, 150, 154, 156–57, 159ff. *See also* Lesbianism
Hooks, Bell 20n, 72–73, 76, 90n

Humanism 99, 103, 111, 133–34
Hume, David 2, 5, 14, 19, 21n, 22n, 28, 31, 34, 36, 39, 47ff, 65n, 66n, 67n, 73, 82ff, 99, 107, 116, 125–26, 134, 137–38, 168, 171, 176
Hume's Enquiries 48, 50–51, 65n, 67n, 127
Hume's fork 52, 56
Husserl, Edmund 97, 108, 111, 140, 168–69
Hysteria 106–7, 136, 140, 152–53
Idealism 97, 104ff, 110, 121, 138, 148, 169
Ideology 15–16, 42, 60–61, 72, 81, 85, 88, 125–26, 149, 161
Imaginary 129ff, 150
Individualism 3ff, 17, 22n, 32–33, 38, 42, 51–52, 63–64, 69ff, 84–85, 90n, 95ff, 114, 117n, 149, 169, 172
In-Itself 108, 110
Innate ideas 29–30, 36–37, 50, 126, 137
Irigaray, Luce 20, 117n, 130–31, 133, 143n, 146ff, 159ff, 163n, 164n, 165n

Jaggar, Alison 5ff, 17–18, 21n, 23n, 32, 38, 45n, 64, 67n, 69ff, 90n, 141, 142n, 151
Jardine, Alice 21n, 22n, 53, 66n, 161, 163n
Johnson, Barbara 45n
Jouissance 112–13, 132, 153–54, 157ff, 162

Kant, Immanuel 5, 9, 18, 22n, 31, 62, 97, 104, 106–7, 121, 135, 170, 173
Keller, Evelyn Fox 18, 23n, 83–84, 90n, 103, 116n, 146
Kierkegaard, Søren 114
Kofman, Sarah 22n, 67n, 133
Krieger, Linda J. 90n
Kristeva, Julia 20, 45n, 99, 114,

123, 147, 151ff, 157, 163n, 164n, 168
Kuhn, Thomas 83

Lacan, Jacques 10, 20, 79, 104, 122, 124, 128ff, 137, 143n, 145, 147ff, 153, 156, 159ff, 168
Lacoste, Louise Marcil 62, 65n, 82
Language 31–33, 50, 81ff, 84, 95, 99, 107, 110, 129ff, 133–34, 138, 146ff, 153–54, 156–57, 159ff, 169, 171
Lesbianism 113ff, 119n, 129, 132, 148ff, 152–53, 159, 162
Lévi-Strauss, Claude 79ff, 122ff, 129, 143n, 145
Liberal feminism 6–7, 17, 38, 70–71, 74, 112, 114, 135, 145, 151, 153, 162
Liberalism 6, 32, 70ff, 82, 88, 112ff, 125–26, 155
Lind, Marcia 65n
Linguistics 11, 121, 129–30, 146, 152
Locke, John 2, 5, 7, 15, 19, 23n, 27ff, 44n, 45n, 46n, 47ff, 53ff, 59–60, 63–64, 71, 73, 83ff, 88, 99, 116, 125–26, 137–38, 155, 170, 176
Longino, Helen 21n
Lugones, Maria C. 20n

MacKinnon, Catherine 8, 21n
Marx, Karl 79, 83, 121, 135, 147–48
Marxism 6, 13, 18, 86ff, 95ff, 109, 111–12, 126, 148–49, 152, 162
Marxist feminism 6–8, 18
Master/slave relationship 109–10, 112, 157
Maternal thinking 88, 100–1, 151, 168, 174
Matricide 53, 61, 66n, 131, 157
McDonald, Christie 141
Mehuron, Kate 117n, 162, 165n

Men's philosophy 2ff, 19–20, 54, 89, 115, 176
Merleau-Ponty, Maurice 19, 96–97, 104ff, 115, 117n, 165n, 168–69
Metaphor 14–15, 122, 156
Metaphysics 8, 14, 16, 20, 28, 31, 33ff, 37ff, 44, 45n, 54ff, 63, 69, 73, 81, 85ff, 95, 110, 112, 138ff, 156, 158, 161
Mill, John Stuart 38, 125, 128, 143n
Mitchell, Juliet 131
Modernity 37, 54, 103–4, 135, 137–38, 142
Moral reasoning 29, 41, 62–63, 100, 114–15
Morality *See* Ethics
Motherhood 45n, 87–89, 100, 113, 152ff, 156–57, 159
Murphy, Julien S. 117n

Naturalization *See* Denaturalization
Nell, Onora 70, 90n
Nelson, Barbara 75
Nicholson, Linda 22n
Nietzsche, Friedrich 97, 114, 151
Nuclear war 173ff

Oedipus myth/complex 53, 66n, 80, 112, 122–23, 129ff, 133, 152, 154
Ontology 69, 87–88, 99–100, 103, 129, 169
Orestes myth 53, 66n, 131, 157
Other minds, problem of 35–37, 44, 108–9

Pascal, Blaise 18
Pateman, Carol 23n, 43, 46n
Patriarchy 28, 31, 70–71, 74, 76, 79–80, 84, 86ff, 103, 109, 125, 131, 135, 139ff
Personal identity 36, 58. *See also* Self
Phallus 112, 122ff, 130ff, 154, 161
Phenomenalism 28, 34–35, 49

Phenomenology 19, 95ff, 105, 113ff, 145, 154, 167ff, 171ff, 174ff
Philosophy of mind 82ff. *See also* Personal identity, Self
Philosophy of science 36, 69, 82ff, 146, 159. *See also* Science
Plato 12, 15, 66n, 160, 169
Political Philosophy 5–6, 28, 31, 43–44, 69, 82, 84, 88
Post-structuralism 11, 14, 20, 95, 107, 117n, 121, 124, 128, 133ff, 145, 150, 152, 157
Pregnancy 6, 9, 36, 76, 87, 152ff, 159, 171ff, 174
Private language argument 33, 84
Protestantism 18, 23n
Psychoanalysis 10, 37, 52–53, 112, 114, 129ff, 133, 140, 146ff, 152–53. *See also* Sigmund Freud
Psychology 2, 48ff, 52, 55ff, 58, 61, 66n, 75, 80, 84, 105ff, 169. *See also* Psychoanalysis
Public/private spheres 41, 63, 70, 162

Quine, Willard V.O. 83, 95

Radical feminism 6–7, 151, 153
Rationalism 29, 137
Rawls, John 43, 46n
Real 129ff, 150
Rich, Adrienne 118n
Rose, Jacqueline 131
Rousseau, Jean-Jacques 13, 15, 18, 23n, 67n, 88
Rubin, Gayle 79ff, 83, 90n, 122ff, 161
Ruddick, Sara 88, 91n, 100–1, 104, 130, 151
Ruth, Sheila 91n
Ryle, Gilbert 8

Sado-masochism 112, 132, 151, 155
Sartre, Jean-Paul 20, 96ff, 101, 105, 108ff, 117n, 118n, 168–69

Saussure, Ferdinand de 11, 22n, 97, 122, 124, 129–30
Scepticism 31, 49–50, 56, 65, 69, 107
Scheman, Naomi 3, 45n, 53, 66n, 84–85, 90n, 117n, 140ff
Science 7–9, 17–18, 36–37, 83, 103, 115, 125, 130, 137, 146–47, 152, 159–60, 168, 173
Searle, John 45n, 65n
Second Treatise on Government 27–28, 32
Sedgwick, Eve 164n
Self 20, 21n, 44, 49ff, 57ff, 110, 127, 129, 136, 141. *See also* Personal identity
Semiotics 20, 31, 117n, 121ff, 127, 133, 138, 152
Sense data theory 106, 138
Sex/gender system 79ff, 83, 149
Sexuality 105ff, 111ff, 135ff, 140 143n, 156–57, 159, 168
Shapiro, Gary 46n, 65n, 168
Siegfried, Charlene Haddock 115, 116n
Simons, Margaret A. 118n
Singer, Linda 114–15, 117n, 118n
Smith, Barbara Herrnstein 43, 46n
Smith, Janet Farrell 177n
Smithka, Paula 175, 177n
Socialist Feminism 6–7, 18
Solipsism 29, 35–37, 85, 108ff, 115
Spelman, Elizabeth V. 20n
Spivak, Gayatri 99, 117n, 163n, 164n
Stereotypes 7, 63, 80, 83, 100–1, 106, 171
Straumanis, Joan 90n
Stroud, Barry 21n, 22n, 54, 66n
Structuralism 14, 20, 95, 107, 117n, 121ff, 133, 138, 163
Subject/object dichotomy 82ff, 103, 107, 110, 146, 152

Substance 17, 28–30, 33ff, 49–50, 125
Symbolic 129ff, 150

Taylor, Harriet 38
Technology, problem of 96, 98–99, 103, 146, 173, 175
Thurschwell, Adam 164n
Tillich, Paul 104
Tong, Rosemarie 77–79, 90n
Treatise of Human Nature 47ff, 127
Tress, Daryl McGowan 141–42, 144n
Tronto, Joan 13–14
Tuana, Nancy 116n

Utilitarianism 55, 171, 173

Vaginal orgasm, 113, 132, 153

Waite, Mary Ellen 20–21n
War *See* Nuclear war

Wawrythko, Sandra 116n
Weber, Max 23n
Weinzweig, Marjorie 76–77, 90n, 101, 117n
Wenzel, Hélène V. 118–19n
Whitbeck, Caroline 87ff, 91n, 96, 109–10, 117n
Wittgenstein, Ludwig 9, 31, 33, 35, 45n, 83ff, 95
Wittig, Monique 20, 114, 118n, 131, 147ff, 152, 155ff, 160, 164n
Wolff, Robert Paul 69–70, 90n
Wolgast, Elizabeth 21n
Wollstonecraft, Mary 38
Women's philosophy 1–4, 19–20, 49, 88, 111, 116, 121, 123, 136, 167ff, 172, 175–76
World 99, 106, 108

Young, Iris Marion 21n, 43, 46n, 164n, 171, 177n

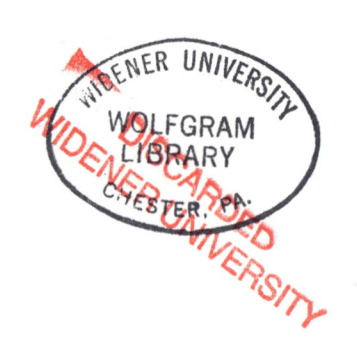